A Pride of Place

A Pride of Place

Rural Residences of Fauquier County, Virginia

EDITED BY KIMBERLY PROTHRO WILLIAMS

Contributing Writers and Consultants: Cynthia A. MacLeod, T. Triplett Russell, Susan Kern,

the Virginia Department of Historic Resources, and Bob Barron

Published for Fauquier County by the University of Virginia Press

Charlottesville and London

University of Virginia Press
© 2003 by the Rector and Visitors of the University of Virginia
All rights reserved
Printed in the United States of America on acid-free paper

First published 2003

1 3 5 7 9 8 6 4 2

LIBRARY OF CONGRESS CATALOGING-IN-PUBLICATION DATA

A pride of place : rural residences of Fauquier County, Virginia / edited by
Kimberly Prothro Williams ; contributing writers and consultants, Cynthia
A. MacLeod . . . [et al.].
 p. cm.
Includes bibliographical references and index.
 ISBN 0-8139-1997-5 (cloth : alk. paper)
 1. Dwellings—Virginia—Fauquier County. 2. Architecture, Domestic—
Virginia—Fauquier County 3. Fauquier County (Va.)—Description and
travel. I. Williams, Kimberly Prothro, 1962–
 F232.F3 P75 2003
 728′.37′09755275—dc21

                                                        2002007438

Contents

Illustrations in Historical Overview

Foreword

Fauquier is a much-blessed county. Its principal blessing perhaps is its landscape. For over two centuries this pastoral scenery has attracted people who care for it deeply. Fauquier's countryside has encouraged the creation of a remarkable legacy of architecture. A history of American architectural forms could be taught using only Fauquier County examples—from log cottages, to antebellum farmhouses, to stately Georgian Revival mansions of hunt-loving plutocrats. Though many wealthy people indeed have been drawn here, especially during the twentieth century, a relatively small number have chosen to erect grand architectural statements. More have elected instead to identify with the established gentry by remodeling and expanding venerable country houses to suit the demands of a sociable country life. The result is an intriguing collection of finely appointed estates reflecting several generations of owners.

Although Fauquier's natives have been good stewards of their heritage, a continuing infusion of discriminating people has bolstered the preservation of the county's gently civilized landscape. Many who move in do so because they like its looks and lifestyle. And they want it to stay that way. As a result, Fauquier boasts some of the Commonwealth's most preservation-minded property owners. Many of the finest farms are permanently protected through voluntarily donated conservation easements. In addition, citizens have supported protective zoning for historic districts. This pride of place and spirit of shared values serves to preserve a treasure for everyone. This catalog of Fauquier's architecture will help us appreciate and safeguard essential elements of this treasure.

CALDER LOTH
Senior Architectural Historian
Virginia Department of Historic Resources

Preface

This publication culminates a two-decade effort by Fauquier County to identify its historically significant resources. Considering the scope of Fauquier's rich heritage of renowned persons, unique structures, natural beauty, and historically significant places, the task of preservation must be accomplished one phase at a time. This phase catalogs the architecture of historic residences in the county outside the corporate limits of towns.

Structures may have many different historical aspects, which could, and should, be included in such a study. But history cannot be completely retold or preserved within the walls of sole structures. The grouping of structures and the relationship of structures to the land and places of historical interest all intertwine and must be considered together to gain a true perspective of the events that shaped the county's history. Each structure's architecture does, however, reflect the cultural, social, economic, and geographical factors influencing life in Fauquier at the time of its construction.

It is the intention of the county, through this publication, to make its readers more aware of this phase of Fauquier's heritage in the hope that everyone may become more conscious of the elements that shaped, and continue to shape, our past, our present, and our future.

Acknowledgments

A project of such duration gradually accumulates the involvement of many persons and organizations that are worthy of recognition for eventually making it possible. Those who have survived the test of two decades of record keeping are named herein, but our thanks extend to everyone who helped finally make this important information more accessible for everyone.

Merle Fallon, for initiating the inventory process as well as following through to assure funding, deserves the credit for bringing about this publication.

The Fauquier County Parks and Recreation Department would like to express its sincere gratitude to those who provided financial support to the project including two very generous but anonymous donors, the Virginia Department of Historic Resources, and the Fauquier County Board of Supervisors.

Just as important are the owners of the sites surveyed who were generous with their information and assistance as evidenced by the wealth of data compiled.

A very special acknowledgment must be extended to Kim Williams, the editor, whose commitment to this project knew no bounds and to Laurie Starke for her work proofreading and indexing the final manuscript.

Gratitude is likewise due to those who helped review the book and provided guidance, including Nancy Baird, John Gott, Edwin Gulick, and Jack Alcott. Particular recognition is also due to Susan Kern for contributing the historical background narrative and to Diane Gulick for her efforts to coordinate the details for submission of the manuscript and those who helped her. Special gratitude is also due to the Traceries staff, Emily Eig, Sujatha Shan, and Lisa Tucker.

The county quadrangle maps were prepared by Fauquier County Geographical Information Systems, and Eugene Scheel drew the map showing the locations of various houses and villages. In the Catalog the photograph of Weston is courtesy of the Warrenton Antiquarian Society, and the photograph of the mantel from Greenview is reproduced courtesy of Colonial Williamsburg Foundation. All other photographs in the Catalog are courtesy of the Archives, Virginia Department of Historic Resources, Richmond.

These acknowledgments would not be complete without recognition of the staff at the University of Virginia Press, especially Cynthia Foote and Dick Holway. Their patience and assistance kept the project alive and pulled together the pieces whenever they seemed ready to fall apart.

Especial acknowledgment is due to the 1995–96 Board of Supervisors, including James Brumfield, Wilbur Burton, James Green, Georgia Herbert, Larry Weeks, and David Mangum, who removed any remaining obstacles to assure the publication of this volume, and the Parks and Recreation Board, Carl Bailey, Richard Bowen, Diane Hughes, Debbie Reedy, James Janoskie, and Ronkeith Kirtley, who made this a priority for the staff.

A Pride of Place

Introduction

We must demonstrate that preserving the cultural heritage is essential to human wholeness. We must move far beyond our present system of conceptualizing and identifying historic resources as parcels of private property and adopt an aggressive model of strategic regional planning, in which individual historic properties are seen as punctuation marks in a much wider conversation: a conversation about community.

W. Brown Morton

In 1978 the National Register of Historic Places was expanded to include properties not only of national significance but also of state and local importance. Soon after, federal grants were given to states to fund inventories or surveys of historic properties. The identification of historic properties was intended to aid planning and preservation efforts at the local, state, and federal levels.

Fauquier County became vitally interested in this program in the mid-1970s when a crisis developed over the replacement of a highway bridge. Although there was general agreement that the Fauquier Springs bridge was in disrepair, different solutions were offered, depending on the historic importance of the bridge. Unfortunately, no inventory existed that suggested any historic priority or supplied credibility for the bridge's preservation on historic grounds. Given only a day's notice, county officials were unable to prevent its demolition and replacement with concrete and steel. Later it was identified as a relatively rare iron-truss bridge, of which only two were left in Virginia.

As a result of this incident, two initiatives emerged. The Virginia Department of Transportation undertook to protect and preserve two bridges of potential significance, and Fauquier County began to review its own historic heritage with renewed interest.

The Fauquier County Board of Supervisors, at the urging of Merle W. Fallon, then Director of the Parks and Recreation Department of Fauquier County (FCDPR), determined to identify and inventory the historic resources of the county in order to make better and earlier planning decisions. The county applied to the Virginia Historic Landmarks Commission (now the Virginia Board of Historic Resources) for funds for a historic resource survey. In 1978 Fauquier County was awarded a grant for this project through the Rappahannock-Rapidan Planning District Commission from the Virginia Historic Landmarks Commission, which had received matching funds from the U.S. Department of the Interior.

The architectural and historic inventory was begun in September 1978. Cynthia A. MacLeod, a Virginian with a master's degree in architectural history from the University of Virginia, was appointed to conduct the survey in Fauquier and to serve as a consultant in historic preservation for the five-county region of the Rappahannock-Rapidan Planning District Commission. Fauquier County employed Bob Barron of Warrenton to serve as her assistant, a position funded by an anonymous donor. Excluded from the survey were nonresidential structures and dwellings within the corporate limits of towns.

In the course of the survey more than nine hundred sites were examined and well over five hundred photographed. These are fully described in reports filed with the Virginia Department of Historic Resources (VDHR) in Richmond, together with photographic negatives and other descriptive material.

Although those findings help to preserve the historic records of Fauquier County, only a small portion of the houses surveyed meet the eligibility criteria to be designated a Virginia Historic Landmark. Those criteria are set forth in legislation as follows:

No structure or site shall be deemed to be an historic one unless it has been prominently identified with, or best represents, some major aspect of the cultural, political, economic, military, or social history of the State or nation, or has had a relationship with the life of an historic personage or event representing some major aspect of, or ideals related to, the history of the State or nation. In the case of structures which are to be so designated, they shall embody the principal or unique features of an architectural style or demonstrate the style of a period of our history or method of construction, or serve as an illustration of the work of a master builder, designer or architect whose genius influenced the period in which he worked or has significance in current time. In order for a site to qualify as an archaeological site, it shall be an area from which it is reasonable to expect that artifacts, materials, and other specimens may be found which give insight to an understanding of aboriginal man or the Colonial and early history and architecture of the State or nation.

The inventory was formally concluded in September 1980, and only minimal updating has occurred since. The fact that the reports and photographs, although available for examination in Richmond, were not easily accessible to the public prompted a decision by the Fauquier County Board of Supervisors to undertake a study of the residential architecture of the county reflecting the socioeconomic history of this section of the Virginia piedmont. In December 1980 T. Triplett Russell, architectural historian, was selected to write this study. The manuscript was completed in 1985, but lack of funding delayed its publication. When funding did finally become available, it was determined that the original intent of making the inventory more accessible to all county citizens would be better served by a catalog of the sites surveyed. This book is the result of that endeavor.

Unfortunately, the delay in publication has not helped to preserve certain notable homes that have been listed but have been lost in the interim. As this planning tool increases awareness of these homes, it is hoped that the next stage of inventory, surveying those structures omitted from the original survey, may be facilitated before they, too, are lost. With these resources in hand the planning and "conversation about community" can then begin in earnest.

Worth Noting

Every effort has been made to ascertain the dates of original construction and subsequent dates of substantial additions or alterations. Dating construction is very difficult, even for a professional architectural historian, and the dates as listed should not be viewed too seriously. However, any ascription of dates of construction before 1800 must be viewed with caution. Not many houses, or even parts of houses, survive from the eighteenth century.

Although history is often widely interpreted, the extensive research of the many trained professionals involved in this project revealed a solid base of valid and credible sources, as indicated in the bibliography.

For more information concerning the survey of homes in Fauquier County, the process for designation of Historic Landmarks, and/or architectural history in general, contact the following organizations:

Fauquier County Parks and Recreation Department
62 Culpeper Street
Warrenton, VA 22186

Fauquier County Historical Society
PO Box 675
Warrenton, VA 22186

Virginia Department of Historic Resources
2801 Kensington Avenue
Richmond, Va. 23221

National Trust for Historic Preservation
1758 Massachusetts Avenue NW
Washington, DC 20036

A Note on Courtesy

Every home listed in this publication should be considered a private residence and treated as such, unless it is now known to be otherwise. Although a few are open by special arrangement or special tours, contacts for accessibility should only be addressed as a result of, and according to, any promotion of those special openings.

Historical Overview

Fauquier's Historical Development: Geographical Setting

Fauquier County is defined, as it was at the time of its settlement, by its geographical features and natural resources. Its character is found in the beautiful rolling countryside contained by the Blue Ridge Mountains and the Potomac and Rappahannock Rivers (fig. 1). The grasslands above the falls of the Rappahannock have been part of Anglo-American descriptions of the area since 1613 when Captain Samuel Argall remarked on the buffalo grazing there. From 1670 comes the earliest and often-quoted passage about Fauquier when explorer John Lederer chronicled the beauty of what was to become Fauquier County: "Having travelled through the shade of the vast forest, come out of a melancholy darkness of a sudden into a clear and open skie. . . . To heighten the beauty of the parts, the first springs of most of these great rivers which run to the Atlantic Ocean, or Chesapeake Bay, do here breakout, and in luxurious branches interlace the flowery meads, whose luxurious herbage invites numerous herds of red deer to feed."[1]

The natural grasses of the lower piedmont provided perfect pastureland for horse and cattle, and fruit orchards soon punctuated steeper slopes. The streams and runs became the power source for many gristmills. The development of the local economies relating to agriculture and small industry soon became an integral part of Fauquier's identity. The mountain gaps on Fauquier's western boundary facilitated settlers' paths west and turnpikes back east that in turn encouraged the agricultural development of the county. As the frontier pushed through and beyond Fauquier, new roads allowed its residents to trade easily in Alexandria and other points east, thereby supporting the agricultural enterprise in a day's travel. Fauquier's road systems, from Indian trails to colonial roads, from turnpikes to railroads to highways, have played a large role in defining the settlement and the cultural patterns on the landscape today.

The rural architecture of Fauquier County reflects three economic forces at every phase of history. The majority of the buildings reflect the revolving needs of localized agricultural and industrial development, at times booming with a new road, railroad, or highway. The second force is seen in the quiet land use of the large horse and cattle farms of the early twentieth century, which continues today to anchor the agrarian image of Fauquier firmly on the landscape. A third economic force is the use of Fauquier as a resort—a hunt country retreat and a healthful escape from the nation's capital, Richmond, Baltimore, and beyond.

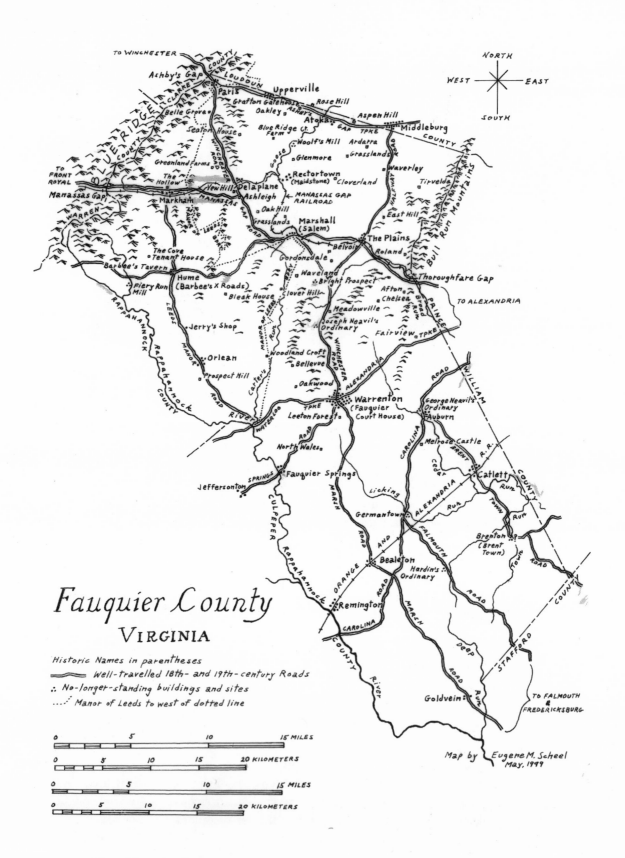

FIG. I. Map of Fauquier County

From the truck farmer to the plantation owner, the house in Virginia historically relied upon an agricultural setting, whether a single house amid garden plots or a great seat among the many agricultural and domestic dependencies demanded by plantation society. Evidence of these agricultural roots is clear in the character of Fauquier's countryside today.

The Roots of Virginia, 1649–1759: Colonial Land Grants and the Founding of Fauquier

The development of Fauquier County was tied to tidewater Virginia and the British colonial land grants that established the county seats and parishes for the settlers of Virginia. The rural character of Fauquier can be seen as a product of the earliest seventeenth-century Northern Neck land grants. Bounded by the Potomac and Rappahannock Rivers, the Northern Neck became the territory administered by Thomas Fairfax, fifth Baron Fairfax of Cameron, at the beginning of the eighteenth century. When settlers began moving west, the sixth baron, Thomas Lord Fairfax, came to Virginia to clarify the western boundaries of his proprietary lands and promote their settlement. Fearful of losing the charter of the proprietary and attempting to salvage as much land as possible should the Privy Council rule against his claim, Lord Fairfax took an individual grant in 1736 in his own name. Called Leeds Manor after his family home, Leeds Castle in Kent, England, the territory contained 122,850 acres of land that spread across what is today the northwestern part of Fauquier, as well as parts of Loudoun, Frederick, and Shenandoah Counties. Leeds Manor was later leased in small holdings of 150 to 200 acres to accommodate the large number of small farmers coming to the piedmont. Although the land was patented in 1736, its leasing did not begin until 1749, when courts had confirmed the validity of the proprietary and Fairfax had established himself at Greenway Court in Frederick County.[2] Because the proprietor preferred to make grants of large tracts of land to land speculators and developers, whom he charged a small yearly quitrent, the majority of land in what was to become Fauquier was held in large tracts until after the Revolution. Some of these tracts were leased out in small parcels, but many settlers passed west through Fauquier to land farther west where freehold settlement enabled a farmer to bequeath developed land to his heirs. With the founding of Fauquier County in 1759 and the proprietor's active promotion of leases on Leeds Manor at the same time, however, a steady influx of immigrants came to the area, and development of the lands accelerated.

The earliest settlement in Fauquier County occurred along the rivers, creeks, and runs, in the manner that most of Virginia was explored and measured. Indeed, the first leases issued in Fauquier were those near Carter's Run in the Manor of Leeds. Although not navigable, these waterways served as important sources of power and food and hence encouraged the development first of large estates and then of smaller farms and mill centers that became the cultural and industrial centers of the county.

The first colonial outposts, initially along the Rappahannock, have left little physical evidence of their existence. Nicholas Hayward's 1687 broadside for enticing settlers to the proposed town of Brenton offers a glimpse of Fauquier's earliest housing: "The proprietor will offer to lease to such persons 100 acres of land for a farm and one acre in the said town for a house and to furnish to each family nails and other hardware in sufficient quantity to build a house in size 26 to 28 feet long and 14 to 16 feet wide, and 15 bushels of indian corn for their subsistence the first year, all an annual rent of 4 ecus (or one pound) sterling."[3] The clearing of the land provided the wood for these average-size two-room frame houses. As further enticement, the town was paled or fortified to defend its location on the Indian Road.

The 1719 Germantown settlement, now an archaeological site listed on the National Register of Historic Places, also provides clues to the early built environment in Fauquier. In 1718 twelve families from Siegen, Germany, who were dissatisfied with conditions at Germanna—Governor Spotswood's established town on the Rapidan River—acquired a warrant to settle 1,805 acres of land in Fauquier County. The land was laid out in an "oblong square" on both sides of Licking Run and was divided equally among the settlers, each lot bordering the stream. By 1748 Germantown had a church and school, though it is described as "like a village in Germany where the houses are far apart."[4]

The Tilman Weaver house (fig. 2), built by one of Germantown's original families, stood as the oldest surviving building in Fauquier until it was torn down in 1924. A description of the house and photographs taken before its demolition indicate that the house was a one-and-a-half-story frame structure measuring 16 by 26 feet. The house was covered with a steeply pitched gable roof and featured two massive stone end chimneys that heated rooms both below and above.[5] One downstairs room had access to a spring in the cellar. Hewn oak beams, secured by wooden pegs, framed the structure, which was plastered on the interior with a mixture of small stones in red clay and straw mortar packed between the studding, then whitewashed. A poplar board which hung over the door of the house in 1899, when it was described by Willis M. Kemper, bore the date of 1721.[6] At some point poplar weatherboard was added, and a small wing was built on either side of the house. A Weaver descendant lived in the house as late as 1899.

The Hall-Parlor House

Like the Tilman Weaver house, other early houses in Fauquier County were single-cell cabins or hall-parlor houses built of local materials. The English tradition of the hall-parlor house was the model for most of tidewater Virginia, though settlements by Germans, French Huguenots, and French Catholics introduced other European traditions. At the same time availability of building materials, climate, and other local conditions affected the final house forms of the area. In the hall-parlor house, the names of the two rooms described their social functions. The hall, which was entered directly from the outside, was considered a public space, while the parlor, entered through the hall, provided an inner or more private room (fig. 3). Within this description based on func-

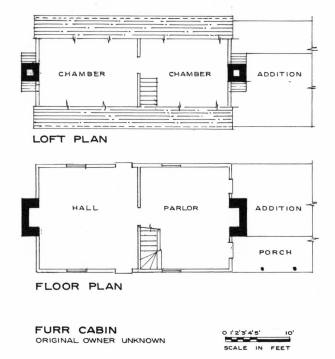

FIG. 3. Architectural floor plan, typical hall-parlor house. (Drawn by T. Triplett Russell)

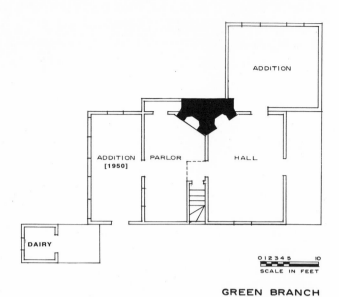

FIG. 4. Green Branch (030-0848), floor plan.
(Drawn by T. Triplett Russell)

tion, many variables could define the specific form of the house, and indeed, no two hall-parlor houses in Fauquier are alike. Almost always one-and-a-half stories tall, the hall-parlor house is usually covered with a steeply pitched gable roof and features one or two end chimneys. Stairs or a ladder to the loft space in the attic level is located in either the hall or the parlor. If a third room is found in the downstairs configuration, as it is in two Fauquier County examples, Yew Hill (030-0060) and Rose Hill (030-0073), it is generally referred to as the chamber and historically implied more private family space.

By the middle of the eighteenth century, Fauquier's English building traditions had been thoroughly adapted to the particular conditions of agrarian life in Virginia. Although most of the early houses continued the tidewater traditions of log or frame construction, and less often brick, soon many more were built in the readily available stone of the area. The local limestone resources also allowed for the production of stucco, often found dressing the rubblestone or log walls

FIG. 5. Green Branch (030-0848), photograph. (Courtesy of Archives, VDHR, neg. 5118-7A)

of the residences. Also common in English precedents, this finished stucco surface is a dominant character-defining feature of Fauquier's built environment.

Several different hall-parlor houses, including Green Branch, Hooewood, Gordonsdale cabin, and The Hollow, each illustrate the different configurations available in a two-room plan. Green Branch (030-0848), a small frame house of 1760–90, provides an unusual version of a two-room plan (fig. 4). Here, instead of extending the depth of the house as in the typical hall-parlor house, the two rooms run laterally, each having a corner fireplace that shares the single chimney on the gable end of the house. The hall is slightly larger than the parlor and is entered on the center of its long side. The parlor is entered through the hall, as is usual, but also has a door leading to the exterior. A stair, located against the central partition wall from the parlor, ascends to the loft level. A steeply pitched gable roof covers the original two-room house, while a later catslide encompasses the front porch (fig. 5).

Hooewood (030-0497), built 1780–90, has a different but more usual division of space (fig. 6). The entry is into a narrow hall which also contains the stair. The parlor, entered through the hall, is the larger room and against the end wall has the only fireplace. The upstairs is lit by a small dormer window and windows in the gable end walls. Three walls of Hooewood are built of stone, while the fourth wall is partially wood frame (fig. 7).

The Gordonsdale cabin (030-0027), ca. 1790, offers yet another configuration of the hall-parlor plan. The house is a log structure, clad with a later stucco fin-

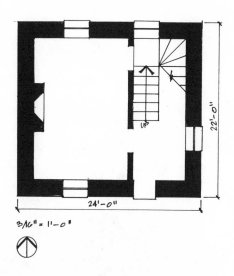

FIG. 6. Hooewood (030-0497), floor plan. (Courtesy of Traceries)

FIG. 7. Hooewood (030-0497), photograph. (Courtesy of Archives, VDHR, neg. 4564-17)

FIG. 8. Gordonsdale cabin (030-0027), photograph. (Courtesy of Archives, VDHR, neg. 4643-26)

FIG. 9. The Hollow (030-0803), photograph. (Courtesy of Archives, VDHR, neg. 5106-24)

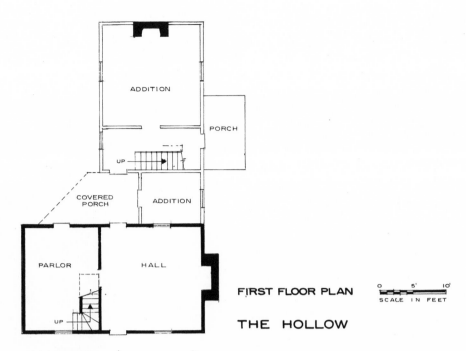

FIRST FLOOR PLAN

THE HOLLOW

FIG. 10. The Hollow (030-0803), floor plan. (Drawn by T. Triplett Russell)

ish and covered with a steep gable roof with stone end chimneys (fig. 8). The two end chimneys heat the similarly sized rooms on both the first floor and loft level. The Hollow (030-0803), built by Colonel Thomas Marshall in 1765, is a small, two-room frame house with a single stone end chimney (figs. 9 and 10). The fireplace at The Hollow is in the larger hall; the stair is located in the parlor room against the central partition wall.

The Foundations of Fauquier County, 1759–1800: Roads, Taverns, and Mills

The 1748 highway act expressed Virginia's needs for well-maintained roads. County-appointed surveyors saw to it that planters and their labor force took responsibility for the upkeep and maintenance of roads passing by their properties. Fauquier Court House, now Warrenton, was the most convenient of area crossroads at which to place the colonial court seat, the anchor for the business of the people and the laws of Great Britain and its colonies. At the juncture of the old Winchester-to-Falmouth Road and the post road from Charlottesville to Alexandria, the major north-south and east-west routes, Fauquier Court House became the geographic and political center of the county upon its founding in 1759. Following the Revolution, most colonial courthouses remained the center of justice and dispensed the new American democracy over the same rural area. Fauquier was no exception.

At other crossroads and along highways, other small communities began with taverns or ordinaries. Because these establishments disseminated news and served as centers of meeting and debate, as well as of horse races and cockfights, they encouraged the settlement of those whose lives were related to the trades that the road supported. The colonial county courts approved the licenses to run ordinaries and preferred to license men, or occasionally women, of substance who could offer room and board for traveler and horse.[7]

Early travelers' accounts are often the only surviving descriptions of the buildings on Virginia's early landscapes. The most commonly noted features of ordinaries were the handbills tacked to the front of the building and the shared accommodations, suggesting the limited space of the hall-parlor floor plan. In the 1780s the marquis de Chastellux commented on the tidewater ordinary: "For lodging there is one large room for all the company. A pallet brought in and laid on the floor for each guest suffices for these country folk."[8] In an early nineteenth-century account, an Englishwoman remarked: "There are always several beds in every room and strangers are obliged to sleep together. The sheets are mostly brown and seldom changed." She also commented on the exterior architectural features: the ordinaries "all resemble one another, having a porch in front, the length of the house, almost all covered with hand bills: they have no sign, but take their name from the person that keeps the house."[9]

Four ordinaries that once served travelers of Fauquier's early highways survive intact today. Owned by the Ashby family, Yew Hill (030-0060), long a landmark at the intersection of the Winchester and Manassas Gap Roads, continued the service offered by the Watts Ordinary, or "Watts" as noted on early maps of the region. The original three-room plan suggests accommodations similar to those described by early travelers, with the first-floor chamber and upper floor probably serving as the Ashby family's more private living quarters (fig. 11). Although sold out of the Ashby family in 1806, Yew Hill continued to serve as an ordinary throughout the nineteenth century and was depicted in Porte Crayon's *Travels through Virginia* in 1853 (fig. 12).

Barbee's Tavern (030-0685) was built ca. 1790 at the intersection of four roads in Leeds Manor that came to be called Barbee's Crossroads (fig. 13). The terms of Joseph Barbee's 1783 lease with Denny Martin Fairfax included the specification that "he will with all expectation erect and build in the said lot . . . one dwelling house twenty feet long and sixteen feet wide with a brick or stone chimney."[10] Every lease executed by the Reverend Denny Fairfax carried this same requirement. These terms suggest that this was Fairfax's attempt to thwart Virginia's 1782 legislation dissolving the proprietary ownership of any vacant lands, thereby turning British holdings over to the Commonwealth. A building of this size probably represents the smallest house that would signify active development of the Fairfax land in Leeds Manor. Originally a hall-parlor plan with a large stone fireplace in the hall, Barbee's Tavern was later enlarged by the addition of another room next to the hall, transforming the house into a central-passage plan. Local tradition holds that Joseph Barbee operated the building as a tavern in the early nineteenth century.

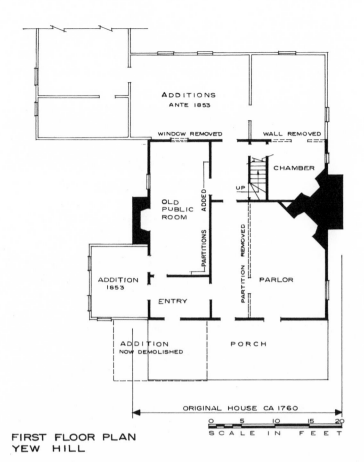

ADDITIONS
ANTE 1853

WINDOW REMOVED   WALL REMOVED

CHAMBER

UP

OLD
PUBLIC
ROOM

ADDED

PARTITIONS

PARTITION REMOVED

ADDITION
1853

PARLOR

ENTRY

ADDITION
NOW DEMOLISHED

PORCH

ORIGINAL HOUSE CA 1760

0   5   10   15   20
SCALE IN FEET

FIRST FLOOR PLAN
YEW HILL

FIG. 11. Yew Hill (030-0060), floor plan.
(Drawn by T. Triplett Russell)

FIG. 12. Sketch of Yew Hill (030-0060) by Porte Crayon from *Travels through Virginia*, 1853. (Reprinted in *Piedmont Virginian*, Jan. 21, 1976, "Yew Hill: George Washington Did Indeed Sleep Here," photo courtesy of Fauquier Heritage Society)

FIG. 13. Barbee's Tavern (030-0685), photograph. (Courtesy of Archives, VDHR, neg. 4865-28)

The town of Maidstone, now Rectortown, incorporated in 1772, was the first town in Fauquier County to be established by an act of the assembly. In 1793 Daniel Floweree received a license to operate an ordinary there. The establishment of Maidstone Ordinary inspired George Washington to claim that the town "originated with and will end with two or three gin shops, which will exist no longer than they serve to ruin the proprietors and those who make the most frequent application to them."[11] Maidstone Ordinary (030-0036) still survives (fig. 14), along with several other residences at the small crossroads community. Another former tavern, Aspen Hill (030-0755), located along the old road between Middleburg and Ashby Gap, has a long public facade and multiple rooms, characteristic of a later period when inns were built to accommodate many guests (fig. 15).

Other tavern buildings no longer standing, such as Ashby's Tavern in Paris, Neavil's Tavern on the Fredericksburg-Winchester Road, Hardin's at the junction of the Shenandoah Hunting Trail and the Falmouth Road, and George Neavil's at Auburn on the crossing of the Carolina and Dumfries Roads, could be found throughout the county during the late eighteenth and nineteenth centuries.

Like the taverns on the area highways that became focal points for travelers and gathering places for locals, mills on the many waterways became the centers of commerce and culture in the late eighteenth and the nineteenth cen-

FIG. 14. Maidstone Ordinary (030-0036), ca.. 1910 photograph. From *Fauquier County, Virginia, 1759–1959* (Warrenton, Va.: Fauquier County Bicentennial Committee, 1959), p. 44.

FIG. 15. Aspen Hill (030-0755), photograph. (Courtesy of Archives, VDHR, neg. 5031-25A-26)

FIG. 16. Mill House (30-0650),
photograph. (Courtesy of Archives,
VDHR)

turies. In the period between 1830 and 1840, seventy-six gristmills were working to capacity in Fauquier. Many of those mills survive intact, while other sites retain mill ruins or other vestiges. At least five of Fauquier's historic residences are previous millhouses, and others are located on important mill sites. The most notable of these, the Mill House, or Chinn's Mill (030-0650), near Atoka, contains many of the buildings that typically made up a mill complex: the mill; the miller's house; the coopery, which provided the barrels for shipping the milled grains; and the cooper's house (fig. 16). Between 1924 and 1929 the stone mill complex was renovated and significantly enlarged to serve exclusively as a private residence.

Another millhouse is that of Millford Mills, formerly Woolf's Mill (030-0713), located on Goose Creek. A landmark on early maps, it was built around 1800. The stone millhouse is all that remains of this once-flourishing mill complex. The Fiery Run Mill was built for James Markham Marshall about 1820. Though the mill is in ruins, the original millrace and miller's house remain. Both the Millford Mills and the Fiery Run miller's house (030-0758) were built into the hillside along a riverbank, responding to unique hillside conditions. Woodland Croft (030-0393), on Carter's Run, may have served as a miller's house, as several mills were located along this stretch of the run in the nineteenth century.

Both the mills and the taverns of Fauquier provided landmarks for early travelers and anchors for those who built nearby, encouraged by some assurance of safe and prosperous settlement and commerce in the region. By the latter part of the eighteenth century, both commercial and domestic buildings were being erected to serve the more permanent economic and social positions of the residents of Fauquier County.

The Central-Passage House

The development of the small hall-parlor house into a larger house with a central-passage plan reflected not only economic stability but social convention. By the middle of the eighteenth century, new demands for personal privacy were firmly in place, and house plans changed to accommodate different roles. The hall, one of the two principal rooms in the hall-parlor house, became the passageway between the two main rooms in the central-passage house (fig. 17). The new hall or hallway ran from the front to the rear of the house and was entered directly from the outside. The house owner thus controlled the transition from the public space of the hall to the more private spaces of the parlor and chamber entered from the hall. The central-passage-plan house resulted from the changing social needs and requirements of the more permanent resident and was thus a deliberate manipulation of space. The central-passage-plan house emerged first as an evolution from one- and two-room dwelling forms and later as a deliberately planned house form. The addition of a single room to an existing hall-parlor structure allowed for the reconfiguration of the interior plan and the evolution of the spaces within. Indeed, once this system of private spaces entered by privilege was in place, it was employed in some form in practically every later house type throughout the nineteenth and early twentieth centuries in Virginia. The hall as public entry and passage to entertaining space or private rooms remained an important element in house building throughout the periods covered here.[12]

Chippewa (030-0426) survived until recent years as the oldest example of a central-passage house in Fauquier County (fig. 18). Chippewa was originally constructed ca. 1760 as a hall-parlor house and later was extended to become a central-passage house (fig. 19). Chelsea (030-0177) was similarly a hall-parlor house that was enlarged in the later nineteenth century to become a central-passage-plan dwelling. Unlike Chippewa and Chelsea, Grapewood (030-0517), built 1780–1800, was specifically built as a central-passage house. Grapewood is covered with a gambrel roof which provided more room in the loft space (fig. 20). Three dormers suggest the improvement of the upstairs for better, well-lighted living area. The entry hall provides access to two different-sized rooms, each heated by a brick end chimney.

An example of the central-passage plan completely supplanting the formerly adequate hall-parlor house can be seen in the Marshall family move from The Hollow (030-0803), their hall-parlor house of 1765, to Oak Hill. Around 1773 Thomas Marshall built Oak Hill (030-0044), a one-and-a-half-story frame house on a stone foundation with brick end chimneys and a four-room plan serviced by a central entry hall (fig. 21). The formality of Oak Hill, compared to The Hollow, can be seen in

FIG. 17. Floor plan representing a central-passage-plan house. (Courtesy of Traceries)

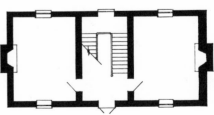

TYPICAL CENTRAL-PASSAGE PLAN

FIG. 18. Chippewa (030-0426), photograph. (Courtesy of Archives, VDHR, neg. 4401-20)

N

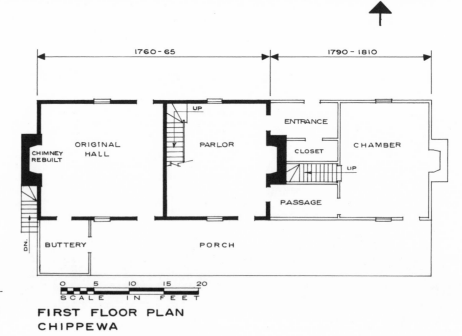

FIG. 19. Chippewa (030-0426), floor plan. (Drawn by T. Triplett Russell)

FIRST FLOOR PLAN
CHIPPEWA

FIG. 20. Grapewood (030-0517), photograph. (Courtesy of Archives, VDHR, neg. 4568-19)

FIG. 21. Oak Hill (030-0044), photograph. (Courtesy of Archives, VDHR)

plan, materials, and details. The small Georgian-era Oak Hill planter's seat was later superseded by the addition of a larger Greek Revival house built next to the original Oak Hill and connected to it by a single-story frame hyphen. The final Oak Hill is a summation of the development of two generations of taste in one of Fauquier's notable families.

Oak Hill is a textbook example of the evolution of social order and building needs in Fauquier County. The move from the hall-parlor house to a small central-plan seat redefined the way Colonel Marshall related to his space and to those who entered into it. The change from hall-parlor to central plan indicated a change in the way of thinking about public and private space by clearly defining a new space through which to control both business and social visitation. The formality of the Georgian-style house and the move to a house detached from its service buildings imposed the same hierarchy of the social order on the landscape as that which occurred on the house interior.

The Georgian-Style House

The Georgian style, a more formal counterpart to this period of building in Virginia and Fauquier, followed British influences in building. More studied in proportion and detailed in an Anglo-Palladian style, the Georgian style disseminated from the great city rebuilding movements in London and trickled into the colonial capitals. The availability of pattern books of architectural styles helped define the details of Great Britain's building trends for consumption in even the remotest corners of the colonial hold. The new seventeenth- and eighteenth-century houses of the minor aristocracy in the British Isles brought about the detached house that became the hallmark of the Virginia plantation setting. The massive block of the Georgian house, standing at the center of the dependencies and quarters of the plantation, is a familiar image in Virginia, with examples like Westover in Charles City County serving as icons of the Old Dominion in the eighteenth century.

North Wales (030-0093) is Fauquier's finest example of the formal Georgian style as adapted to rural Virginia (figs. 22 and 23). Built 1773–81, the substantial stone house features all of the form, massing, and details characteristic of the style, including the rigidly symmetrical five-bay facade, the pairs of end chimneys, and the central-hall, double-pile plan.

The Federal Style

By the end of the American Revolution, the details of the Georgian era had been refined in England and Scotland by the Adam brothers, who applied the classical elements in a new way. The graceful, attenuated lines and more delicate massing of the Adamesque style were adopted in the American Federal period as a replacement for the robust and corpuscular Georgian. The Federal house often appears more vertical, especially in a town setting, or is broken into a five-part Palladian plan in a country setting, in response to the block form of the Georgian. The details, including finer dentil work and moldings than previ-

FIG. 22. North Wales
(030-0093), photograph.
(Taken by T. Triplett Russell)

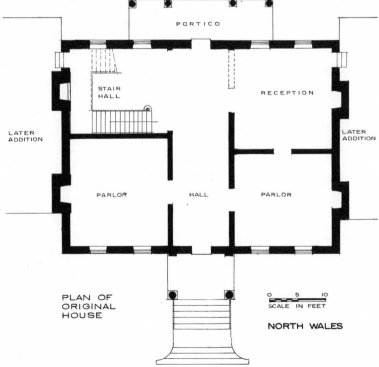

PORTICO

STAIR
HALL

RECEPTION

LATER
ADDITION

LATER
ADDITION

PARLOR

HALL

PARLOR

PLAN OF
ORIGINAL
HOUSE

0   5   10
SCALE IN FEET

NORTH WALES

FIG. 23. North Wales
(030-0093), floor plan.
(Drawn by T. Triplett Russell)

FIG. 24. Fairview (030-0550), photograph. (Courtesy of Archives, VDHR, neg. 4642-2A)

ous classical derivations, give the Federal style its elegant restraint and cosmopolitan feel.

Fairview (030-0550), built ca. 1810, bears Federal-style detailing on both the exterior and interior that survives as a fine example of the style in Fauquier (fig. 24). The central-passage, double-pile plan fills the same social requirements established with the Georgian style. The Flemish bond brickwork with its jack-arched lintels and the interior details including molded baseboards, chair rails, mantels, and cornice trim enliven the spaces and provide an elegance not seen in the earlier Georgian style (fig. 25).

Other examples of Federal woodwork can be seen at Belle Grove (030-0008) (fig. 26), built around 1812, and at Chestnut Lawn (030-0088), built in 1832. La Grange (030-0200), built around 1830 and recently renovated, is a large five-bay brick house overlooking the town of Paris (fig. 27). The carved cornice with dentils and jack-arched lintels add a restrained elegance to the unornamented facade.

Grasslands (030-0781), built 1820–50, has subtle Federal features, seen in the form and massing of the building and in the only exterior decoration, an elliptical fanlight over the central entry. Although Afton Farm (030-0519) appears to be a late nineteenth-century I-house, the interior trim on the mantels, windows, and doors dates the original single-cell house to the Federal period (fig. 28). Another I-house with late Federal details is Roland (030-0075), built 1840–50, whose cornice with dentils, pedimented porch, and interior details are refinements unusual on rural farmhouses (fig. 29). Carrington (030-0017), built in 1830, has similar Federal form and massing but lacks the refined exterior details often associated with the style (fig. 30).

FIG. 25. Mantel in
Fairview (030-0550),
photograph. (Courtesy of
Archives, VDHR, neg. 4642-
0A-1)

FIG. 26. Detail of mantel in Belle Grove (030-0008), photograph.
(Courtesy of Archives, VDHR, neg. 4863-9A)

FIG. 27. La Grange (030-0200), photograph. (Courtesy of Archives, VDHR, neg. 1609-36)

FIG. 28. Mantel in Afton Farm (030-0519), photograph. (Courtesy of Archives, VDHR, neg. 4578-11)

FIG. 29. Detail of mantel in Roland (030-0075), photograph. (Courtesy of Archives, VDHR, neg. 5023-28)

FIG. 30. Carrington (030-0017), photograph. (Courtesy of Archives, VDHR, neg. 5109-34)

The Traditions of Agriculture and the Ideals of a New Democracy, 1800–1850: Turnpikes, the Virginia Farmhouse, and the Greek Revival Style

By the end of the eighteenth century, the need for better roads brought about the turnpike, a private venture chartered for the public good. The turnpikes that traversed Fauquier County established routes to the markets on Duke Street in Alexandria, which controlled the east-west trade routes across northern Virginia after the American Revolution. In 1806 the Little River Turnpike Company opened an artificial road from Alexandria to Aldie, just beyond the eastern boundary of Fauquier. From this main route other turnpikes forked to the Shenandoah Valley through every major gap: Ashby, Manassas, and Thornton's in Fauquier County and to the north Snickers's or Williams's Gap in Loudoun County. The southern end of the county was tied more directly to Fredericksburg, which sought trade with lower Fauquier, Culpeper, and Louisa in central Virginia.

Many of Fauquier's towns were incorporated in the early nineteenth century as a result of the prosperity that these direct routes to markets ensured. The

FIG. 31. A tenant house on the Rumsey house (030-0668) property, photograph. (Courtesy of Archives, VDHR, neg. 4861-8)

county entered a period of growth and building that has been called the Golden Age of Fauquier County. In 1810 the census of Fauquier counted 22,689 people living in the county. Population peaked at 26,086 in 1830, the beginning of the county's most prosperous decade, when the majority of economic activity was firmly based in agriculture. From 1830 on, the population fell, in 1910 reaching what it had been a century before, 22,526. The largest number of Fauquier's historic residences were built during these decades of economic development and prosperity. Those who did not build new houses often enlarged and updated existing structures to fit their growing needs.

The evolution of the small cabin or hall-parlor house into a more permanent house for life in the nineteenth century can be seen in a variety of ways. One is through additions, where the original small log or stone dwelling is buried within subsequent structures, or where the original structure is significantly enlarged or extended, or perhaps even connected to other buildings by covered walkways or hyphens. Many of Fauquier's historic houses contain the cells of their earliest houses. A second way is more an evolution of buildings, where the early log or frame house is supplanted by a more substantial and larger house on the same property and is itself turned into quarters, a tenant house, or a domestic outbuilding. A third manner in which houses evolved was more cosmetic, whereby the original house was simply updated, by hanging the latest fashion on the outside—such as a Greek Revival portico or Classical Revival door surround. This type of evolution is seen most predominantly during the period when the Greek Revival style was popular and again during the early twentieth century when the Classical Revival style firmly installed itself on the Fauquier landscape.

Examples of early houses significantly enlarged by later additions are found throughout the county. A two-story wing addition to a tenant house on the Rumsey house (030-0668) property converted this small, one-room frame farmhouse to a more comfortable dwelling for later nineteenth-century life (fig. 31). The Meadows (030-0529), originally a one-room house, was enlarged by an additional four rooms and front porch on the first-floor level (fig. 32). A similar enlargement evolved at Easthill (030-0595), originally a one-room stone house built by John Finch around 1840. Within ten years the roof of the stone house was raised, and a two-story frame addition was attached (fig. 33). A year later the house was enlarged again by the addition of a frame wing. Outbuild-

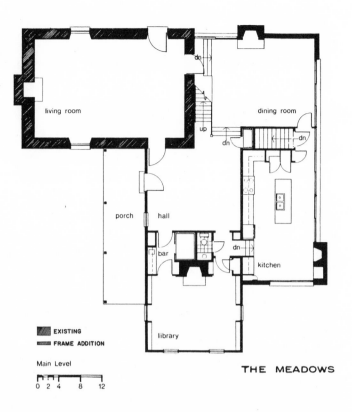

THE MEADOWS

FIG. 32. The Meadows (030-0529), floor plan. (Drawn by T. Triplett Russell)

ings to serve the domestic needs of a dairy and smokehouse still stand as part of this farm.

The Virginia I-House

The quintessential Virginia farmhouse, the I-house, developed in this period as an improvement to the small central-passage-plan house. Like the central-passage house the I-house has a central passage and is one room deep, but it is two stories tall. The downstairs hall provides entry to the dining room and parlor and houses the stair to the second-floor hall. The plan is repeated on the second floor where the upstairs hall provides access to the two upstairs chambers. The I-house is generally of frame or brick construction with end chimneys of stone or brick. Although many examples of random additions to the small, one- or two-room-plan house can be found, the evolution of a smaller house into an I-house was the most common type of house enlargement during this period in Fauquier. Originally built as a hall-parlor house, the log Fletcher-Graves house (030-0043) was enlarged into an I-house plan by raising the roof to two stories and increasing the number of bays from two to three by the addition of a frame wing.

Eventually I-houses were erected in their own right and can still be seen today throughout the county. Seaton Farm (030-0049), near Upperville, is an example of a brick I-house from around 1840 (fig. 34). The Cove tenant house (030-0756) is representative of the later nineteenth-century I-house, which has windows on the end (as opposed to chimneys) and is heated by a wood-burning stove instead of fireplaces (fig. 35). A one-and-a-half-story wing at the rear

FIG. 34. Seaton Farm (030-0049), photograph. (Courtesy of Archives, VDHR, neg. 5367-18A-19)

FIG. 35. The Cove tenant house (030-0756), photograph. (Courtesy of Archives, VDHR, neg. 5031-28A-29)

Historical Overview 31

FIG. 36. Russell house (030-0719), photograph. (Courtesy of Archives, VDHR, neg. 4872-28)

FIG. 37. Payne house (030-0720), photograph. (Courtesy of Archives, VDHR, neg. 4872-31)

FIG. 38. Glenmore cabin (030-0593), photograph. (Courtesy of Archives, VDHR, neg. 4652-19)

of this house predates the main I-house, again illustrating the evolution of the small house to the larger I-house dwelling form. Outside of Orlean, the Russell house (030-0719) and the Payne house (030-0720), which stand across the road from each other, were built ca. 1872 by Alfred Russell and his brother-in-law, W. Wood Payne (figs. 36 and 37). This pair of I-houses, like the many others in Fauquier, are a familiar vernacular image on the rural landscape of Virginia.

The evolution to better living space by moving from a simple house to a more substantial one has already been illustrated at Oak Hill and can be seen again at Glenmore, on Goose Creek. The Glenmore cabin (030-0593) (fig. 38), built between 1800 and 1810, may have been the main dwelling for this farm complex while the more substantial Federal-style house, Glenmore (030-0025) (fig. 39), was being constructed. The Glenmore house, built 1810–20, with its array of outbuildings became the fine country seat for the Glascock family.

Slave/Servant Quarters

In addition to the small, self-sufficient farms of Fauquier were the larger landholdings that were generally dependent upon an array of outbuildings, including slave quarters. Those quarters that survive, whether as part of a domestic complex or in outlying fields no longer associated with the original farm, are testaments to the period of Virginia history when the plantation economy was inextricably intertwined with slave labor, and housing for this labor force was an integral part of the visual landscape. While many of the main houses stand as examples of high-style architecture, the collections of related dependencies are equally important as models of agricultural systems and as the documents of a now-alien social structure, in addition to their important record as building types and technology.

Fauquier County has a number of former slave quarters that were adapted for single-family use following the Civil War. The early to mid-nineteenth-century Acorn Farm cabin (030-0782) was originally a two-family quarter, with two entrances and a central partition on the interior of the log building. Around 1870 the two entrances were closed, and a single entrance was cut into the log structure, converting the building to a single-family farmhouse (fig. 40). When the main house at Fieldmont (030-0630) burned down ca. 1858, the slave quarters were converted into the property's primary residence. The Brady-Downs cabin (030-0594) (fig. 41) may have been built as quarters for the adjacent Easthill Farm.

FIG. 40. Acorn Farm cabin (030-0782), photograph. (Courtesy of Archives, VDHR, neg. 5040-10A)

FIG. 41. Brady-Downs cabin (030-0594), photograph.

Other farms retain former slave quarters as part of the domestic outbuilding complex. At Greenland Farm, or Belmont (030-0250), a tightly knit group of
outbuildings including a stone slave quarters, a stone kitchen, and other outbuildings flank the main house. Originally built in the late eighteenth century
for John Ashby, this farm complex asserts an antebellum character with the
main house standing among dependencies (fig. 42). Rose Hill (030-0073), built
in the 1770s, offers an important collection of domestic outbuildings representative of the eighteenth- and nineteenth-century Fauquieran landscape. The
assortment of dependencies illustrates the specialized spaces that were created
outside the house for a variety of activities. The slave quarters remain as part
of this eighteenth-century complex.

The Classical Revival

In this period of prosperity, Fauquier joined the celebration of American
democracy that was seeking roots beyond the immediate post-British heritage
and was looking to the first Western democracies for ideas. The revival of
Greek and Roman precedents for building forms, town names, and especially
public architecture swept through America in the early to mid-nineteenth century. The classical temple-form building, as adopted by Thomas Jefferson for
the Virginia State Capitol and as promulgated by him, became the icon of

democracy, an image of stability and permanence in the still-new Republic. Banks, businesses, and institutions of higher learning also saw the temple form as architecture fitting the image they wished to portray. By the 1830s and 1840s the form had virtually permeated all building types and could be found throughout the country in a variety of settings.

The Greek Revival house differed from previous house styles in massing as well as detail. The building was often turned so that the facade was on the gable end, and the gable was enclosed by the cornice and raking cornice, thereby alluding to or suggesting the temple-front public architecture of antiquity. The identifiable elements of the Greek Revival style were based on simple forms: cubes, blocks, and triangles, as seen in the articulation of the pediment above the mass of the building walls, a portico with columns, or perhaps more restrained pilasters. Symmetry became an important feature for both the building elevation and molding details. Regardless of the major change in orientation of the building and the reconfiguration of interior space that followed, the room use remained the same as that established by the mid- to late eighteenth century. A hall, whether a central-passage or side-passage hall or a transverse hall that extended the width of the building, remained the entryway and division between public and private space. The hall led into the downstairs rooms and generally housed the stairs leading to the second-floor rooms above.

This period of architecture, which occurred during Fauquier's Golden Age, brought the county's first signed works in building: at least two master builders tried their hands at Greek Revival, designing and building several residences that survive today. As was the case during the Georgian and Federal periods, pattern books of British and American buildings helped establish the formality of the style and the elements proper to it. The master builder in this period was the unlicensed equivalent of the professional architect at the end of the century. In this period of prosperity in Fauquier, these Greek Revival houses were built as secondary residences and houses for entertaining. A wide entry hall across the front of the house provided the transitional access to the double parlors, facilitating the social scene in these fashionable country dwellings. The siting of each of these residences was considered in the overall design, evident in the approach road or landscaping surrounding the house.

A large group of Fauquier's Greek Revival houses built between 1819 and 1840 are similar in plan and form and are, in some cases, the work of a single builder. The typical plan has three rooms, composed of an entry and stair hall extending the width of the building, with two rooms behind, each heated by a fireplace on the rear wall (fig. 43). The typical elevation consists of the entry on the gable end of a masonry structure, with a pedimented gable with a lunette window articulating the facade. The almost indistinguishably designed houses Woodbourne (030-0322), Bellevue (030-0493), and Oakwood (030-0083) (fig. 44) are attributed to a builder named Clarkson, while Oak Hill (030-0044) was built by John Armstrong of Jeffersonton, Culpeper County. Given their de-

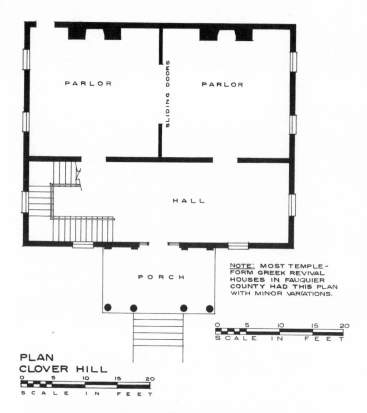

PLAN
CLOVER HILL
0 5 10 15 20
SCALE IN FEET

NOTE: MOST TEMPLE-
FORM GREEK REVIVAL
HOUSES IN FAUQUIER
COUNTY HAD THIS PLAN
WITH MINOR VARIATIONS.

0 5 10 15 20
SCALE IN FEET

FIG. 43. Clover Hill (030-0516), floor plan. (Drawn by T. Triplett Russell)

sign similarities, Clover Hill (030-0516) (fig. 45) and Waveland (030-0512) may possibly have been built by one of these two builders.

Before falling to ruins and then being demolished, the small and charming Bright Prospect (030-0577) offered a more subtle adaptation of the Greek Revival style in the county (fig. 46). Built around 1829, the single-cell, story-and-a-half stone building had its entrance in the gable end and a large chimney at the rear. The returns of the cornice ends at the modest Bright Prospect made a clear, if indirect, gesture to a temple pediment, illustrating the pervasiveness the Greek Revival style had attained in Fauquier County.

Although Ashleigh (030-0005) is not representative of the typical Greek Revival house in Fauquier County, it is considered one of the premier Greek Revival houses in Virginia and is listed on the National Register of Historic Places. Ashleigh was built ca. 1840 by local builder William Sutton for Margaret Marshall, granddaughter of Chief Justice John Marshall, to designs that she appar-

FIG. 44. Oakwood (030-0083), photograph. (Courtesy of Archives, VDHR, neg. 4399-21)

FIG. 45. Clover Hill (030-0516), photograph. (Courtesy of Archives, VDHR, neg. 4567-21)

FIG. 46. Bright Prospect (030-0577), photograph. (Courtesy of Fauquier Heritage Society)

FIG. 47. Ashleigh (030-0005), photograph. (FCDPR)

ently had prepared herself. The low massing and columnated portico of Ashleigh are said to reflect her travels though the Deep South, as these architectural treatments are more representative of the Greek Revival style as seen in the southern plantation houses of Alabama and Mississippi (fig. 47).

The builder of Ashleigh, William Sutton, was also responsible for the construction or renovation and reconstruction of several other residences in Fauquier in the period between 1830 and 1850. Glenville (030-0026), Waverly (030-0057), and Woodside (030-0059), all attributed to Sutton, are among the more elegant estates in the county.

Constructing an entirely new building during this building boom was not always practical; for those persons wishing to update their already existing residence, it was far more practical to add a portico, a cupola, or some other Greek or Roman detail that would "classicize" the building. Much of the Greek Revival architecture in Fauquier County, in fact, is the result of this type of refurbishing.

Waverley (030-0226), on Route 626 near Halfway, for instance, clearly reflects the changing architectural modes and tastes from the late eighteenth century to the mid-nineteenth century. Its core, a late eighteenth-century

stone cottage, was expanded during antebellum times to more appropriately reflect the changing tastes and needs of its occupants. The double-story hexastyle portico across the front elevation (fig. 48) was made in keeping with the Greek Revival tradition and gave the vernacular house a more stylish and up-to-date look. This portico qualifies the house as an architectural highlight of the scenic road between Middleburg and The Plains.

Similarly altered to reflect the fashion of the time is Bleak House (030-0191), located near Jerry's Shop. Originally a small hall-parlor house, Bleak House was extended in the early to mid-nineteenth century by the addition of two rooms. In 1853 the house and its addition were completely encased and encompassed by a two-story frame structure with classical details (figs. 49 and 50). An elegant Doric porch, recessed into one side of the front elevation, opens onto a double entry door framed by Greek moldings. A wide frieze with a Greek fret motif, broken by grilled vents over the window and protected by a projecting cornice, is found on three of the four elevations of the house.

FIG. 48. Double-story portico of Waverley (030-0226), photograph. (Courtesy of Archives, VDHR)

FIG. 49. Bleak House (030-0191), photograph. (Courtesy of Fauquier Heritage Society)

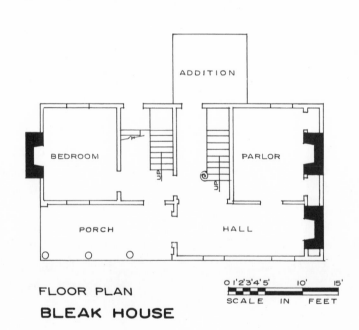

FIG. 50. Bleak House (030-0191), floor plan.
(Drawn by T. Triplett Russell)

A Pride of Place

Industry and Commerce, 1850–1900:
Railroads and Romantic Revivals

Just as the turnpikes offered new opportunities of prosperity for those who were smart to plan, the railroads quickly changed the economic landscape, favoring some while leaving others to the increasingly sleepy roads that once supported them. Fauquier's only major venture in canals along the Rappahannock was cut short by the opening of the Orange and Alexandria Railroad in 1852. The Manassas Gap Railroad quickly replaced the east-west turnpikes as the carrier of most goods through the mountain gaps to the Shenandoah Valley, and the Orange and Alexandria replaced north-south routes through the county. The Baltimore and Ohio Railroad, which developed lines to the Shenandoah Valley through Harpers Ferry, once again changed the orientation of trade routes from the Valley. Just as Alexandria had replaced the tidewater as the focus of trade around the time of the Revolution, the railroads brought competition from the northern cities such as Baltimore. In addition, small, privately financed rail lines brought the influence of connecting cities to rural Fauquier.

The Romantic Revival

Though the fashions in house building influenced by the new connections and new money of the railroads were interrupted by the Civil War, Fauquier has a sampling of the Romantic Revival styles of the second half of the nineteenth century. This period of revivals, Gothic, Italianate, Romanesque, and Egyptian, reflected a romantic fascination with ancient or mythical cultures. The attraction was the simplicity of life before technology, a medieval innocence in unspoiled gardens, inspired in part by romantic epic literature. The picturesque quality of these styles was a departure from the symmetry and formality of the previous classically defined tastes. Publications of these styles, including Andrew Jackson Downing's *Cottage Residences,* 1842, and *The Architecture of Country Houses,* 1850, spread the image of home as a comfortable retreat in a woodland or garden setting. The popular details, such as trimmed gables, turned posts, towers, or turrets are all indicative of the eclectic character of these styles.

Two of Fauquier's best-known houses, Oakley (030-0046) and Melrose Castle (030-0070), were built in this period and are listed on the National Register of Historic Places. Oakley was built in 1857 to be Richard Henry Dulany's Italian villa in the Virginia countryside, a place suitable for entertaining the horse culture in which he was so involved (fig. 51). The front of the house has a familiar central entry and three-part division, decorated with a refined Italianate bracketed cornice, stylized window surrounds, large glazed entry doors, and a lacy balustrade atop the front veranda. The site at the rear of the house drops off sharply and supports the soaring three-story veranda, wrapping around the T-extension of the central portion of the house. A projecting bay with numer-

FIG. 51. Oakley (030-
0046), photograph. (Tak-
en by T. Triplett Russell)

ous arched windows on one end of the house lightens the mass of the building.

Melrose Castle (030-0070), commissioned in 1857 for Dr. James Murray of
Baltimore, illustrates the castellated mode of the Gothic Revival style. The
house and its name, taken from Murray's ancestral home in Scotland, may also
have been influenced by the works of Sir Walter Scott, who used Melrose
Abbey in several of his popular romantic novels. One of Virginia's most picturesque houses of the Romantic Revival period, Melrose Castle offers a distinctly
Gothic image despite the symmetry and balance of classical styles, as seen in
both plan (fig. 52) and elevation. The house was designed by Edmund George
Lind of Baltimore and constructed by local builder George Washington Holtzclaw. In 1862 Melrose was occupied by Union troops, one of whom left his
mark in an inscription in a closet at Melrose (fig. 53).[13]

New styles, especially the Italianate, became symbols of new wealth in
many of the small towns that developed along the Manassas Gap Railroad.
The John Delaplane house (030-0591), a two-story brick house designed in the

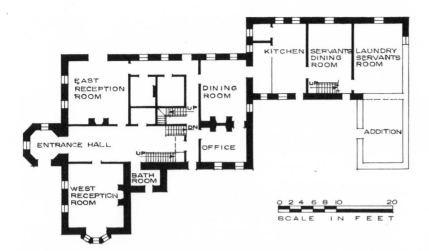

FLOOR PLAN
MELROSE CASTLE

FIG. 52. Melrose Castle (030-0070), floor plan. (Drawn by T. Triplett Russell)

FIG. 53. "Dr. Murray's House, Fauquier County, Virginia, with Tents. November, 1863." Vintage photograph of Melrose Castle (030-0070) by T. H. O'Sullivan. (Courtesy of the Library of Congress, Prints and Photographs Division, T. H. O'Sullivan Collection)

FIG. 54. Curtis house (030-0377), photograph. (Courtesy of Archives, VDHR, neg. 4397-7)

FIG. 55. Walnut Hollow (030-0718), photograph. (Courtesy of Archives, VDHR, neg. 4872-19)

Italianate style, was built with a store and warehouse to serve Piedmont Station, now Delaplane, in 1852. Delaplane survives as a model of the small depot town that grew up in this period. The town of Markham, founded 1854, was the home of Edward C. Marshall, first president of the railroad. Marshall built his Italianate house, Rose Bank (030-0101), around 1875 to replace an earlier farmhouse which burned. Popularized as an ideal architecture for healthful country life, the Italianate style was a fitting image for the prosperity of Marshall's new town and new commerce.

The so-called Queen Anne style appeared among Fauquier's relatively few Romantic Revival houses. A handful of rural houses were composed of the light domestic elements of the Queen Anne style: projecting polygonal bays and turrets, accentuated gables, shingle siding, porches, and spindle columns. The picturesque qualities of the style relied on the asymmetrical form and broken rooflines. Queen Anne details can be seen on the Curtis house (030-0377) (fig. 54), Walnut Hollow (030-0718) (fig. 55), and, most notably, the gatehouse (fig. 56) at Grafton (030-0712)—once the entry to an exuberant house of the same style that was destroyed by fire in 1903.

FIG. 56. Gatehouse at Grafton (030-0712), photograph. (Courtesy of Archives, VDHR, neg. 4870-3)

Fauquier's Country Life, 1900–1960: Colonial Revival Retreats

In the early twentieth century, trains and automobiles assured Fauquier's easy accessibility from Washington, Baltimore, Philadelphia, and New York. With the center of the hunt country firmly entrenched in Upperville, Fauquier became a popular country retreat. The county saw the largest period of building since the Golden Age in the previous century. Just as that era of prosperity can be defined in architectural terms by the Greek Revival style, the new era of wealth is illustrated by its Colonial Revival architecture.

The Colonial Revival

The Colonial Revival style developed in the early twentieth century as a wave of nationalism and perhaps nostalgia led American architects to revive indigenous American building traditions. A search for a truly national style resulted not in the development of a single new style but in the revival of several historic American styles from the colonial era. Fauquier, which idealized the country-seat landscape of Virginia's tidewater roots, readily embraced the Colonial Revival movement in architecture. Books on early American buildings popularized the elements of Westover, Carter's Grove, Monticello, and particularly Mount Vernon. Fiske Kimball's 1922 book *Domestic Architecture of the American Colonies and of the Early Republic* and Thomas Tileston Waterman and John A. Barrow's *Domestic Colonial Architecture of Tidewater Virginia*, published in 1932, were among the many publications that made familiar the images of early American architecture, especially of colonial New England and early Virginia.

The Colonial Revival tended to borrow from the large and familiar or even mythologized American past. The country houses of this period were stately and convenient, a product of modern architectural training. Colonial Revival houses in plan did not acknowledge the roots of Virginia's settlers in the small, impermanent log dwelling but incorporated a formal, modern plan, with wide halls connecting airy rooms dressed in elements styled after "olde" colonial images. Kitchens and other services were incorporated into the house itself and no longer occupied a separate building. The entertaining spaces of the Colonial Revival house extended to the exterior of the house to include the formally designed landscapes and garden terraces. An emphasis on gardens, in part sparked by the founding of the Garden Club of Virginia, became an important feature in the built environment of these new country seats.

The period of Colonial Revival in the first half of the twentieth century brought the designs of professional architects to Fauquier. William Lawrence Bottomley of New York, one of the country's most celebrated Colonial Revival architects, designed at least four Fauquier County residences. His work often involved major rebuilding or renovations of existing structures, as illustrated most notably at Dakota (030-0300), Clovelly (030-0318), Tirvelda Farm

FIG. 57. Clovelly (030-0318), photograph. (Courtesy of Archives, VDHR, neg. 4388-26A)

(030-0626), Whitehall (030-0542), and Cloverland (030-0768). Bottomley produced designs for at least forty-eight Virginia buildings, many in Richmond. He remarked of his work, "I believe we should do everything possible to preserve this old southern ideal of country-house architecture because it is one of the finest things we have and it is still vital."[14]

Bottomley appropriated familiar colonial elements, including the Mount Vernon portico, probably the most popular element replicated in Colonial Revival America. At Clovelly (030-0318) (fig. 57), Bottomley used a Mount Vernon–type portico on the east elevation, while on the west front elevation of the house, he incorporated an engaged broken pediment surround adapted from the James River plantation house Westover. Like Clovelly, Ardarra (030-0742), designed by George Stout in the Colonial Revival style, sports an engaged broken pediment surround on one side and a double-height Mount Vernon portico on the other (figs. 58 and 59). The Colonial Revival was all-pervasive; even the most vernacular buildings were embellished with adaptations of the style. Over-the-Grass (030-0620), a two-story stone building originally constructed in the nineteenth century, was enlarged in the mid-twentieth century and dressed in a portico like that of Mount Vernon.

Directly inspired by Thomas Jefferson's Monticello, another architect, Wad-

FIG. 58. Ardarra (030-0742), front elevation, photograph. (Courtesy of Archives, VDHR, neg. 5027-23)

FIG. 59. Ardarra (030-0742), rear elevation, photograph. (Courtesy of Archives, VDHR, neg. 5027-24)

dy Butler Wood, designed his own house in Fauquier County, Leeton Forest (030-0308), with an impressive Doric portico (fig. 60). Although he made his reputation in Washington, D.C., Waddy Wood was born and educated in Virginia and returned to the area to design several Fauquier residences, including Belvoir (030-0080) (fig. 61), Ridgelea (030-0084), and the main residence at Blue Ridge Farm (030-0894).

FIG. 60. Leeton Forest (030-0308), photograph. (Courtesy of Archives, VDHR, neg. 4387-3)

Though the Anglo-Palladian version of early America was by far the most pervasive in the Colonial Revival movement, colonial elements of other places and eras, including Dutch and Jacobean, also served as models, as did English country houses. Elway Hall (030-0317), built in 1908, interpreted an English manor house with a medieval feel and eclectic details in a number of styles. Waverly (030-0337) promoted the half-timbered mode of the English manor house revival (fig. 62). Recalling New World precedents, Prospect Hill (030-0926) (fig. 63) revived the earliest extant brick house in the British colonies, Bacon's Castle in Surry County.

Washington businessman H. W. Hilleary celebrated the appeal of the new colonial house on the landscape. His 1920s real estate flyer promised: "This illustrated brochure will convey some idea of the very handsome country homes, the pleasing pastoral scenes, the high grade stock and the inspiring pleasures of the sportsman in the great counties of Fauquier and Loudoun."[15] The same physical characteristics of the region noted by its first surveyors in the seventeenth century remained its most desirable features well into the

FIG. 61. Belvoir (030-0080), photograph. (Courtesy of Archives, VDHR, neg. 4680-31)

FIG. 62. Waverly (030-0337), photograph. (Courtesy of Archives, VDHR, neg. 4392-1)

A Pride of Place

twentieth. Small or large, the country house and the nearby rural landscape have defined Fauquier's taste since the first permanent settlement. That these have been maintained as standards through every phase of economic development and stylistic trend speaks of the relationship of the house to the land and of the people to their rural country homes in Fauquier.

FIG. 63. Prospect Hill (030-0926), photograph. (Courtesy of Archives, VDHR, neg. 5371-32A)

NOTES

1. From "The Discoveries of John Lederer . . ." (1672), quoted in Fairfax Harrison, *Landmarks of Old Prince William* (1924; rept. Berryville, Va., 1964), 26.

2. John K. Gott, *High in Virginia's Piedmont: A History of Marshall (Formerly Salem), Fauquier County, Va.* (Marshall, Va., 1987), 6.

3. *Voyages d'un Français,* 1687, translated in Harrison, *Landmarks,* 180–81.

4. Brother Gottschalk, "Moravian Diaries of Travels through Virginia," *Virginia Magazine of History and Biography* 11:3 (Jan. 1904): 241.

5. The description of the Tilman Weaver house is by Henry I. Hutton, in H. C. Groome, *Fauquier during the Proprietorship* (Richmond, 1927), 130. Hutton stated that the house had two rooms separated by a partition on the lower floor, but he also said that the north chimney had two fireplaces "side by side," which may imply three rooms below originally. Hutton described a frame structure built of hewn sills, plates, studs, and joints. The inclusion of studs suggests that this was a frame building and is contrary to every other passing account of the Weaver house as a log structure.

6. Willis M. Kemper's 1899 description, quoted in T. Triplett Russell, "Country Places in the Northern Virginia Piedmont," manuscript prepared for the Fauquier County Board of Supervisors, 1985, p. 8.

7. For ordinaries and their social role, see Rhys Isaac, *The Transformation of Virginia, 1740–1790* (Chapel Hill, N.C., 1982). Harrison, *Landmarks,* chap. 17, details Fauquier's ordinaries.

8. Marquis de Chastellux, *Voyage dans l'Amerique Septentrionale, 1780–82,* quoted in Harrison, *Landmarks,* 485.

9. *Excursions in North America* (1806), quoted in Harrison, *Landmarks,* 485–86.

10. Fauquier County Land Records, Liber A, folio 267, Warrenton, Va.

11. As quoted in "Fauquier's 200 Years," *Virginia Cavalcade* 9:1 (Summer 1959): 26.

12. According to probate inventories between 1721 and 1730, twenty-seven of thirty-four of Virginia's wealthiest decedents lived in a house with a two-room plan. By the middle of the eighteenth century, the central-passage plan with a more formal facade was taking precedence. Dell Upton, "Vernacular Domestic Architecture in Eighteenth-Century Virginia," in *Common Places: Readings in American Vernacular Architecture,* ed. Dell Upton and John Michael Vlach (Athens, Ga., 1986), 317.

13. Melrose, National Register of Historic Places Inventory Nomination Form (U.S. Department of the Interior: May 10, 1982).

14. John Taylor Boyd Jr., "The Country House and the Developed Landscape: William Lawrence Bottomley Expresses His Point of View about the Relation of the Country House to Its Environment in an Interview," *Arts and Decoration* 31 (Nov. 1929), as cited by Richard Guy Wilson, "Waverly Hill," in Charles E. Brownell et al., *The Making of Virginia Architecture* (Richmond, 1992).

15. *Fauquier County* (Washington, D.C.: H. W. Hilleary & Co., n.d.). Hilleary also noted Fauquier's proximity to rail lines and markets.

The Catalog

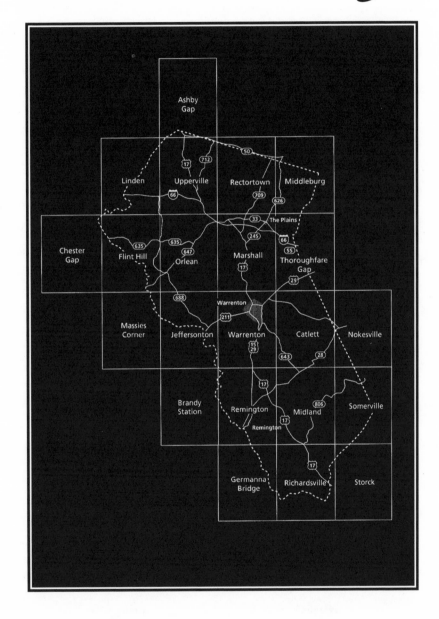

*T*he information found in this catalog of rural residential historic properties in Fauquier County was assembled between 1978 and 1980 as part of a historic architectural survey conducted for the Virginia Historic Landmarks Commission by architectural historian Cynthia A. MacLeod. Additional research and documentation of the properties was prepared by T. Triplett Russell. The catalog includes the following information: property name(s), a Virginia Department of Historic Resources identification number, a location identifier in the form of the U.S. Geological Survey quadrangle map name, the date(s) of construction, and a brief narrative overview discussing the history and architecture of the property. This information has been updated from 1980 in the case of major changes. However, none of the photographs in the catalog was taken after 1980.

Names have been assigned to all of the properties in the catalog. In many cases a property has been known by two or more names. In general and when known, the most common name for the property appears first with former or alternate names listed next in no hierarchical order. If a property is not currently referred to by a name, a name was selected for the property based upon the original owner of the property or the owner of the property at the time that the principal residence on the property was constructed.

Each property holds an identification number; all of the individual properties in Fauquier County share the prefix of 030 and have a suffix which ranges in number from 0003 to 0999. This number refers to the Virginia Department of Historic Resources file in which information on the property is stored.

The catalog is arranged geographically and chronologically. It is first organized geographically according to U.S. Geological Survey quadrangle maps of Fauquier County (arranged from west to east and from north to south). Within each of the quadrangles, the properties are listed in chronological order, based upon their original or most pertinent date of construction, and then alphabetically when two or more properties bear the same date. (Note that the construction dates given in the entry headings and the appendixes are sometimes supplemented within the entries with dates for other additions and alterations.)

Appendix A provides a convenient index of the properties by date of construction, and Appendix B indexes each property by its preferred name. Both appendixes also include the quad name and VDHR file no. for each property, as well as the page number for the property's entry.

Ashby Gap

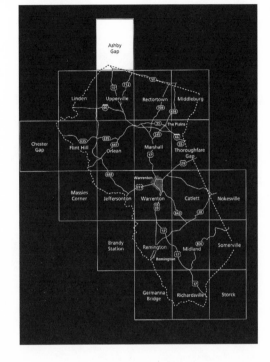

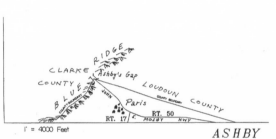

ASHBY

La Grange (030-0200), *Ashby Gap,* ca. 1830. Named for the French estate of the marquis de Lafayette, La Grange stands on a mountainside overlooking the village of Paris. The substantial brick dwelling is said to have been built by Peter Glascock before his death in 1838. The house in its massing and detail presents an excellent local example of the Federal style of architecture.

Linden

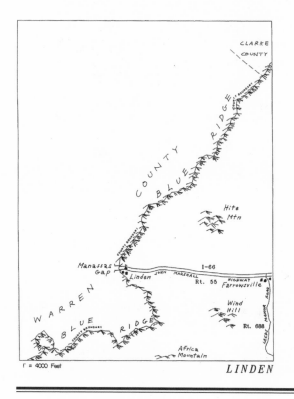

LINDEN

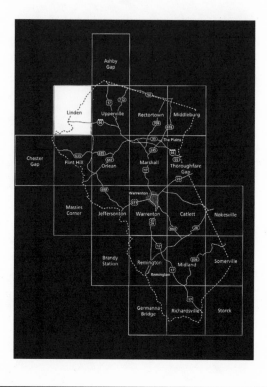

Laurence House (030-0748), *Linden*, ca. 1810. The Laurence house was named for the original builders of the property, either Peter Laurence or Mason Laurence, who leased the land on which the house stands from the Fairfax proprietary. The stone dwelling, built ca. 1810, probably was originally one and one-half stories tall and was raised to its full two-story height in the mid-nineteenth century. Two frame wings have been added to the historic stone house in recent years.

Mountain View (Stribling House) (030-0132),

Linden, ca. 1810; ca. 1850. Located off Route 688, the large frame dwelling known as Mountain View or the Stribling house was originally built in the early nineteenth century but was added onto over the next 100 years. The earliest part of the house is the south parlor and hall of the central-hall house and was built as early as ca. 1810. The stone side hall and parlor addition was made to the modest residence in the mid-nineteenth century. At that time another frame structure was built on the property for Dr. Robert Stribling who used the first floor as his doctor's offices. Local history holds that the upper level of the building was used by the Masonic Lodge, its first meeting place in this area.

Mountain View Log Building (Red Oak Farm Log House) (030-0863), *Linden*, ca. 1820.

This log house, called the Red Oak Farm log house, was built ca. 1820. According to local tradition, this house, along with other now-demolished log buildings in its proximity, was used to house field hands from nearby Mountain View Farm before the Civil War.

Valley View (Gibson House, Linden Goose Creek Farm, The Anchorage, Belle Meade Farm) (030-0836), *Linden*, ca. 1820; 1938.

The large stone section of Valley View was originally built ca. 1820 by William Gibson who owned a mill on nearby Goose Creek. In 1938 the entire house was gutted, remodeled, and added onto on both the front and rear elevations. The imposing double-story projecting portico, which serves as a porte cochere, gives the original vernacular house its current Classical Revival appearance. In addition to the primary residence, there is a tenant house which dates to the original period of construction.

Elmore (030-0751), *Linden*, 1826–27.

Located on Goose Creek, Elmore was built 1826–27 for John Tutt on seventeen acres of land near the old village of Farrowsville. The large two-story frame house was built around an earlier log building which now serves as the living room. Of particular architectural note is the double-story pent closet between the pair of stone and brick end chimneys.

Littleton-Saffell House (030-0746), *Linden,* ca. 1842 [demolished]. The Littleton-Saffell house in Rectortown was built, along with the Littleton Tanyard house, by Richard K. Littleton about 1842. In 1889, when then-owner of the property Thompson Palmer died, he left his house and land to his former "Colored Servants," John Tucker, Alfred Tucker, and Nannie Lawson. The three sold the property to William Saffell. The house was built in phases but unified by a central entry and, at one time, a full-length porch.

Littleton Tanyard House (030-0747), *Linden,* ca. 1842. The Littleton Tanyard house was built along with the Littleton-Saffell house by Richard K. Littleton about 1842. The vernacular stone and frame house possibly was built for the operator of the tanyard on the site. The house is particularly noteworthy for its high stone foundation and frame walls. Since the survey the then-ruinous house has been restored.

Hartland (030-0840), *Linden,* 1850. Hartland was built near Markham for Dr. William Stribling by local architect-builder William Sutton in 1850. The two-story, side-passage stone house was designed in the Greek Revival style and presents an elegant front entry porch with columns supporting a pedimented roof. The original stone kitchen dependency was joined to the main house about 1860; another stone kitchen was then built some distance away from the main house. In 1940 this second kitchen was also joined to the main house by a covered walkway. Several mid- to late nineteenth-century outbuildings survive on the property, including a stone meat house and dairy (located close to the original kitchen), a stone springhouse (in ruins), two barns, and a log structure whose original use is not known. Hartland offers a fine illustration of a mid-nineteenth-century farm complex.

Clifton (030-0923), *Linden,* 1870–90. The main house at Clifton was built as a dwelling but served as a boarding school for boys from the late nineteenth century until 1920. The entire property consists of the main dwelling, a kitchen with a smokehouse attached to it by a covered walk, a schoolhouse, a log dwelling, and several frame sheds. The main dwelling is a large two-story, five-bay frame building with a rear ell, all raised upon a high stone foundation. A bracketed cornice has ornamental incisions in the woodwork. A Mount Vernon–type double-story portico was added across the front and rear elevations which continues the decorative cornice of the main block. The schoolhouse is a square building with a hipped roof and cupola.

Triplett House (030-0105), *Linden,* ca. 1889. The Triplett house, on Route 55, is noteworthy for its elaborate two-story scrollwork porch. The house was constructed ca. 1889 by Theodore M. Triplett and upon his and his wife's death was left to their daughter, Mary Foote Triplett. After her death in 1965, the house and property were sold out of the Triplett family.

Upperville

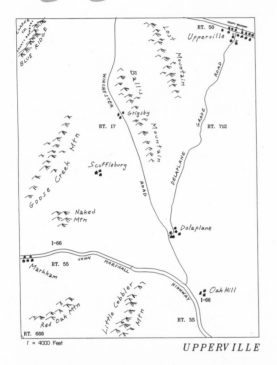

UPPERVILLE

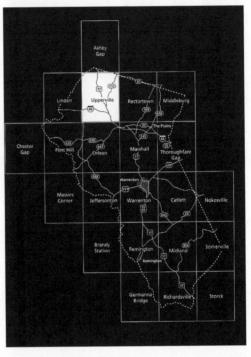

Rose Hill (030-0073), *Upperville*, 1750–70. Located four miles south of Paris, Rose Hill stands on a tract of land granted to Major James Ball in 1731. This house, if erected before the Revolutionary War as thought, would be the second-oldest surviving house in Fauquier County (the oldest being Yew Hill). Rose Hill remains in a remarkably intact and unaltered state. Built by John Rout, a resident active in local affairs, Rose Hill was later the home of Captain Hezekiah Turner, appointed by George Washington in 1777 as paymaster to Colonel Thomas Marshall's regiment. Characteristic of the eighteenth-century vernacular Virginia dwelling, Rose Hill is a one-and-a-half-story frame structure featuring a steeply pitched gable roof, stone end chimneys, and a three-room interior plan. The house is surrounded by an important collection of domestic outbuildings, including a kitchen, office, icehouse, smokehouse, springhouse, dairy, stable, and slave quarters.

Yew Hill (Watt's Ordinary) (030-0060), *Up-perville,* ca. 1760. Located on a 320-acre land grant to Thomas Ashby, Yew Hill was built in the pre-Revolutionary era and served from its earliest years as a private dwelling and ordinary. Yew Hill was operated by Thomas Watts who applied for a license to operate an ordinary in 1753. Yew Hill became known as Watt's Ordinary or simply Watts. In 1758 Benjamin Ashby, the son of the original owner, sold the property to his brother, Robert Ashby. In 1766 Robert Ashby moved to Yew Hill and continued to operate the ordinary established by Watts. In the spring of 1769, George Washington, who had purchased land in the region and was out surveying it, stayed at Yew Hill for nine days. In 1806 the Ashby family sold the property to Edward Shacklett whose daughter Kitty eventually inherited the place. Kitty Shacklett continued to run the ordinary until her death in 1880. In depicting Yew Hill in his book *Travels through Virginia,* Porte Crayon called it "Miss Kitty Shacklett's Quaint Old Fashioned Cottage" (see fig. 12). Yew Hill survived the Civil War years and stands today as an important architectural and cultural resource of Fauquier's historic past. Characteristic of the early vernacular buildings of Virginia, the one-and-a-half-story frame structure is set upon a stone foundation and features a steeply pitched gable roof with two end chimneys. The interior of Yew Hill is divided into three rooms: one long and narrow room with a fireplace on the side wall extends along one side of the house, while the other side is divided into two smaller rooms with corner fireplaces that share a common chimney. Although Yew Hill has been somewhat altered over the years, its original form and configuration remain intact, and the building survives as one of the oldest and most intriguing properties in Fauquier County.

The Hollow (030-0803), *Upperville, 1765.* The Hollow was built in 1765 by Captain Thomas Marshall on a 300-acre tract of land on Goose Creek that Marshall leased from Thomas Ludwell Lee and Richard Henry Lee. Thomas Marshall and his family lived at The Hollow until 1773 when they moved to Oak Hill. The original section of The Hollow consists of a one-and-a-half-story frame dwelling with a gable roof and a stone end chimney. The interior features a hall-parlor plan; the interior wall partitions are sheathed with horizontal beaded paneling fastened with handmade rose-headed nails. A box stair leads to the loft level above. A rear wing with a full second story was added to the original structure in the late nineteenth century.

Oak Hill (030-0044), *Upperville, ca. 1773; 1819.* Oak Hill, near Delaplane, consists of two principal dwellings, from ca. 1773 and 1819, that were joined together by a hyphen. The original Oak Hill was built ca. 1773 by Thomas Marshall, father of Supreme Court justice John Marshall. John Marshall lived at the farm from 1773 to 1785 with his family and eventually inherited the property when his father moved the rest of the family to Kentucky lands given to him for his military service in the Revolutionary War. Although John Marshall primarily lived in Richmond and Washington during his years as a legislator and justice, he maintained an interest in his Oak Hill property, enlarging and improving it and using it as a secondary country residence. In 1819 Marshall built a large Greek Revival temple-form house next to the small frame house built by his father and connected the two with a single-story hyphen. After the death of both John Marshall and his son Thomas Marshall in 1835, the property passed into the hands of Thomas Marshall's son John Marshall II. Financial ruin from overindulgence and generosity forced him to sell the house to his brother Thomas. After Thomas Marshall's death during the Civil War, the Oak Hill property passed out of Marshall family hands. Oak Hill is a Virginia Historic Landmark and is listed on the National Register of Historic Places.

Aspen Dale (030-0007), *Upperville,* ca. 1795; 1907. Located near Markham, Aspen Dale consists of two principal parts dating from the late eighteenth and the early twentieth centuries. The original section may have been built as early as 1795 by Thomas Adams who had inherited the property from his father, John Adams, in 1781. This section of the house is a one-and-a-half-story structure covered with a side-gable roof that features a pair of brick end chimneys. In 1907 a large two-and-a-half-story addition was built to abut the end of the original portion, while a porch erected across the entire front elevation helped to connect the two individual buildings visually.

Locust Grove (Triplett House) (030-0838), *Upperville,* ca. 1800 [main house destroyed]. The original house at Locust Grove was built ca. 1800 but was completely destroyed by fire during the twentieth century. Several nineteenth-century farm buildings are still extant on the property, but they do not appear to have been erected as early as the original house.

Mount Independence (030-0674), *Upperville,* ca. 1800; ca. 1825; ca. 1890. Originally the home of Major John Thomas Chunn, an officer in the Revolution, Mount Independence was built ca. 1800 and was later enlarged and remodeled. The house is on Crooked Run and evolved from a modest one-and-one-half-story dwelling to a large two-story frame and brick farmhouse. The original part of the house is the first floor of the frame center section with a stone chimney. Around 1825 a two-story brick wing was added to the north end of the original house. Toward the end of the nineteenth century, the roofs of the one-and-a-half-story sections were raised to two full stories, making the house a long, six-bay-wide building. A gable was placed on center of the building in an effort to unify the brick and frame facade. In recent years the frame section of the house was removed, and an addition was made to the brick section.

Bollingbrook (Waterloo) (030-0010), *Upperville, ca. 1810; ca. 1854.* When originally built (ca. 1810), this property was named Waterloo. About 1854 then-owner Robert Bolling greatly enlarged the house and changed the name of the property to Bollingbrook. The original house, nearly square in plan, is constructed of brick and features a four-room interior with a fireplace in each of the rooms. The addition made in 1854 more than doubled the original house size, while porches added in 1877 further enlarged the dwelling. Despite all of these additions, the house appears today as one large, unified building with a central block flanked by recessed wings, all covered with a hipped roof. In addition to the main dwelling, the Bollingbrook property contains an impressive array of nineteenth-century outbuildings including a kitchen-laundry, smokehouse, schoolhouse, two stone buildings of undetermined use, and a building now used as a barn but probably originally built as a carriage house. In addition to these and other buildings is an extensive 512-foot barn and cannery designed with classical proportions and massing. Local tradition holds that following a lawsuit over the sale of Bollingbrook in 1859, the purchaser of the property, Gustavus Lesner, boasted that if he won the suit and gained ownership of the property, he would build a pyramid of champagne bottles as high as the top of the barn. Lesner won the suit, but on his way to take possession of the property, he died. Charles R. Harrison of Baltimore bought the property, planted 125 acres in peach trees, and built the cannery that is now part of the large barn on the property.

Edmonds House (Yerby, Simpers's Mill)

(030-0246), *Upperville*, ca. 1810; ca. 1870. Known alternatively as the Edmonds, Yerby, and Simpers's house for several of its owners, this property lay within the original boundaries of Belle Grove (030-0008) and in 1810 was the home of William Edmonds. By 1823 William G. Yerby was leasing 200 acres, including the house, and was running a gristmill on the site. After 1856 the property came into the possession of Henry Simpers, who operated the farm and built a stone mill on the site that was taken down in the 1940s. Simpers remained owner of the property until 1911. During his ownership a large section with a polygonal end tower was added to the original two-story, three-bay farmhouse, significantly increasing the overall size. At the same time a single-story porch was erected to unite the original part of the house to the new section. Northeast of the house is a substantial bank barn measuring approximately 100 by 45 feet, constructed of stone on the lower level and timber frame on the upper level.

Fountain Hill

Fountain Hill (030-0896), *Upperville*, ca. 1810; 1973. The original house at Fountain Hill was built by Joshua Fletcher about 1810. It is an impressive two-story, four-bay stone house, set upon a full basement. The four-bay facade and rear elevation originally had two side-by-side doors on center; these were altered in 1973 when the house was substantially enlarged to the designs of architect William Bland Dew.

Gibraltar

Gibraltar (030-0092), *Upperville*, ca. 1810; ca. 1890. At one time owned by the Marshall family and supposedly named by Chief Justice John Marshall, Gibraltar is actually two individually constructed houses that were later joined together. The oldest part of the house appears to be the two-story, two-bay stone house. Its thick stone walls apparently inspired Justice Marshall to name the place after the Rock of Gibraltar. Shortly thereafter, the one-and-a-half-story, hall-parlor frame house was built perpendicular to the stone house. By the late nineteenth century, both sections of the house had been joined by a stair hall, giving the house its rambling L-shaped plan.

Mount Pleasant (The Meadows) (030-0567),

Upperville, ca. 1810; 1840; 1890. Although the original dwelling now known as The Meadows (formerly Mount Pleasant) and located near Delaplane may have been built as early as 1810, it was enlarged, first ca. 1840 and later by then-owner John Delaplane in 1890, leaving little of the original building intact. The 1840 addition includes the two-story Greek Revival section of the house that now serves as the main block. In 1890 a second floor was added to the first floor of the original house, and a two-story projecting bay was built at the corner of the house. A series of mid-nineteenth-century outbuildings including a kitchen and slave quarters are located in proximity to the main house.

Oakwood (030-0837), *Upperville,* ca. 1810. Built ca.

1810, Oakwood presents an excellent example of an early nineteenth-century farm complex. The primary residence is a substantial two-story farmhouse with a central-hall plan. An exceptionally large stone meat house stands in good condition just behind the main residence. Other stone buildings that formed part of the original farm complex, including a dairy and a springhouse, also survive on the site.

Pleasant Vale (030-0680), *Upperville,* 1810–20. On a

tract of land that was originally part of the James Ball land grant, the house at Pleasant Vale was built around 1810–20 by James Adams whose father, John Adams, had purchased the land in 1770 from Ball's heirs. James Adams lived at Pleasant Vale until he built Spring Valley in the mid-nineteenth century. The house at Pleasant Vale is a typical one-and-a-half-story, hall-parlor house with a steeply pitched gable roof and stone end chimneys. A one-room log structure was built ca. 1830 approximately six feet from the southwest corner of the house and later was joined to the hall-parlor house by a shed-roof hyphen. The front porch of the house dates from the late nineteenth century.

Belle Grove (Settle) (030-0008), *Upperville*, ca. 1812; ca. 1830; 1970s. Built by Isaac Settle ca. 1812, Belle Grove is an elegant two-story Federal brick house. The original and principal block of the house sits upon a raised stone foundation and features a five-bay front elevation. The house has a side-gable roof with a large but shallow chimney built flush with the end walls. The central-passage plan opens onto two front rooms and one large rear room with much of the interior woodwork intact. The one-and-a-half-story wing abutting the main block of the house was added ca. 1830. Additions, including the porch across the smaller wing, were made in the 1970s. Tradition holds that during the Civil War, Colonel John Singleton Mosby's soldiers sought refuge in the low basement of Belle Grove. The house remained in the Settle family for several generations and was once the home of local historian B. Curtis Chappelear.

Rutledge (030-0514), *Upperville*, ca. 1812; 1856. The house known as Rutledge was built in two principal phases. The original part of the house, now the center section, was built ca. 1812 on property then owned by Richard B. Buckner. This house was a typical hall-parlor house with two massive stone end chimneys. At Buckner's death in 1856, the property was inherited by his daughter Ella, who married E. Jaquelin Smith. The couple built the larger two-story, three-bay frame house that is attached at a perpendicular angle on the west end of the original house. At the same time a two-story frame addition was built east of the original house, enclosing it in the center of the new dwelling.

Waverly (Turner Adams House) (030-0057), *Upperville*, ca. 1812; 1851. Originally built ca. 1812, the simple one-and-a-half-story frame house known as Waverly was significantly enlarged by 1851 to reflect the fashionable Greek Revival style. The house was erected on part of the Oak Hill tract that was sold by Colonel Thomas Marshall to Turner Adams in 1803. By 1851 William Curlett had bought the house and property and had local builder William Sutton build the large two-story brick house against the original one-and-a-half-story structure. The front elevation of the house features an elegantly designed porch with fluted Doric columns. The long and narrow windows are topped by delicate lintels having scroll-like ornamentation.

Baird House (030-0675), *Upperville*, ca. 1820; ca. 1880. The Baird house consists of a ca. 1820 log house with several later nineteenth-century additions appended to it. The house is on land that was owned in 1820 by Joseph Carr, the founder of Upperville, who probably built the original portion of the house for an overseer. This was a hall-parlor plan house constructed of log; a mid-nineteenth-century log addition extended the house an additional bay to the north, while a one-and-a-half-story rear wing was placed perpendicular to the dwelling in 1880. In the early twentieth century, the interior was completely remodeled. The house stands in deteriorating condition.

Montana (030-0883), *Upperville*, ca. 1820; ca. 1890. Now in dilapidated condition, the farmhouse at Montana was built in two distinct phases on land owned by Nimrod Farrow ca. 1820. The oldest part of the house at Montana is the one-and-a-half-story frame structure covered with a steeply pitched roof that extends over the front porch. This original house was heated by the central stone chimney on the end elevation. The shed-roof extension and its chimney at the rear of the house were added during the mid-nineteenth century. Then, toward the end of the nineteenth century, a taller two-story frame structure was built against the original house, more than doubling the dwelling's original size.

Wolf's Crag (030-0097), *Upperville*, 1822. Wolf's Crag is a tall and imposing stone structure majestically perched upon a steep escarpment overlooking the village of Markham. The house was built in 1822 on land originally owned by Nimrod Farrow. Wolf's Crag was so named by Turner Ashby, later a Confederate general, who bought the property in 1853 when his mother sold Rosebank, located nearby. Several frame additions have been made to the house since its construction, but the original form and massing remain apparent.

Montmorency (030-0039), *Upperville*, ca. 1825; 1946.
Located near Upperville, Montmorency was built by
John Kerfoot ca. 1825 on land he had purchased from
Charles Landon Carter in 1822. In 1826 John Kerfoot's
son Daniel married Maria Carr of Upperville. Although the couple inherited a house called Greenville
in Clarke County from Kerfoot's father, Maria wanted
to live near her father, Joseph Carr, and was so home-
sick that Daniel Kerfoot exchanged houses with his
brother who had inherited Montmorency. The couple
thus came to live in Fauquier. The two-story Federal
brick Montmorency is covered with a long gable roof
and features a five-bay front elevation and projecting
front porch. In 1946 a new kitchen was built, and the
entire house was renovated. At that time interior cornices and shutters were installed, and paneling was
added in the dining room and along the staircase.

Carrington (030-0017), *Upperville*, 1830. Carrington
was built in 1830 for Edward Carrington Marshall, son
of Chief Justice John Marshall, and his new bride, Rebecca Courtney Peyton Marshall. The house provides
a good example of a Fauquier County farmhouse that
combines vernacular architectural qualities with more
formal classical traditions. The two-story stuccoed
house features Federal massing and symmetry but
lacks the architectural details and refinements generally associated with the style. From 1834 to 1838 Edward
Carrington Marshall served as a delegate from Fauquier County to the Virginia legislature. In 1850 he
sold Carrington to Thomas J. Adams and moved to Innis, one mile north of Markham. Edward Carrington
Marshall was president of the Manassas Gap Railroad
and spent a great deal of his time lobbying for the
completion of the railroad through Fauquier County.

Avoka (Ovoka) (030-0048), *Upperville,* 1830–40. Located near Paris, Avoka stands on part of the land patented by George Carter in 1731. The site was the home of Charles Stevin who had a racetrack for his horses on the level land in front of the present house on the property. In 1768 the property was sold to John Young, and following the Revolutionary War it passed through several hands. In the period 1830–40, then-owner John Rust built the present house at Avoka. The house originally stood as a large two-story, five-bay brick house with a two-story rear ell forming a T-shaped plan. Over the years the house was enlarged to include the one-and-a-half-story wings and the double-story front portico.

Colvin House (030-0763), *Upperville,* 1830–60. The house known as the Colvin house was built in the mid-nineteenth century on land that had originally been part of the large land grant to John Ball. The main house at Colvin Farm is representative of the rural vernacular buildings of Virginia and Fauquier County from the period. It is a two-story, three-bay-wide frame structure with a gable roof and two stone end chimneys. The three-bay symmetrical exterior elevation corresponds with the interior plan: a central passage opens onto flanking rooms with fireplaces on the end wall of both rooms. A stairway along the wall of the central hall leads to two rooms upstairs, similarly having fireplaces. Renovations have significantly altered the integrity of the original house.

Ashland (030-0006), *Upperville,* 1831. Located near Delaplane on land that was originally part of the Landon Carter grant, Ashland is sited with a spectacular view through the Paris gap. The rear wing of Ashland appears to have originally been a ca. 1820 hall-parlor house that was later enlarged to become a central-passage-plan house. In 1831 Dr. James Withers added the Greek Revival temple-form house and connected it to the original house by a short passageway. Windows and door openings have been altered in the twentieth century, along with the addition of the wraparound porch. In 1846 Hezekiah Shacklett, a brother of Kitty Shacklett of Yew Hill, bought the property. It remained in Shacklett family hands until it was sold in 1901. Ashland includes a cohesive complex of outbuildings: a meat house, slave quarters, and kitchen are tightly and symmetrically organized around the main dwelling on the property.

Sky Meadows (Mount Bleak) (030-0283),

Upperville, ca. 1835. Now a house museum at Sky Meadows State Park near Paris, the large two-story stone house known as Mount Bleak was built by Isaac Settle of Belle Grove for one of his sons, Abner Humphrey Settle. Built ca. 1835, the house is a traditional two-story, five-bay stone structure featuring a central-hall plan. Behind the house and in close proximity to it is a series of domestic outbuildings including a frame kitchen and servant quarters. This domestic complex at Sky Meadows State Park is open for tours and provides a living example of life in the early to mid-nineteenth century in rural Virginia.

Belle Grove (Armistead, Woodside) (030-0791),

Upperville, ca. 1836; ca. 1870. Built on land that was once part of the Carter estate and was sold ca. 1836 to John Armistead, Belle Grove consists of two principal parts, initially built in the mid-nineteenth century and added onto ca. 1870. The oldest section is a two-story stone structure covered with a gable roof and featuring a massive stone inside end chimney. The side-passage-plan house has Greek Revival details including cornice returns on the exterior and paneled doors and corner block details on the interior woodwork. The large two-story wing with projecting bay window was added ca. 1870. Also on the property are the original stone springhouse, a stone bank barn, and a kitchen and meat house. Belle Grove survives as a good example of a mid-nineteenth-century agricultural complex with many of its farm buildings still intact.

The Grove (Woodlawn) (030-0053), *Upperville,* 1837; ca. 1960. Originally known as Woodlawn, the Grove was erected ca. 1837 on property historically associated with the family of Revolutionary War veteran Thomas Marshall and his son Chief Justice John Marshall. Although accounts of when and for whom the now altered Federal-style house was built vary, the property was owned by members of the Marshall family until 1873, when Henrietta Randolph Pendleton purchased the 9¾-acre property for her husband, a retired Episcopal minister. Since that time, the property has been known as The Grove, for the grove of oak trees that once surrounded the property but unfortunately succumbed to a blight. The property remained in the Pendleton family until 1944. The house was restored in 1960 but was gutted by fire in 1978. It has since undergone extensive remodeling and has been added onto significantly.

Ashleigh (030-0005), *Upperville,* 1840. Ashleigh is a remarkably elegant Greek Revival–style house which was originally the home of Margaret Marshall, granddaughter of Chief Justice John Marshall. Margaret received a portion of the family's Oak Hill estate and had the house built ca. 1840. Tradition holds that she designed the house herself after traveling through the Deep South where she was inspired by the architecture. The house was built by local builder William Sutton, who erected many of Fauquier County's finest country estates. In 1845 she married John Thomas, and the property remained their home until 1860 when the impending Civil War forced her to sell the property. Her brother and trustee wrote of the sale at the time: "The war coming on, she sold this most valuable estate (her husband, to his credit, never encouraging the sale) to Gray Carroll [a relative] for $25,000. She received $12,000 down and was so confident of our success in the war, as to urge Mr. Carroll to pay the balance in Confederate money which promised six percent." In 1929 Ashleigh was renovated by then-owner Dr. Edmund Horgan, who obtained pine paneling removed from the White House during the Hoover administration and installed it in one of Ashleigh's lower rooms.

Jackson Place (Stonebourne) (030-0678), *Upperville,* ca. 1840. The Jackson house, at the foot of Naked Mountain, is a symmetrically designed two-story, three-bay stone structure covered with a side-gable roof and featuring stone end chimneys. A stuccoed section in the middle of the front elevation of the house indicates the onetime location of a double-story porch.

Seaton Farm (030-0049), *Upperville,* ca. 1840. The Seaton house on Gap Run stands as an example of a typical mid-nineteenth-century Virginia I-house of brick construction. The two-story, three-bay house originally featured a front porch. The kitchen wing that abuts the main house appears also to date from the mid-nineteenth century. Significant alterations, including an interior remodeling, took place during the twentieth century.

Western View (Castle of Hope) (030-0253), *Upperville,* ca. 1840. Western View once was owned by Henry Fielding Marshall who called it Castle of Hope. It is a two-story, two-bay log house raised upon a high stone foundation. The two-story frame wing across the rear of the house was added in the mid-twentieth century.

Marshall Wine House (030-0817), *Upperville*, ca. 1840 [ruins]. The stone ruins atop Red Oak Mountain near Markham are all that remain of Marshall Wine's farm. Edward Carrington Marshall of Carrington probably built the house and barn for Marshall Wine and his family before the Civil War. In 1868 Wine purchased the 147-acre property. Although little remains of the house and related buildings today, the ruins provide a good illustration of a remote mountain farm layout.

Courtney (Buena Vista) (030-0796), *Upperville*, 1840–50. Courtney was built by Henry Thomas Dixon, a resident of Fauquier County who supported the Union during the Civil War. Toward the latter part of the war, Dixon went to Washington and was given the commission of colonel of Federal troops. Shortly following the war, Dixon was killed in a street duel in Alexandria, undoubtedly a result of his Unionist sympathies. The house, built before the war, is a large two-story dwelling covered with a hipped roof and designed in a Greek Revival style. It features a five-bay front elevation with a central entry door surrounded by an early twentieth-century fanlight and sidelights.

The Hill (030-0054), *Upperville*, 1840–60; 1941. Built on part of Landon Carter's enormous Goose Creek tract of land, The Hill consists of a large two-story brick house built between 1840 and 1860 that was significantly enlarged in 1941. The original part of the house is the two-story central section and the first floor of the flanking wings. In 1941 the house was remodeled and enlarged to the designs of architect William Lawrence Bottomley. At this time a second story was added to the wings, and the interior was remodeled.

Holland's Mill (030-0801), *Upperville*, 1840–70. The house known as Holland's Mill consists of three principal parts and began as a miller's house in connection with Holland's Mill. The mill, operated by John Holland on Charles L. Carter's Ridgeville estate, was burned during the Civil War. The original part of the house consists of the low two-story stone structure at the northeast end of the building. A two-story brick addition was built onto the stone house shortly after its erection. After the Civil War a two-story, central-passage-plan house was built perpendicular to the existing buildings.

Spring Valley Farm (030-0679), *Upperville*, 1840–50. Located on a tract of land that was originally part of the James Ball grant above Markham, the house known as Spring Valley was built in the mid-nineteenth century by James Adams who had inherited the land from his father, John Adams of Pleasant Vale. The two-story house was enlarged during the late nineteenth century but still retains its mid-nineteenth-century massing and detail. Several domestic outbuildings, including a stone meat house bearing an inscription that reads "1843" and two log buildings of unknown use, are located on the property.

Jeffries House (030-0759), *Upperville,* 1850. Built in 1850 by John B. Jeffries, the Jeffries house provides a good example of a two-story, two-bay frame dwelling in Fauquier County. Set upon a raised stone foundation, the side-passage house features a massive stone end chimney. A three-story wing was added about 1900 to one end of the original structure.

Apple Manor (030-0807), *Upperville,* ca. 1850; ca. 1910. Built during the mid-nineteenth century and later enlarged, the house at Apple Manor was built at the edge of extensive apple orchards. The frame house with a pair of massive stone end chimneys was erected in sections over a long period of time. The oldest part is probably the one-and-a-half-story front section, while the two-story shed-roof section extended this original house to the rear. The original roofline appears to have been raised, along with the chimney stack.

Highfield (030-0247), *Upperville,* ca. 1850; ca. 1925. High on a small hill close to Route 17, this house is a local landmark that has been noted by travelers on the old Virginia highway from Warrenton to Ashby Gap. Although primarily built ca. 1850, Highfield incorporates part of an older log building into its structure. This original house appears, based upon construction evidence, to have been a one-and-a-half-story, hall-parlor-plan house. The house was raised to two full stories and greatly enlarged to become a three-bay house with a central-passage, double-pile plan. In 1925 a rear wing was added to the house, the interior was refinished, and the windows were altered.

Hill Farmhouse (030-0790), *Upperville*, ca. 1850. The Hill farmhouse is a two-story rubblestone dwelling with massive end chimneys. Originally built in the mid-nineteenth century, it has been extensively altered and added onto over the years. A stone springhouse and some of the barns date from the original period of construction.

Woodside (near Delaplane) (030-0059), *Upperville*, ca. 1850. Woodside is located near Delaplane on part of the tract of land Colonel Thomas Marshall purchased from Thomas Turner in 1773. In 1835 Anne Lewis Marshall, granddaughter of Chief Justice John Marshall, received Woodside as her part of the Oak Hill estate. Although Woodside includes a rear wing of frame construction that dates from the early nineteenth century, the main block of the house was built ca. 1850 for Anne Lewis Marshall Jones and her husband, James Fitzgerald Jones, and their family by local builder William Sutton. They lived at Woodside until 1881 when Colonel Robert Beverley purchased the property for his daughter Rebecca. The two-story house was designed in an elegant local interpretation of the Greek Revival style; it features brick pilasters on either side of the recessed front entry door. Several domestic outbuildings including a log kitchen, a log smokehouse, and several sheds and barns are located near the main dwelling.

Ferguson House (Beverly Place) (030-0677), *Upperville*, 1850–70. Formerly known as the Beverly place, the Ferguson house was built on a branch of Gap Run on the east slope of the Blue Ridge Mountains by James Ferguson. His son, Sydnor G. Ferguson, who was born at the house, was a prominent Methodist minister and one of the youngest of Mosby's Rangers. Local history recounts that as a ranger Sydnor Ferguson single-handedly captured Captain Richard Blazer, who had been chosen by General Philip Sheridan to command a body of Federal troops ordered to "clean out Mosby's Gang." The Ferguson house is an L-shaped house raised upon a high stone foundation. The principal wing features a rather austere three-bay front elevation with little ornamentation save for the central door surround with its Greek key motif. Also on the property is a mid-nineteenth-century drive-through crib barn with two log rooms or pens separated by a pass-through, all under a single gable roof.

Fleetwood Farm (030-0206), *Upperville, 1850–70.*
The house at Fleetwood is located near the stone Fleetwood Mill on Crooked Run and probably was built by Henry Simpers who came to Fauquier County from Maryland to take over operation of the mill. Although Fleetwood has been altered and added onto over the years, the original two-story brick dwelling still manifests an imposing presence. This house was designed in a transitional style, showing a combination of influences from the Fauquier County standards. It presents the characteristic Greek Revival three-bay front elevation located in the gable end with a lunette window piercing the attic level. The overhanging roof with bracketed eaves and the windows set within round-arched recesses and holding long and narrow 2/2 sashes, however, are features more often associated with the later Italianate style of architecture. The frame wing to the rear of the house appears to have been a mid-twentieth-century addition.

John Delaplane House (030-0591), *Upperville,* ca. 1852. The John Delaplane house, built ca. 1852, is one of the focal points of the small hamlet of Delaplane. The village, first known as Piedmont Station, originated as a stop on the Manassas Gap Railway that entered Fauquier in 1852. At the time of the establishment of the station stop, B. C. Shacklett built the general store and warehouse next to the railroad tracks, as well as the house on the hill, fronting the tracks. John Delaplane, who came from Ohio in 1873, purchased the two-story brick Italianate house, along with the warehouse and the general store. He took over the operation of the store, and in 1874 the village was renamed Delaplane in recognition of the merchant. A nineteenth-century stone smokehouse is located at the rear of the main house.

Anderson House (030-0731), *Upperville,* ca. 1854. The Anderson house was originally built by Thomas Anderson, one of four of Mosby's Rangers executed near Front Royal on September 28, 1864. On land inherited from his father, Anderson built a single-room log structure with a stone chimney. In 1854 he expanded his one-room house to include the two-story frame section with a side-hall plan. About 1885 the log portion was raised to two stories, and the entire house was modernized to include a kitchen wing, a projecting bay in the living room, and new window sash.

Elmwood (Elmington) (030-0717), *Upperville,*
1857. Located near Upperville on land purchased by
Robert Singleton in 1847, Elmwood was erected ca.
1857. The large two-story brick house with a typical
central-passage, double-pile plan was renovated and
added onto in the mid-twentieth century. A small
frame outbuilding on the property is traditionally
known to have been used as a school.

Bendermeer (030-0282), *Upperville,* ca. 1860; ca. 1890.
Built ca. 1860, Bendermeer features the two-story,
three-bay I-house form with stone and brick end chimneys. The original central-passage plan has been altered, and the center hall has been eliminated. A two-
story rear wing was added to the main block of the
house in the late nineteenth century. An early nineteenth-century log structure with an end stone chimney may have been the kitchen–slave quarters or
could have been the primary dwelling on the site before the large house was built.

McCarty Home (Old Switchboard House)

(030-0252), *Upperville,* ca. 1868. The McCarty house,
built ca. 1868 in Delaplane, is one of the first houses to
have been built in this small crossroads community.
The house and lot were strategically located near the
depot of the Manassas Gap Railroad and two branches
of the turnpike. In 1872 the original owner, Thomas S.
Wine, sold the property to W. E. Delaplane, after
whom the community took its name.

Gaskins Log House (030-0788), *Upperville,* 1870.
The Gaskins log house is a one-and-a-half-story, one-
room dwelling with later additions. The house is characterized by its large rubblestone chimney.

Sumption-Shacklett House (Shacklett-Hatcher Property) (030-0536), *Upperville*, 1874. The Sumption-Shacklett house is a large two-story, side-passage frame dwelling with a single-story frame wing abutting one end. The house was built in two separate phases during the late nineteenth century and is representative of the vernacular domestic architecture of the region. The house stands in poor condition.

Rose Bank (Rosebank) (030-0101), *Upperville*, ca. 1875. Located near Markham and built ca. 1875, this Italianate-style house occupies the site of an earlier house that probably was built by Colonel Turner Ashby ca. 1812. That first house constructed on the property was the birthplace of Colonel Ashby's son, General Turner Ashby of Confederate fame. Colonel Ashby died in 1834, leaving Rosebank to his wife and family. In 1853 Mrs. Ashby sold Rosebank to Edward C. Marshall, the first president of the Manassas Gap Railroad. Following a destructive fire in the first house in 1863, Marshall built the present house sometime after the Civil War. Although the two-story, two-bay frame house retains a form and massing typical of the Fauquier County farmhouse of the mid- to late nineteenth century, the bracketed cornice and 2/2-light windows are indicative of the Italianate style of architecture that was becoming fashionable in the 1870s in both rural and urban settings.

Bergen (030-0942), *Upperville*, 1890. Located on the western slope of Naked Mountain, near Markham, is the rambling Victorian house called Bergen. The irregular plan, asymmetrical massing, and decorative details, including the bracketed cornice, projecting bays, and double-story porch with spindle columns and scroll-saw details, are all characteristic of the Queen Anne style of architecture.

Greenland Farm (Belmont) (030-0250), *Upperville*, 1890. Off Route 724 across from Pleasant Vale Church stands a tightly knit and cohesive group of buildings forming the small Greenland Farm complex. Originally built in the late eighteenth century as the home of Captain John Ashby, the main house at Greenland has been so significantly altered and enlarged throughout the nineteenth century that it appears today as a late nineteenth-century farmhouse with forms and details typical of rural Victorian design. John Ashby was the son of Robert Ashby who came to Fauquier and built Yew Hill. John Ashby also came to Fauquier and settled on the south side of Goose Creek near what is now Delaplane. In 1770 he moved to Greenland where he died in 1815. John Ashby's son, Colonel Turner Ashby, was the father of Confederate general Turner Ashby, the noted cavalry leader. The two-story frame building is three bays wide and features an intricately sawn front porch, a double-story polygonal bay, and a central gable with fish-scale shingles, all characteristic of Victorian craftsmanship and design. Surrounding the main house is a series of domestic outbuildings that were built at various times throughout the farm complex's use. Of particular note are the stone kitchen and the stone slave quarters, located in close proximity to the house itself.

Fallingbrook (Heronwood) (030-0881), *Upperville*, ca. 1890; 1956; 1988. The land upon which Fallingbrook stands was purchased in 1906 by J. G. Oxnard from the trustees of H. Grafton Dulany Jr. The land was part of Grafton, or no. 6 lot, purchased by Dulany in 1881. When Oxnard bought the sixty acres, the house, valued at $2,000, was known as Seldom Seen. In 1956, under the ownership of Admiral and Mrs. Neill Phillips, the farmhouse was remodeled by architect William N. Bowman of New York, whose idea it was to transform the house into a French provincial villa. More significantly, the design involved the transformation of the overgrown grounds into ornate gardens including a topiary garden with statuary.

Ridgeville (030-0882), *Upperville*, ca. 1890. Located on the site of an early nineteenth-century house and incorporating part of it into its structure, Ridgeville was basically rebuilt ca. 1890. The original Ridgeville was inherited by Charles Landon Carter from his father, the second Landon Carter, at his death in 1801. The present Ridgeville stands in ruinous condition today.

Ivanhoe (030-0789), *Upperville,* ca. 1900. Ivanhoe is located on the site of an earlier house, built ca. 1844, that was also called Ivanhoe. That house was built by Fielding Lewis Marshall and burned down a few years after the Civil War. About 1900 A. J. Singleton built the present Queen Anne house. It has an irregular plan, asymmetrical massing, projecting bays and towers, and wraparound porches that are all characteristic of the Queen Anne style. Certain architectural details such as the pedimented dormers, window moldings, and classical columns supporting the porch are more classically inspired.

Rock Cliff (030-0846), *Upperville,* 1910. Built from the gutted shell of a mid-nineteenth-century dwelling, Rock Cliff was erected by Dr. Wheat, grandson of the owner who built the first house on the site in the mid-nineteenth century. Dr. Wheat gutted the original house, quadrupled its size, and designed the new house in a grandiose Classical Revival temple-form style. A double-story pedimented portico supported by Ionic columns projects from the center of the house and stands out as the character-defining feature of the imposing residence.

Mount Airy (030-0042), *Upperville,* 1911. Built in 1911 by John Baker, Mount Airy is an imposing Georgian Revival stone dwelling. The almost square footprint, the five-bay front elevation, the hipped roof with paired end chimneys, the dormer windows and the window and door treatment, and the central-hall, double-pile plan are all characteristic of the Georgian Revival style of architecture.

Saint Bride's Farm (030-0857), *Upperville, 1916.* Located south of Upperville, Saint Bride's was built in 1916 for Dr. Cary D. Langhorne, a naval doctor from Greenwood, near Charlottesville, who founded a chair in architecture at the University of Virginia. Langhorne hired noted architect Nathan Wyeth to design his large two-and-a-half-story brick house in Fauquier County. The house was designed in an elegant Classical Revival style with careful attention paid to the workmanship of details, such as the engaged pediment around the front entry and the garland swag in the tympanum above. The interior of the house was remodeled in the 1960s by architect Walter Macomber.

Blue Ridge Farm (030-0894), *Upperville, 1935.* The main house at Blue Ridge Farm was built in 1935 for Admiral Cary T. Grayson on land that was originally part of the Landon Carter land grant. The stone house, designed in a neo-Georgian style by Washington, D.C., architect Waddy B. Wood, is built into a hillside so that it rises a full two stories at the rear, while presenting an unassuming single-story facade. The entrance is articulated by a projecting porch supported by paired Doric columns. Also on the property is a one-story stone house from ca. 1815 that was moved to its present location from an adjacent property during the latter part of the twentieth century.

Rectortown

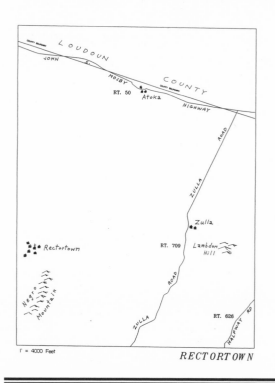

RECTORTOWN

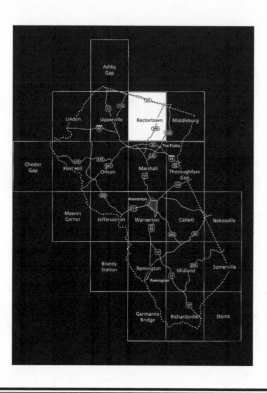

Lynn House (030-0603), *Rectortown*, ca. 1780 [demolished]. The Lynn house, located on a parcel of the property historically known as Over-the-Grass, was a one-room log structure erected in the late eighteenth century. The modest-sized dwelling had been remodeled significantly over the years but was vacant for most of the twentieth century.

Charles Chinn House (030-0780), *Rectortown,* 1780–1840. Located on the same property as the Mill House (Chinn's Mill), the picturesque Chinn house consists of several individual buildings connected together in a progression from small to large. The largest part, the two-story stone section with massive end chimneys and steeply pitched roof with shed-roof dormers, is probably the oldest section and dates to the late eighteenth century. A single-story log structure, originally a kitchen dependency, is connected to this two-story section by a one-and-a-half-story central hyphen; both are later additions. Both the mill and the house were built by Charles Chinn, a prominent Fauquier County citizen of his day.

Fields House (Pearle House) (030-0774), *Rectortown,* 1785; 1840 [demolished]. Until its recent demolition the Fields house had survived as one of the oldest log structures in the county. The house was built in two separate phases. The oldest part was built ca. 1785 by William Pearle for his daughter Margaret, wife of John Fields. It was a one-and-a-half-story log structure with mortise-and-tenon rafters joined at the peak with wooden pegs and an end chimney built of stone. The Fieldses lived on the property and farmed the 100 acres of land that were deeded to them at William Pearle's death. In 1803 the Fieldses sold the property. In 1840 the log house was extended by a two-story log addition (it may have been raised to two stories at a later date) covered with a gable roof. A stone kitchen, set immediately next to the house, at one time was linked to the log house by a covered walk. The interior of the kitchen featured a large fireplace with a huge beam serving as a lintel over the opening.

Maidstone Ordinary (Floweree Tavern)

(030-0036), *Rectortown*, 1790–1810. Maidstone Ordinary is in the small crossroads village of Rectortown, historically known as Maidstone or Maidstone's Ordinary for this former tavern building. The building, now a single-family residence, is one of only a few surviving tavern buildings in the county. The building probably was built by Daniel Floweree ca. 1793, the year he obtained a liquor license to operate a tavern on the site. The oldest part of the building is the stone section, while the two-story log section, covered with weatherboarding, was a slightly later addition. The barroom apparently was located in the basement of the log section and may have been fed directly by a natural spring. The tavern remained in the Floweree family until the late nineteenth century, when it was purchased at auction by A. J. Sampsell. Since then, Maidstone Ordinary has served as a dancing school, telephone exchange, and barbershop, among other things. It is reputed that during the Civil War, Mosby visited the barroom at Maidstone more than once.

Mill House (Chinn's Mill) (030-0650), *Rector-town*, 1790–1820; 1924–29. The Mill House or Chinn's Mill consists of a cohesive group of Federal-period mill buildings integrated with twentieth-century additions sensitively made to create an impressive hunt country estate. Charles Chinn operated a mill on the site as early as 1768, while Leven Powell, the founder of Middleburg, was responsible for the construction of many of the buildings of the complex. The historic property includes the miller's house, the cooper's house and shop, the millowner's house, and what was probably a dairy-smokehouse. During the twentieth century John S. Phipps, son of Henry Phipps, a partner of Andrew Carnegie and founder of the U.S. Steel Corporation, purchased the former mill complex. From 1924 to 1929 Phipps enlarged the millowner's house, renovated several of the outbuildings as guest quarters, and added a stable and swimming pool, tying them harmoniously together with landscaping. The Mill House is a Virginia Historic Landmark and is listed on the National Register of Historic Places.

Green Dale (030-0741), *Rectortown, 1800; 1820; 1920.*
The house at Green Dale consists of three distinct and
separate parts built at three different periods. The oldest part of the house is the one-and-a-half-story log
section that is a single room deep. This log house was
built ca. 1800 and has a later log addition. In 1820 a
two-story brick house with a gable roof and brick end
chimneys was built approximately twenty feet from
the small log structure. The large brick house and the
small log house were connected in 1920 by a two-story
frame section containing a stair. Other alterations
were made at the time the frame hyphen was added.

Jeffries House (Glenmore Tenant House)
(030-0568), *Rectortown,* ca. 1800. Located near Rectortown, the two-story, two-bay dwelling known as the
Jeffries house was built ca. 1800. The house is constructed of logs, covered with stucco, and features elegant interior trim including chair rails and a mantel
with spiral columns.

Mann House (Lake Place) (030-0833), *Rectortown,* ca. 1800. In 1792 George Mann of Loudoun
County began accumulating land west of Rectortown,
and about 1800 he built this two-story stone house directly over a spring. Shortly after the construction of
the main house, a smaller stone kitchen wing was attached to it. In 1979 the house was renovated to the
designs of architect Joseph H. Orendoff.

Millford Mills (Woolf's Mill) (030-0713), *Rectortown*, ca. 1800. Owned by Mr. and Mrs. Paul Mellon at the time of the survey, the once-flourishing Woolf's Mill or Millford Mills on Goose Creek near Rectortown was built ca. 1800 by Caleb Whitacre. The mill was later sold to the McClanahans whose daughter married Frank Woolf, who then operated the mill. The stone millhouse is all that remains of the mill complex. The house was built in two sections: the eastern part of the house consists of a single room with a large fireplace and a loft area above; the western section was built into the bank of a hill and rises a full two stories on the south side. A screen porch across the rear of the eastern side of the house was added during the mid-twentieth century.

Shirland Hall (030-0706), *Rectortown*, ca. 1800; 1833. Shirland Hall consists of two individually built houses that were attached to form one long dwelling. The oldest part of the house is the two-story, three-bay brick section erected ca. 1800. In 1833 the two-story stone section was built against one end wall of the original brick house. A stone with the initials W.F. for William Fletcher and the date 1833 was found on this house but was moved during the renovation of the house in the 1970s. In 1850 another stone addition, recessed slightly from the main block and set at a lower height, extended the overall length of the house to 77 feet. At one time the entire structure was stuccoed and scored to give it a unified appearance. This stucco finish was removed during the 1970s renovation.

Glenmore Cabin (030-0593), *Rectortown*, 1800–1810. Local history says that this log cabin at Glenmore served as the living quarters for the Glascock family as they were building the main house on the property, known as Glenmore. Because the cabin predates the larger Federal-style house on the property, this theory is well substantiated. The cabin—a tall, two-and-a-half-story log building covered with stucco and featuring a stone end chimney—provides a fine example of the vernacular domestic architecture of Fauquier County from the nineteenth century. The stone lean-to and the shed-roof porch are not original to the house.

Western View (030-0571), *Rectortown*, 1800–1810. Western View, off Route 626, was historically part of a 117-acre tract of land patented in 1757 by Simon Miller. The house located on the property was built by the mid-eighteenth century as a typical I-house with a large stone end chimney.

Rosemont (Orange Hill) (030-0652), *Rectortown*, 1801; 1848; 1935; 1977. The original house at Rosemont was a one-room rubblestone dwelling with an accompanying one-room stone kitchen located nearby. A stone on the kitchen bears the date 1801 and the initials R.S. for Reuben Strother, then owner. Andrew Wolf purchased the property in 1848 and erected a two-story, central-hall-plan brick house which he connected to the older house by a frame passage. In 1935 several additions enlarged the house, and in 1977 the interiors were extensively remodeled.

Montrose (030-0518), *Rectortown*, ca. 1805; 1822; 1870. Originally built ca. 1805 by John Fishback, the house at Montrose has been significantly enlarged over the years. The original part of Montrose is the three-bay section of the now four-bay main house. This three-bay section features a central stair hall with rooms opening off it to either side. In 1822 a single-story stone wing was added to one end of the three-bay house. In 1870 this lower wing was raised to a full two stories, creating the four-bay elevation. The house was further extended by a lower two-story wing. The entire house, including the original section and later additions, is constructed of stone and clad with a stucco finish.

Brenton (030-0636), *Rectortown*, 1810. Brenton was originally constructed in the early nineteenth century on land owned by Hugh Chinn, whose family owned and operated a gristmill on Cromwell's Run in the eighteenth century. The stone Brenton was built in 1810 but was significantly altered in 1870. At that time the gambrel roof was added, a one-and-a-half-story stone wing was built to the north of the house, and a porch was erected across the east facade. Although other alterations have occurred since 1870, the building provides an important example of the use of stone and its architectural treatment. The corner quoining and the splayed lintels represent the dying art of stone craftsmanship.

Mount Defiance (030-0775), *Rectortown,* 1810; 1930. The house known as Mount Defiance is located at the intersection of Routes 50 and 709. According to local tradition, this intersection was named Mount Defiance in the 1760s by the Chinn family who lived on the south side of the road in defiance of the Powell family who lived on the north side. Although the house known as Mount Defiance may include part of an older eighteenth-century structure, the existing stone house dates from the early to mid-nineteenth century. Tradition holds that the house once served as a tavern and that what is now the garage was formerly a blacksmith shop. In 1930 a two-story stone wing was added to the main house to accommodate a kitchen-dining area.

Aspen Hill (030-0755), *Rectortown,* ca. 1810. Aspen Hill, located close to the old road between Middleburg and Ashby Gap, historically served as an inn or tavern building. Aspen Hill is an imposing two-story stone building covered with a side-gable roof and visually buttressed by large end chimneys. An immense cooking fireplace is found in the basement of the house, while a meat house occupies a secondary outbuilding. The kitchen and porches were added in the mid-twentieth century.

Murray House (030-0767), *Rectortown,* ca. 1810; 1840–50; ca. 1851. Located in Rectortown, this house has evolved over the years from a small brick building to a substantial dwelling of brick, stone, and frame construction. The three structurally different sections were all covered with stucco to give the house the appearance of being a single unified building. The first known owner of the house was George Mann who built the original one-and-a-half-story brick section of the house. Between 1840 and 1850 a new owner, John Murray, raised the roof of the brick section to two stories and extended the building to the west with a two-story stone addition. The addition significantly enlarged the dwelling and altered it from a hall-parlor house to a five-bay, central-hall house. Around 1851 a frame addition was made to the masonry structure. For fifty years during the twentieth century, the Murray house served as the Rectortown Post Office.

Porter Log House (Weaver Cabin) (030-0639), *Rectortown*, ca. 1810. Located on the Tilman Weaver land grant of 1741, this property is a fascinating complex of early nineteenth-century buildings. The main house, built ca. 1810 and referred to as the Porter log house or the Weaver cabin, is a two-story log structure set upon a raised foundation. The house has a steeply pitched gable roof and is clad with a stucco finish. An early nineteenth-century stone kitchen, a stone springhouse, and a mid-nineteenth-century barn are located behind the house.

Rumsey House (Bishop-Glascock House, Smith House) (030-0668), *Rectortown*, ca. 1810. Located on a tract of land granted to Tilman Weaver in 1741, this house was built by Captain Joseph Smith following his marriage to Weaver's daughter Susannah, who inherited part of the original grant. Built ca. 1810, the modest-sized frame house is set upon a high stone foundation and features stone end chimneys, clad with a stucco finish. A smokehouse, dairy, and two barns survive as nineteenth-century auxiliary buildings to the main dwelling.

Craine House (Middleton) (030-0744), *Rectortown*, 1810–40. The Craine house actually consists of two separate buildings erected at least fifty years apart and owned by John Craine. The older building, set upon a raised stone foundation, is a single-story log structure with a massive stone end chimney. The house appears to have been a single-room structure with a boxed stair leading to a loft above. A two-story frame house was built ca. 1880 immediately next to the log cabin. The two buildings have been connected by a small hyphen.

Glenmore (030-0025), *Rectortown,* 1810–20. Glenmore is an elegant Federal house on Goose Creek near Rectortown. Built 1810–20 by John Glascock, the original central block of the house survives, in plan and detail, as a fine example of the Federal style of architecture in rural Virginia. The property comprises several historic outbuildings, including a meat house, cornhouse, barn, and springhouse. A log building, referred to as the summer kitchen, was moved to the site. The property, with its dwelling and outbuildings, provides an excellent example of an intact mid-nineteenth-century complex of domestic buildings.

Kelvedon (030-0034), *Rectortown,* 1810–50. Kelvedon, located east of Rectortown, was built in the early nineteenth century by William Rector. He received the land from John Rector, founder in 1772 of Maidstone, which was later named Rectortown in his honor. Since its original construction the house has been added onto several times. The oldest part of the house is the two-story, three-bay central section with stone end chimneys. A long one-and-a-half-story wing was added to the west end of the main section in the mid-nineteenth century. In 1920 the west wing was extended further, and a new north wing was added. The interior of the house has been completely remodeled so that none of the original interior details survive. A stone meat house and dairy-springhouse are probably contemporaneous to the original construction.

Palmerstone (030-0601), *Rectortown,* 1813; 1850; 1881; 1930. The name Palmerstone was derived from Edward Palmer Turner, who purchased the property in 1881. The house was originally built in 1813 and was significantly enlarged and altered ca. 1850 and again in 1881. The two-story, three-bay main block of the house dates to ca. 1850, while the mansard roof was added in 1881. In 1930 a Classical Revival front porch replaced a turn-of-the-century entrance porch.

Owen House (030-0667), *Rectortown*, 1815; 1850.
Named for a recent owner, the Owen house was originally built ca. 1815 as a one-and-a-half-story, single-cell
log house. In 1850 the roof was raised to a full two stories, and a two-story frame wing was added, transforming the house into a three-bay, central-passage-
plan house.

Atoka (030-0704), *Rectortown*, 1816; 1930s; 1976. Located on land that was owned throughout most of the
nineteenth century by Joshua Hogue and his heirs, the
house at Atoka consists primarily of a 1930s house
which incorporates a nineteenth-century dwelling into
its structure. Judging from a stone located in the 1930s
addition that bears an inscription date and name, the
original hall-parlor-plan house was built by Joshua
Hogue in 1816, although not necessarily on this site.
None of the original woodwork in the nineteenth-
century section of the house remains intact. In the
1930s the house was greatly expanded by stone additions made by then-owner William C. Langley. The
frame section to the west of the house contains the
present kitchen and was added in 1976 by then-owner
Senator John Warner of Virginia, who sold the house
to Jack Kent Cooke, then-owner of the Washington
Redskins.

Delacarlia (Walnut Grove) (030-0387), *Rectortown*, 1818. Known as Delacarlia or Walnut Grove, this
house was originally built by Dr. Thomas Triplett in
1818. According to local history, he built the house for
his wife so that she could live in the country near the
mountains and perhaps be cured of the tuberculosis
that was plaguing her. Dr. Triplett is known as the
founder of the first sanitorium in Washington, D.C.,
located near the Delacarlia Water Works. Although
the house was renovated in the mid-nineteenth century and again in the twentieth century, its low and horizontal massing and U-shaped plan remain intact. The
one-and-a-half-story stone house, set upon a raised
foundation and built into the hillside, has a three-part
plan consisting of a central block and projecting wings
that form a U-shaped footprint. A covered porch fills
in the area between the two projecting wings. Foundations of symmetrically placed outbuildings are located
to either side of the house. The entire site and house
plan recalls the property known as Huntley in Fairfax
County, also built by Dr. Triplett.

Whitewood (030-0561), *Rectortown*, ca. 1818. Built near The Plains by Isaac Foster ca. 1818, Whitewood is a two-story stone house with a central-hall plan. Already a substantial dwelling, Whitewood was further significantly enlarged in the 1960s. Despite these alterations, Whitewood retains much of its original interior woodwork.

Armistead-Glascock House (030-0700), *Rectortown*, 1820. The Armistead-Glascock house is an early to mid-nineteenth-century hall-parlor house. It was built on land that belonged to John Carter of Sudley by John B. Armistead who married Carter's daughter, Anne Byrd Carter. The house was bought before 1860 by Aquilla Glascock. The main house features a three-bay front elevation, a steeply pitched gable roof with rear catslide and shed extensions, and three massive stone end chimneys. A chimney pent which at one time opened into the interior is now entered from the front porch.

Anderson Farm (030-0606), *Rectortown*, ca. 1820. The Anderson farmhouse, one long building today, actually consists of several distinct sections that were built in separate phases. The oldest section, built ca. 1820 by Henry Priest, is a one-and-a-half-story log structure with a massive stone end chimney. A second building, erected in 1870 as a store, is a one-and-a-half-story, three-bay stone structure with a massive stone end chimney. A single-bay, single-cell stone addition extended the original store along one end, while the other end was connected to the original house by a frame passageway. A frame kitchen, off the stone store section, was built in 1927. A meat house, springhouse, and log corncrib appear to be contemporaneous to the original 1820 frame section of the house.

Balthorpe House (Marly) (030-0769), *Rector-town*, ca. 1820. Originally built ca. 1820, the Balthorpe house is said to have been built by Jeremiah Balthorpe, a Dutchman and brickmaker. Although the interior of the house was destroyed by fire in 1910 and then entirely rebuilt, the exterior walls survived intact and display impressive brick detailing, especially under the eaves and on the parapet. The frame wings and front and rear porches were added about 1950.

Crossroads Farm (Rector House) (030-0705), *Rectortown*, 1820–30. Crossroads Farm is located on Route 50 at Rector's Crossroads, between Middleburg and Upperville. Currently occupying a half-acre lot, this farmhouse sat on 425 acres in the nineteenth century. Its first resident was Caleb Rector, who in 1830 and 1831 bought land described as "the same on which he now lives." During the Civil War, General J. E. B. Stuart and his cavalry brigades camped at these crossroads on several occasions. Caleb Rector himself was a member of the Sixth Regiment Cavalry Brigade, was captured at Yellow Tavern, and died at Point Lookout Prison.

Grasslands (030-0781), *Rectortown*, 1820–50. Although Grasslands has been enlarged by two-story side wings, the original two-and-one-half-story central block remains intact. This house, built by Samuel Tebbs in the mid-nineteenth century, was designed in a late Federal style of architecture. The five-bay front elevation with its central-passage entry is flanked by symmetrically aligned windows. The elliptical fanlight over the central entry is an elegant and refined feature of the period and adds a touch of grace to the otherwise undecorated elevation.

Mount Airy Farm (Robert Morf House)

(030-0209), *Rectortown*, 1820–60. Originally built in the mid-nineteenth century, Mount Airy has been significantly enlarged by the addition of several wings to the house. The original house is the two-story midsection, sandwiched between later additions. This two-story house featured a typical hall-parlor plan and two end chimneys (one of which was removed). All of the one- and two-story appendages to the original house were added in the mid-twentieth century. A stone bank barn, which dates to the period of the original house, is located near the dwelling.

Pleasant Valley

(030-0024), *Rectortown*, 1820–40. Pleasant Valley was built 1820–40 on land bequeathed by Colonel Leven Powell to his widowed daughter, Sarah Powell Chilton, and her children. The house is an imposing two-story, five-bay, center-hall stone house with stone end chimneys. A one-and-a-half-story kitchen immediately next to the main house was raised to two stories in the late nineteenth century and was incorporated into the house as a bedroom. In 1975 a large living room was added to the north of the house, and the interior and exterior of the house were remodeled.

Hale House

(030-0773), *Rectortown*, 1825; 1974. Built primarily in 1974, the Hale house combines two historic houses on either end of its large central block. The oldest section, the stone house, was built in 1825 by Henry D. Hale and was added onto in the 1870s to include a frame section. In 1974 the frame addition was demolished, while the dilapidated stone house was completely rebuilt and connected to a new large brick house. At the same time a log structure was brought from Winchester to the site and appended to the other end of the new house.

Locust Grove (Lake House, Polk-a-Dot Farm) (030-0740), *Rectortown,* 1827; ca. 1840; 1937. The main residence at Locust Grove near Rectortown was built in several distinct phases in the 110-year period from 1827 to 1937. The original builder of the house was Isaac Lake, one of several Lake family members who owned property in the northern part of Fauquier County in the early nineteenth century. The first part of the long house to be constructed was the single-story stone kitchen that now forms part of the north wing of the main house. Shortly after the construction of the kitchen, the larger two-story, central-hall house with large stone end chimneys was built. Before 1840 the main house and the kitchen were joined by a two-story hyphen that stands slightly lower than the main section of the house. In 1937 a new stone kitchen was built and was connected to the original kitchen by a narrow enclosed passageway, also of stone. At that time the entire house was remodeled, and the interior was completely redone.

Stoneleigh (030-0904), *Rectortown,* 1830. Stoneleigh was originally a one-and-a-half-story stone structure that was built by Isaac Gibson in 1830. The name "I Gibson" and the date 1830 are carved on a stone on the east chimney of the house. Toward the end of the nineteenth century, the one-and-half-story house was raised to two stories, and later, in the first decades of the twentieth century, the house was enlarged and renovated. The general massing of the original house remains intact.

Byrnley (030-0013), *Rectortown,* 1830–40. Known as Byrnley since 1923, the property is located near The Plains on a rise overlooking the Little River valley and facing the Bull Run Mountains. Byrnley is said to have been built ca. 1760 by George Byrne but probably more likely was constructed in the mid-nineteenth century and added onto significantly over the years. The house today consists of a central two-story block with a lower two-story wing attached to either end, with smaller one-story wings attached to those. The central block, the oldest part of the house, was originally built as a side-passage-plan house designed in a vernacular Greek Revival manner. A stone wing added in 1939 was designed by Arthur C. Holden of New York.

Tannery Farm (Tan Yard Farm) (030-0660), *Rectortown, 1830–50.* Tannery Farm, referred to as the Tan Yard Farm in deed references, served as a tanning yard during the nineteenth century. Old hides affirming the property's historic use were excavated on the farm in the 1950s. Today, Tannery Farm survives as a compact domestic complex consisting of three individual buildings of either log or stone arranged in an L-shaped plan that encloses a central courtyard area. The oldest building, which dates from the mid-nineteenth century, is the one-and-a-half-story log section with a single dormer window and a stone end chimney. Shortly after its construction, a stone wing was added to the end of the log structure. The stone structure has a frame second floor which may have been a later addition. Another stone wing added to the end of the stone section further lengthened the overall house size. In 1950 a nineteenth-century log building brought from Paris, Virginia, was placed perpendicular to the existing buildings.

Puller House (030-0609), *Rectortown, ca. 1831.* Built by Samuel Puller ca. 1831, the Puller house was sold in 1860 to John R. Crupper. Crupper gave his name to the small late nineteenth-century community known as Cruppertown, which was located at the intersection of Zulla Road and a road leading to Long Branch Church. The Puller house, which was originally built as a one-room stone dwelling and later expanded, is the sole surviving building of what was once Cruppertown. The house occupies an overgrown site and is currently in dilapidated condition.

Eastern View (Salem House) (030-0715), *Rectortown, 1832; 1880s.* Eastern View Farm consists of a two-story farmhouse, a stone bank barn, and a stone outbuilding whose original use is unknown. The house itself comprises two sections. The older section was built in 1832 and consists of a long, four-bay brick building with one central and one end chimney. In the 1880s the house was considerably improved by the addition of a three-bay, central-passage-plan section placed perpendicular to the old house.

Hitt-Halley Place (030-0800), *Rectortown*, 1833. The Hitt-Halley house was built in 1833 by Benjamin Hitt and sold in 1854 by the Hitt heirs to Dr. Samuel Henry Halley. Despite some additions and alterations to the original structure, the main house provides a good example of a Federal dwelling form in Fauquier County. The two-story brick house features a three-bay front elevation and exterior end chimneys. The one-and-a-half-story wing was added onto the original block of the house around 1849. A frame building in the front yard of the main house was built as an office by Dr. Halley after he purchased the property.

West View (030-0893), *Rectortown*, ca. 1835; 1910. West View is located on a tract of land that was granted to Landon Carter, son of Robert "King" Carter, in 1724. The house was built ca. 1835 by owner Daniel Hitt. The property was acquired before the Civil War by Robert Fletcher and at the time of the survey remained in Fletcher family hands. Designed in the Greek Revival style, the nearly square one-and-a-half-story house has the entrance in a wide gable end with pilasters articulating the corners. An elegant entrance porch features paired fluted columns. The double-story portico on the side of the house was added in 1910.

Benvenue (Kincheloe House) (030-0635), *Rectortown*, 1840. Benvenue is an elegant two-story Federal brick house. The exterior of the house presents a symmetrical five-bay front elevation with a central entry. This Federal exterior would normally indicate a central-passage, double-pile plan. The interior, however, is more typical of the Greek Revival style, being divided into a front transverse stair hall and two nearly square reception rooms at the rear. The stair hall is partitioned by two convex curved walls, behind one of which is a spiral stair.

Edgehill (030-0572), *Rectortown*, 1840; 1881; mid-20th century. Originally a one-and-a-half-story log dwelling erected ca. 1840, the house at Edgehill was later extended by a one-and-a-half-story stone wing. A stone in this wing bears the inscription "Ballard 1881." Because the owner's name at the time was John Gregg, it seems likely that Ballard was the builder. During the twentieth century the entire house was raised to two full stories, and half-dormers were built into the roofline. At the same time a lower concrete-block wing was added onto one end of the house.

Glen Welby (030-0914), *Rectortown*, 1840; 1920. The house at Glen Welby consists of a two-story central block flanked by two-story end wings. The central block is the original house that was erected in 1840 by Richard Henry Carter, son of Edward Carter of Meadow Grove, while the end wings date to a 1920 extension of the house. The central block is a typical rural Virginia I-house with a symmetrical three-bay elevation and end chimneys.

Altman-Triplett House (Edge Hill) (030-0605), *Rectortown*, ca. 1840; 1928. The original portion of the now-expanded Altman-Triplett house is a one-and-a-half-story log structure raised upon a high stone foundation that was built into the hillside. This original one-room log structure is sheathed with wide pine boards and covered with a gable roof. The house was almost doubled in size in 1928, and a frame garage was added. The original mid-nineteenth-century springhouse remains on the property.

Chestnut Hill (030-0637), *Rectortown*, ca. 1840. Chestnut Hill is a long two-story log structure with stone end chimneys. The house is actually composed of two parts, including an older side-passage-plan house with a boxed stair leading to the second floor and a single-room addition next to it. Several frame additions were built during the later nineteenth century.

Mount Seclusion (030-0859), *Rectortown*, ca. 1840. Built ca. 1840 by Peter Adams, Mount Seclusion survives as an intact and relatively unaltered example of the Greek Revival style in Fauquier County. Raised upon a high basement, the two-story stone house features a five-bay front elevation with massive end chimneys. The house retains its original central-hall interior plan and woodwork. A front porch with scroll-sawn brackets and balustrade and a screened-in side porch are the major additions and alterations to this well-preserved dwelling.

Kinross (Reid Place) (030-0753), *Rectortown*, 1850; 1964. Built in 1850 by Alfred Reid, Kinross is an imposing two-story Federal brick house. The house was later the home of Major Daniel Cocke Hatcher of the Confederate army. The house sits on a 208-acre estate near Atoka and features a five-bay front elevation with a central entry, a gable roof, and brick inside end chimneys. Jack-arched lintels and a cornice with dentils add subtle refinement to the exterior of the house. In 1964 a one-and-a-half-story wing was added, and the original building was renovated.

Locust Hill (south of Rectortown) (030-0860), *Rectortown,* 1850–80. Known as Locust Hill, this house, located south of Rectortown, was built by Mandley Pierce of Mount Seclusion during the mid-nineteenth century. The original part of the house is the familiar two-story, three-bay house with end chimneys. In the early twentieth century, the house was extended along one end by a two-story, two-bay wing. At the same time the house was ornamented with bargeboard detailing at the cornice line and an elaborately carved porch to give the building greater stature.

Oakley (030-0046), *Rectortown,* 1853–57. Built near Upperville by Richard Henry Dulany in the years just before the Civil War, Oakley is a large and exotic country house designed as an Italian villa. Dulany was the founder of the Upperville Colt and Horse Show, the oldest in the country and the principal center of equestrian activity in Virginia's hunt country. Completed in 1857, Oakley was the site of cavalry skirmishes during the Civil War, and the house was occupied successively by Confederate and Union troops. Oakley is now a Virginia Historic Landmark and is listed on the National Register of Historic Places.

Edgewood (Rockburn Stud Farm) (030-0622), *Rectortown,* 1854–58. Edgewood, located on the site of an earlier house, was built by James E. Murray between 1854 and 1858 and was given the name Edgewood by John T. Moffett who inherited the property in 1884. The property consists of a brick dwelling and a stone kitchen, smokehouse, and dairy-springhouse, all from the mid-nineteenth century. The house is a two-story brick structure designed in a late Federal style. In 1927 John S. Phipps bought the farm and changed its name to Rockburn Stud Farm to distinguish it from his residence known as Rockburn.

Western View (Denton) (030-0570), *Rectortown,* 1857. Built near The Plains by James Hathaway, a merchant of the no longer surviving small village of Landmark, Western View is a substantial brick dwelling. Erected in the years just before the Civil War, it has elements of both the Greek Revival and the Italianate styles of architecture. Local history contends that during the war, James Hathaway hid John Singleton Mosby in his house. When Federal troops searched the house, Mosby managed to escape out a second-floor window and hide unnoticed in a tree. Although the overall plan and massing of the house adhere to the early to mid-nineteenth-century Greek Revival style, the architectural details such as the overhanging hipped roof and the bracketed cornice reflect the influence of the then-popular Italianate style.

Farmington (Whitewood) (030-0573), *Rectortown,* 1858; ca. 1940. Originally built in 1858, the house known historically as Farmington but now known as Whitewood was extensively renovated ca. 1940 to the designs of architect William Lawrence Bottomley. The original house on the property was built by members of the Fishback family on land that had been granted to them in the eighteenth century. The property remained in Fishback hands until the mid-twentieth century, at which time the house was greatly enlarged and renovated. Despite the extensive renovation and the addition of bay windows, entry porches, and more, the general boxlike massing and the central-passage, double-pile plan of the mid-nineteenth-century house remain intact.

Rockburn (030-0214), *Rectortown,* ca. 1867. Located near Rectortown, Rockburn was once part of a 257-acre tract of land that was sold by John Rector to George Glascock in 1771. Glascock built a two-story frame house on the site whose foundation has been incorporated into the garden wall of Rockburn. The current house on the site was completed ca. 1867, to replace a ca. 1828 stone house that burned during the Civil War. During the construction of the new house, the Glascock family moved into a temporary house in the woods near Goose Creek where Colonel John Singleton Mosby recuperated after being shot by a Union sniper at Lakeland, near Atoka. The name of the property, Rockburn, is said to have come from an old method of quarrying stone that involved burning brush over the rock and slaking it with water. The ca. 1867 house was originally built as a one-and-a-half-story stone building that was later raised to a full two stories. Other alterations to the house include joining the detached kitchen to the main house and adding a grandiose two-story portico set upon a high stone base and a large two-story wing, connected to the main dwelling by a curved walkway.

Cloverland (030-0862), *Rectortown,* 1869. Cloverland Farm provides an excellent example of a mid-nineteenth-century farm complex, complete with a primary residence and several intact nineteenth-century associated outbuildings, such as servant quarters, a stone meat house, schoolhouse, icehouse, and remains of a springhouse or dairy. The primary residence, a two-story frame building with an L-shaped footprint that is set upon a raised stone foundation, is a good example of a typical mid- to late nineteenth-century rural farmhouse form.

Heathfield (Beaulieu) (030-0892), *Rectortown,* ca. 1870; 1950s. The original one-room frame farmhouse known as Heathfield and built ca. 1870 was altered beyond recognition in the 1950s. The owner added a fanciful Mediterranean-style guest wing, a corner turret, and a kitchen and dining room to what had been a modest structure.

Utterback-Foster House (Turnby) (030-0608),
Rectortown, ca. 1870; 1950s. The Utterback-Foster house was originally built ca. 1870 as a small, two-room log tenant house. In 1873 Bryant Utterback, who had been living in the house, purchased it from Thomas R. Foster of The Plains, along with seventy-three acres of land. In the 1950s the house was completely renovated and enlarged. The living room and dining room of the present house are the original rooms.

Herringdon House (030-0562), *Rectortown,*
1880–1900. The Herringdon house is a modest Fauquier County farmhouse that has survived fires, bad weather, and several renovations and additions. It appears to date from the late nineteenth century but contains certain interior details and elements from an earlier period. A stone springhouse is the sole surviving outbuilding of this small farm complex.

Maizemoor (030-0669), *Rectortown,* 1883; 1945.
Maizemoor, on Route 691 leading from Rectortown to Marshall, was named by the Whiting family who bought the property in the late nineteenth century. Although historic records indicate that a house existed on the property as early as 1805, the existing house appears to date from the late nineteenth century. This large stone house may have been built as early as 1850 by Jeremiah Balthorpe who owned Maizemoor just before the Civil War, but it was significantly altered or rebuilt in 1883 when the Whiting family bought the property. Again in 1945 the house was altered and enlarged. At that time the original stucco finish was removed, and the cornice and porches were replaced. A two-story wing was also added to the house at that time.

Fairview (030-0754), *Rectortown*, 1888. Built in 1888 by Samuel A. Woolf on land northeast of Rectortown, the house at Fairview replaced an earlier house around which numerous outbuildings once stood, including a mill, servant quarters, a blacksmith shop, meat house, and barn. A log barn currently on the property was brought to the farm from another Woolf property on Goose Creek. The form and details of the existing house at Fairview provide a good example of typical late nineteenth-century farmhouse building trends and techniques. It is a two-story, three-bay frame dwelling with a central gable projecting from the roofline and a single-story porch with scroll-saw brackets extending across the central entry bay of the front elevation.

Grafton (030-0712), *Rectortown,* 1906. Grafton is a large Classical Revival–style house built in 1906 on the site of an earlier house. The property was originally part of the Landon Carter grant of 1731 and upon its division in the nineteenth century was referred to as tract no. 6. In 1884 the tract came into the possession of Henry Grafton Dulany, who built a large Queen Anne–style house, which was destroyed in a fire in 1903. Three years later the present house was erected to replace it. In direct contrast to the exuberance of the Queen Anne style, this house was designed in a symmetrical and balanced Classical Revival style. A gatehouse built at the time of the 1884 house is still standing at the entrance to the property and presents an ornate and picturesque example of its building type and style (see fig. 56).

Ardarra (030-0742), *Rectortown,* 1932. Ardarra is a large Colonial Revival–style house designed by architect George Stout on land that was once part of Charles Burgess's Goose Creek tract. Typical of the mid-twentieth-century Colonial Revival style, the house is a large five-part-plan house with a two-story central pavilion flanked by two-story end wings connected by one-and-a-half-story hyphens. A double-story portico inspired by Mount Vernon and meant to recall the grand architecture of the colonial era extends the full length of the house and faces south.

Cloverland (030-0768), *Rectortown, 1932.* Designed by architect William Lawrence Bottomley in 1932 and built by locally known builder William Hanback, Cloverland is an immense farmhouse having the general form of a rural Palladian villa. The house consists of a two-story central block flanked by lower wings and connected to remote dependencies by walls and arcades. The central block, built of stone, is seven bays wide and is covered with a hipped roof. The central entry is surrounded by an engaged architrave with a classical entablature.

Locust Hill (near Middleburg) (030-0752), *Rectortown, 1934; 1979.* Built for William A. Phillips of New York in 1934, Locust Hill stands as a grandiose example of the twentieth-century Georgian Revival style of architecture as found in Fauquier County. The large brick structure with its central pavilion and wings was designed by New York architect Horatio W. Olcott. In 1979 a rear porch and glazed breakfast room were added to the house to the designs of William Bland Dew of Middleburg. Stables and other supporting farm buildings also were built at that time.

Little Cotland (030-0743), *Rectortown, 1940.* The property known as Little Cotland is on land owned in the early nineteenth century by Colonel George Love, commander of his own company in the Virginia militia. Love is also credited with surveying the county line between Loudoun and Fauquier, as well as the villages of Paris and Upperville. Primarily built in 1940, the house at Little Cotland may incorporate into its structure parts of a pre–Civil War dwelling that was on the site. The original house was destroyed by fire, leaving two stone chimneys which are likely those located on the end elevations of the present house. This house is a large two-story brick structure with lower one-story lateral wings. In addition to the main house, the property consists of several historic outbuildings including a bank barn inscribed with the date 1851 and a mid-nineteenth-century stone smokehouse that now serves as a pool house.

Over-the-Grass (030-0620), *Rectortown,* 1950. Although part of this house may have mid-nineteenth-century materials incorporated into it, the house has been extensively altered and presents a mid-twentieth-century appearance. The oldest part is the two-story stone section with stone end chimneys. A third story and side and rear wings were added to the house in the twentieth century, and the interior layout was reconfigured. In addition, a double-story portico, inspired by Mount Vernon, and bay windows not typical of local building traditions have been added, greatly altering the vernacular qualities of the structure.

Middleburg

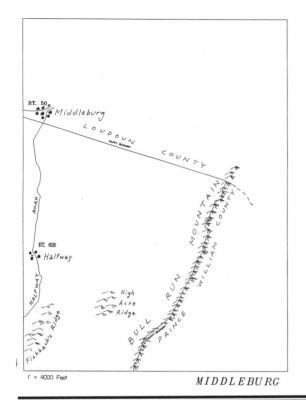

MIDDLEBURG

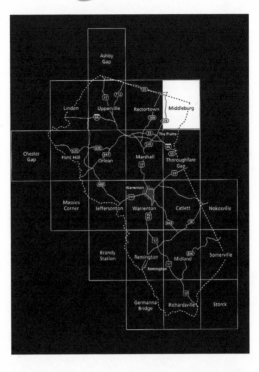

Waverley (030-0226), *Middleburg*, ca. 1790; ca. 1830; 1940s. Located along the scenic Halfway Road connecting Middleburg and The Plains, Waverley proudly presents its imposing double-story portico to the passerby. During the pre–Civil War era, the original eighteenth-century section of the house was significantly enlarged and altered to reflect the changing stylistic trends and tastes of the era and region. The most notable addition, the double-story portico, was designed ca. 1830 in the popular Greek Revival style that added grace and elegance to the vernacular house behind it. In the 1940s Waverley was restored to the designs of Chicago architect David Adler. The property, listed on the Virginia Landmarks Register and the National Register of Historic Places, currently serves as the home of Piedmont Vineyards.

Hatherage (030-0629), *Middleburg, 1790–1810.* Hatherage, built in the late eighteenth to early nineteenth century, was originally the home of John Hathaway, an officer in the Revolutionary War. The original one-and-a-half-story section of the house still stands as the central block. The lower one-story flanking stone wings and the dormers and the porch on the original section were all added in the mid-twentieth century. The interior of the house was also altered during that time.

Springfield (030-0810), *Middleburg, ca. 1805.* The stone center section of Springfield is the original part of the house and dates to the early nineteenth century. Raised upon a high basement, the house stands one and a half stories high and features inside end chimneys. The side wings flanking the central section of the house were added in 1952. At that time other alterations, such as the interior remodeling and the replacement of the dormer windows and the front door, were also made to the house.

Greystone (Rock Hill) (030-0079), *Middleburg,* ca. 1807. Located off Route 626 near Halfway, Greystone was built ca. 1807 by Minor Winn Jr. Winn inherited the property from his father who had significant landholdings in Fauquier County at his death in 1778. Although older buildings may have existed at Greystone, they have since been torn down, leaving the present Greystone house the oldest structure on the property. Greystone is a two-story stone house with a double-story porch across the front elevation that was added during the late nineteenth-century Victorian era.

Glen Ora (030-0078), *Middleburg,* ca. 1810; ca. 1930. Although Glen Ora was substantially enlarged and altered during the twentieth century (ca. 1930), the original part of the house, built ca. 1810, is still clearly visible. The original section of the house is located in the center and consists of a one-and-a-half-story stone building with a stone end chimney. The original hall-parlor plan has been altered, along with the window and door treatments and interior woodwork and trim.

Redman House (030-0547), *Middleburg,* ca. 1810.
This substantial stone house, called the Redman
house, is sited on a high knoll above Burnt Mill Run.
The original part of the house consists of the two-
story, three-bay section with large end chimneys. A
two-story frame wing was added to the east end of
the house later in the nineteenth century. The rather
slender and delicate porch with turned posts contrasts
abruptly with the solid stone walls and was most likely
added to the house toward the end of the nineteenth
century.

Peake House (030-0599), *Middleburg,* 1810–40.
Named for John Peake, the original owner of the land
in 1772, the Peake house consists of two sections. The
oldest part of the house is a single-room log structure
with an enclosed stair leading to the loft level. By 1840
a two-story frame house with a hall-parlor plan was
built immediately next to the log structure. Later the
two houses were connected by a frame hyphen. The
house stands in ruinous condition today.

Fieldmont (Fruit Farm) (030-0630), *Middleburg,*
1817. Fieldmont is located on a tract of land that was
bought in 1774 by William Sanford Pickett and later inherited by his great-grandson, the Reverend John Sanford Pickett. In the 1850s the Reverend Mr. Pickett ran
the Long Branch Female Seminary in an old schoolhouse that is still standing. The property also contains
a large frame and stone house that was built in two
separate phases. The oldest part of the house is the
two-story stone section, originally built as slave/ser-
vant quarters by William S. Pickett in 1817. In 1858
when the ca. 1774 main house burned down, the slave
quarters were converted into the property's primary
residence. In 1914 a large two-story frame addition
with a double-story portico was appended to the stone
house. This addition, designed in a Colonial Revival
style, now appears to be the main block of the house.

Halfway Farm (Haines House) (030-0359), *Middleburg*, ca. 1820. This property, now called Halfway Farm because of its location halfway between The Plains and Middleburg on Route 626, was originally owned by the Haines family and was historically known as the Haines house. The house was built ca. 1820 and has been greatly enlarged and modified over the years. The original two-story stone section with its two end chimneys was extended, making one end chimney a central chimney. The interior plan and exterior window and door openings were altered in the twentieth century.

Creel House (030-0600), *Middleburg*, 1820–60. The Creel house is located in rugged land on the western side of the Bull Run Mountains near the former town of Landmark. Built in the period 1820–60 by John Creel, the house consists of a massive one-and-one-half-story stone structure with a smaller single-story stone addition abutting one end of the building. The main block of the house, featuring a central entry flanked by two windows, most likely consisted of a hall-parlor plan originally but today consists of one large open space. The building has been renovated and currently stands in excellent condition.

Boxwood (Gen. William "Billy" Mitchell House) (030-0091), *Middleburg*, 1826; 1925. Originally containing a small one-and-one-half-story stone farmhouse built by William Swart in 1826, Boxwood evolved to become the gracious 120-acre estate and home of General Billy Mitchell. The foremost advocate of air power as an essential element in the nation's defense, Mitchell had been court-martialed for criticizing the military's disdain of aviation; it was from his Fauquier estate that he continued his work and writing, living here until his death in 1936. Mitchell also took part in foxhunts with neighbors, rode in horse shows, and sold well-trained hunting dogs. Boxwood, L-shaped in overall plan, was built in three distinct sections: the original one-and-a-half-story central block dates from 1826; a two-and-a-half-story northeast wing and ell were added before the Mitchells' ownership of the house; and a two-and-a-half-story southeast wing was added by the Mitchells in 1925. The house, combined with a collection of outbuildings, is an intriguing architectural complex whose association with the nationally significant figure of Billy Mitchell makes it worthy of distinction. Boxwood is a Virginia Historic Landmark, is listed on the National Register of Historic Places, and is recognized as a National Historic Landmark.

Easthill (Finch-Squires House) (030-0595), *Middleburg*, ca. 1840. The house known commonly as Easthill and now consisting of various connected parts was originally built by John Finch who bought the property on which it stands in 1833. Constructed ca. 1840, the oldest part of the Finch house was built as a one-room stone structure. A loft level above the single room possibly was reached by a ladder, as no indications of a stair remain. In 1850 Finch added the two-story frame section to the stone house. In 1951 a two-story stone wing and another frame addition abutting the wing doubled the size of the house. In addition to the house, a rubblestone dairy and a log springhouse, both from the mid-nineteenth century, still stand on the property. With all of its additions, the Finch house provides an excellent local example of how small, one-room dwellings evolved over time to reflect the changing physical and social needs of the residents.

Toll House (030-0624), *Middleburg,* ca. 1840. Originally built as a private residence around 1840, this small house on the road between The Plains and Middleburg became a tollhouse for the Middleburg and Plains Turnpike Company, formed in 1855–56 to grade the road. The house thus assumed the name Toll House.

Garrison House (030-0596), *Middleburg,* 1840–60; 1979. The Garrison house was built by William Garrison on a spur of the Bull Run Mountains known as Mount Garrison. The house, which has grown over the years, includes two mid-nineteenth-century sections and one large late twentieth-century addition. The oldest part of the house is the central portion of the building. This section, raised upon a stone foundation, is a log structure sheathed with weatherboard siding and covered with a steeply pitched gable roof. A two-story frame section with board-and-batten siding was added to the original house ca. 1860. The remainder of the house, which practically doubles the overall size of the first two sections, was built in 1979. The older sections seem to have been remodeled and altered at that time.

Kirkpatrick House (030-0598), *Middleburg,* 1840–60. The Kirkpatrick house was built 1840–60 by William Kirkpatrick Jr. on land inherited from his father's estate. The house is a two-story rubblestone structure. Its original hall-parlor plan has since been altered. The house is covered with a gable roof and has stone end chimneys.

Brady-Downs Cabin (030-0594), *Middleburg,* ca. 1850. The rustic Brady-Downs cabin actually consists of two log cabins connected by a narrow breezeway, often referred to as a dog-trot plan. Similar in form to slave cabins found on neighboring farms, the Brady-Downs cabin may, at one time, have been a dependency of Easthill, adjacent to the cabin.

Crain House (Stonehedge) (030-0809), *Middleburg, 1919.* The Crain house is a rambling structure designed in an English Cotswold cottage tradition and consisting of several parts. Each part is covered with separate and individual roofs with several projecting chimney stacks that make the house appear from a distance to be a clustered hamlet or village, rather than an individual house. The house was designed in 1919 by William Hulbert and actually incorporates two early nineteenth-century log structures built by then-owner James Crain.

High Acre (030-0645), *Middleburg, 1920–30.* The main house at High Acre Farm was built in the mid-twentieth century on a spur of High Acre Ridge. The house was designed with towers and parapet walls reminiscent of a medieval castle. A stone kitchen and a large frame barn are also located on the property.

Tirvelda Farm (High Meadows) (030-0626), *Middleburg, 1931.* Built for Norman de R. Whitehouse in 1931, Tirvelda, formerly called High Meadows, was designed in a Georgian Revival style by New York architect William Lawrence Bottomley. The mid-twentieth-century dwelling is said to have been built on the site of a house occupied by Simon Kenton, celebrated Indian fighter and Kentucky pioneer. Several early nineteenth-century houses on the property have been restored.

Highbury (030-0642), *Middleburg, 1950–70.* Highbury was built by Robert De Lawrence in the period 1950–70 on a spur of the Bull Run Mountains known as Mount Garrison. Although primarily a modern building, the house incorporates a nineteenth-century log building that was moved from its original location about a half mile to the northwest.

Chester Gap

WARREN COUNTY

Chester's Gap

RAPPAHANNOCK COUNTY

1" = 4000 Feet

CHESTER GAP

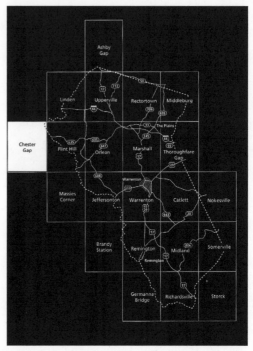

Ashby Gap

Linden   Upperville   Rectortown   Middleburg

Chester Gap

Flint Hill   Orlean   Marshall   Thoroughfare Gap

The Plains

Massies Corner   Jeffersonton   Warrenton   Catlett   Nokesville

Brandy Station   Remington   Midland   Somerville

Germanna Bridge   Richardsville   Storck

Flint Hill

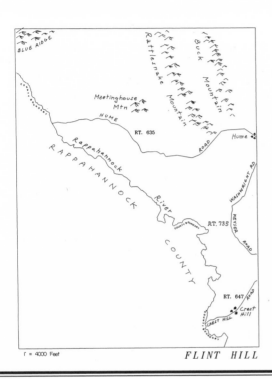

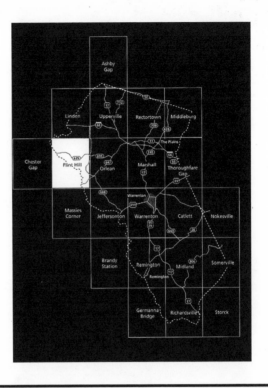

FLINT HILL

ɪ' = 4000 Feet

Barbee's Tavern (030-0685), *Flint Hill*, ca. 1790. Located at Barbee's Crossroads and probably built by Joseph Barbee ca. 1790, Barbee's Tavern is one of the oldest hall-parlor houses in the county. Fauquier County records indicate that Denny Martin Fairfax leased 57 ½ acres of Leeds Manor to Joseph Barbee in 1783 with a clause stating that he "will with all expectation erect and build in the said lot of ground . . . one dwelling house 20 feet long and 16 feet wide with a brick or stone chimney." The house, still standing, is a one-and-a-half-story frame dwelling that originally had a hall-parlor plan. Tradition holds that Joe Barbee operated the building as a tavern in the early nineteenth century.

Fiery Run Miller's House (030-0758), *Flint Hill,* ca. 1820. The Fiery Run Mill and miller's house were built for James Markham Marshall of Fairfield about 1820. The mill remains only as ruins, but the millrace and miller's house survive relatively intact. The miller's house, built into the hillside, was constructed in two phases. The oldest part of the house was built as a one-and-a-half-story, one-room building set upon a high stone foundation. An addition, made ca. 1860, extended the original house and its raised foundation to one end. A shed-roof porch, supported by wood posts, projects from the addition to the house. The Fiery Run miller's house is an excellent surviving example of a now-disappearing building type that was at one time a common feature of Fauquier County's landscape.

Canaan (030-0873), *Flint Hill,* ca. 1830. Thomas Marshall Ambler of Morven was awarded the tract of land known as Canaan from Chief Justice John Marshall as part of a chancery suit but did not gain possession until 1838, after Marshall's death. Set upon a stone foundation, the deteriorating Canaan is a one-and-a-half-story log structure covered with beaded weatherboard siding and featuring large stone end chimneys. The front elevation presents an asymmetrical arrangement of openings: the entrance door, which at one time was sheltered by a small pedimented porch, is set off-center, while windows placed at unequal distances from both the entrance door and the end walls flank the door opening. In 1876 Ambler's will gave this tract to H. B. Kerrick, who maintained ownership until his death in 1894, at which point the property changed hands several times.

Briarpatch (030-0217), *Flint Hill,* ca. 1840. Located in Marshall, this charming cottage was designed over a fifty-year period. Briarpatch actually consists of two individual parts. The oldest section is a single-cell, one-and-a-half-story log structure covered with a gable roof. The loft level is reached by a boxed stair in the southeast corner of the first-floor room. A two-story, hall-parlor-plan house similarly constructed of log was built to abut the small, one-room house at a perpendicular angle. The two wings share a stone chimney that originally served as an end chimney to the one-room house. The log walls of both wings are covered with a stucco finish.

The Dell (030-0917), *Flint Hill,* 1840–60. Built near Fairfield by James Markham Marshall for his daughter Susan and her husband, Dr. Cary Ambler, The Dell is a large two-story brick building with architectural treatment and details characteristic of the Greek Revival style. The house features a three-bay front elevation with a flat wall surface elegantly articulated on the first floor by window openings set within recessed arches and a refined porch projecting from the central entry door. The porch is supported by pairs of Tuscan columns and carries a plain entablature above. The arched window bays and the porch present details from the Greek Revival style and add architectural intrigue to the simple massing of the structure. The Amblers' son, Dr. James Markham Ambler, was assistant surgeon on the Arctic steamer *Jeannette,* which was crushed in ice in 1881. Dr. Ambler remained on board with the wounded, eventually losing his own life. His body was returned to Leeds Cemetery in Fauquier County. The Dell remained in the Ambler family until 1934.

Fairfield (030-0696), *Flint Hill,* 1840–50. The land on which Fairfield was built was originally part of Lord Fairfax's personal estate known as Leeds Manor. The Fairfield tract was later sold to John and James Markham Marshall and Raleigh Colston and eventually came into the sole ownership of James Markham Marshall. Having given his home Happy Creek in Warren County to his eldest son, James Markham Marshall then built his personal residence at Fairfield in 1812. When the house was rebuilt in 1840–50, it was designed in a transitional Greek Revival–Italianate style that combines form and details from the two styles. The original part of the house, the main block, is a two-story brick structure with a square footprint. While the flat front elevation and the flat lintels with corner blocks recall the earlier Greek Revival style, the overhanging roof with the exposed rafter ends is more characteristic of the mid-nineteenth-century Italianate style. In 1890 a two-story end pavilion was connected to the main block by a lower two-story hyphen. Both the pavilion and the connecting hyphen were designed in sympathy to the main block of the house, having similar details and features. Fairfield has been home to several notorious souls including Robert Ford who shot Jesse James.

Mount Welby Farm (030-0183), *Flint Hill,* ca. 1850. Built on the western slope of Rattlesnake Mountain near Hitch, the house known as Mount Welby is an imposing two-story frame house built ca. 1850 and featuring characteristics of the Greek Revival style. The house stands upon a raised basement, is covered with a low-hipped roof, and features a front porch with coupled and fluted columns. The house has since undergone renovation.

Cleaveland (030-0874), *Flint Hill,* 1850–70. Standing in deteriorating condition, Cleaveland survives as a good example of a large two-story, double-pile farmhouse from the mid- to late nineteenth century. The imposing frame building is set upon a stone foundation and features perfectly symmetrical five-bay front and rear elevations. Pairs of stone end chimneys flank both ends of the dwelling, while a low-hipped roof is supported by wooden brackets. The building's symmetrical massing combined with ornate details, such as the brackets, indicates the transition from the Greek Revival to the Italianate style of architecture.

John Downing Farm (Cold Hill) (030-0687), *Flint Hill,* 1857 [destroyed]. At the time of the survey, the ruins of the John Hitch Downing mansion, built in 1857, were located near Chester's Gap in the foothills of the Blue Ridge Mountains. A stone meat house, standing northwest of the ruins, was at that time the sole surviving intact structure from the mid-nineteenth-century farm complex.

Anderson-Green House (030-0280), *Flint Hill,* ca. 1867 [demolished]. The Anderson-Green house, which stood in ruinous condition at the time of the survey, was built in two sections, a log section and a frame addition. The log section, with its square-notched corners and stone chimney, formed the original core, while a frame addition extended the house's overall length.

Clairemont (030-0726), *Flint Hill,* 1870–80. Located on land that was originally part of the Marshall family holdings, Clairemont is a large two-story frame dwelling built in the late nineteenth century. The house is raised upon a stone foundation, is covered with a hipped roof, and features a three-bay front elevation and interior end chimneys. The interior of the house has a central-passage, double-pile plan.

Houynhym Farm (David Carper House) (030-0278), *Flint Hill,* 1877. The property including Houynhym Farm in the eighteenth century was located in the Manor of Leeds and was later purchased by John Marshall et al. In 1877 an overseer of 5,000 acres of Leeds Manor purchased 378 acres on which he built this house and its associated outbuildings. Though added onto over the years and completely remodeled on the interior in the 1960s, the house has a typical Virginia I-house form and features Italianate detailing. The smokehouse, of log construction with square-notched corners, has been converted into a doghouse.

The Cove Tenant House (030-0756), *Flint Hill, 1880–1910.* The Cove tenant house is a two-story frame dwelling that is representative of the late nineteenth-century vernacular domestic buildings of rural Virginia. The house form, called an I-house, features a three-bay front elevation and a single-pile, central-passage plan. Earlier examples of the I-house form feature brick or stone end chimneys; here the end chimneys have been replaced by a central wood-burning stove, and windows are located on the end elevations. The one-and-a-half-story wing at the rear of the house predates the main section and is similarly representative of the area's vernacular architecture of the period.

The Cove (030-0757), *Flint Hill, 1885.* Named for its location in a natural cove between Oven Top and Buck Mountains, The Cove is a large house designed in the exuberant and elegant Queen Anne style of architecture. Characteristic of the style, the house features an irregular plan and roofline, asymmetrical massing and fenestration, and an eclectic display of projecting towers, gables, and bays, wraparound porches, and decorative wall treatments. Most of the wood used in the construction of the house was cut, dried, and sawed on the farm, while the detailed millwork probably was executed off the property.

Orlean

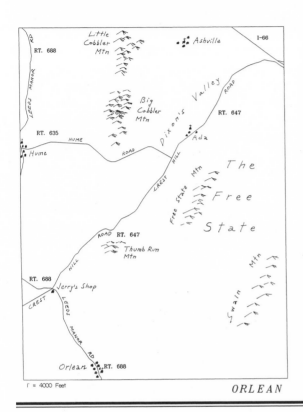

1' = 4000 Feet

ORLEAN

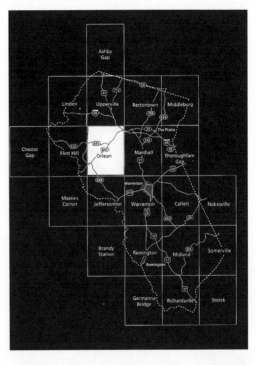

Ball House (Eric Sevareid House) (030-0243),
Orlean, 1807. The Ball-Sevareid house probably was
built in 1807 by Benjamin Ball the younger on land his
father leased in Leeds Manor. In the early 1980s at the
time of the survey, the house was being used as a
shooting box by the well-known news commentator
Eric Sevareid. The one-and-a-half-story frame structure sits upon a stone foundation and is covered with a
steeply pitched gable roof with a pair of massive stone
end chimneys on one end, a single stone chimney on
the other end, and a porch extending across the front
elevation. The house contains two rooms on the
ground floor, accessed by two individual doors, but
may originally have been a single-room house that
was extended to two rooms in the later nineteenth
century.

Hunterleigh (Moreland, Turner House)

(030-0658), *Orlean*, 1810; 1850. In 1810 the land on which Hunterleigh stands was owned by James Keith Marshall and was known as Moreland. At that time Marshall built a one-and-a-half-story frame house that forms one wing of the expansive house today. In 1850 James T. Turner built a two-story, three-bay, hall-parlor stone house twenty-five feet south of the original house and connected the two by a single-story frame wing. Another wing south of this section, added in 1968, extended the house to its current five-bay width. Also located on the property is an early nineteenth-century bank barn. The property was given the name Hunterleigh in the twentieth century.

Orlean Farm

Orlean Farm (030-0086), *Orlean*, 1812; ca. 1850. Orlean Farm is located on land in Leeds Manor that appears to have originally been part of a 588-acre tract granted to John Winn Smith by Denny Martin Fairfax. Smith and his eldest son, John Puller Smith, moved to Fauquier from Fredericksburg in 1795. John Puller Smith, a merchant, became a magistrate of Fauquier County and by 1812 had built the house at Orlean Farm, which was later added onto and enlarged. The oldest section of the house appears to be the frame part; this was probably a one-and-a-half-story structure that was later raised to two stories. In the mid-nineteenth century the stone wing was added to the frame structure, and the interior arrangement of rooms was reorganized. Minor renovation work on the house took place during the twentieth century.

Morven (030-0864), *Orlean,* ca. 1819; 1835; 1950. The long and rambling plan of Morven is the result of several building campaigns that began in 1819 and continued to the mid-twentieth century. Located on land deeded by John and James Markham Marshall to their brother-in-law John Ambler, the original part of Morven was built ca. 1819 and apparently was named for a Scottish song, "The Windy Hills of Morven." The original part of the house is a single-story frame structure with a central chimney projecting from the long gable roof. Shortly after 1820 a second house, of stone, was constructed about thirty feet north of the original dwelling. The floor plans of both of these dwellings were similar, offering two rooms on either side of a central fireplace. About 1835 a third house, with a pedimented portico (*shown*), was built between the two detached dwellings and was connected at a right angle to them. In plan, these three buildings formed the three sides of an open court. In 1950 this courtyard was filled with new construction designed by architect Washington Reed, including space for a dining room and kitchen.

George W. Shacklett House (Myers House)

(030-0657), *Orlean,* ca. 1819; ca. 1830. The log house known as the George W. Shacklett house for its original builder was built in two separate phases. The oldest part of the house, from ca. 1819, is the one-and-a-half-story, one-room section raised upon a rubblestone foundation. The original stone end chimney was replaced by a concrete-block chimney during the twentieth century. The two-story, two-bay section, also of log, was built against the end wall of the one-room house ca. 1830. A porch was added to this section of the house in the late nineteenth century. Both sections of the log structure are covered with weatherboard siding. The Shacklett house survives as a good example of a mid-nineteenth-century log structure that evolved from a one-room house.

Cobbler Mountain (Mont Blanc) (030-0653), *Orlean*, 1820 [destroyed]. The original house on the property known alternatively as Cobbler Mountain or Mont Blanc was built by John Marshall for one of his sons in 1820. That house was destroyed by fire, though several of the original outbuildings from the estate survived into the 1930s. An estate office was enlarged and converted into a single-family dwelling after the main house burned down. As built, the office was designed in a Greek Revival style with a front gable; its remodeling also used Greek Revival detailing. The dwelling, approximately seven miles south of Delaplane on Route 720, has been demolished since the time of the survey.

Bleak House (030-0191), *Orlean*, ca. 1820; 1853 [demolished]. Originally a modest one-and-a-half-story, hall-parlor-plan house built ca. 1820, Bleak House was extended in the early to mid-nineteenth century by the addition of two rooms. In 1853 the house and its addition were completely encased by a two-story frame structure with Greek Revival details that was erected as a screen to the modest house behind it. An elegant Doric entrance porch was recessed into one side of the front elevation and crowned with a high Doric entablature. The original columns are shown in figure 49. Three of the four elevations of the house had a wide frieze with a Greek fret motif, broken by grilled vents over the window and protected by a projecting cornice.

Glanville (030-0210), *Orlean*, ca. 1820; ca. 1900. Sited high upon a hill near Marshall, Glanville is a large stone antebellum house that has been enlarged since its original construction. Probably built ca. 1820 by Benjamin Harrison who owned the land at that time, the house was designed as a traditional side-passage-plan house. About 1900 a two-story frame addition with a stone veneer on the facade was added to the original house, which was also renovated.

Manor Farm (030-0649), *Orlean*, ca. 1820; 1950; 1970. The property known as Manor Farm incorporates both nineteenth- and twentieth-century constructions. Originally the property consisted of two log buildings: a log dwelling and a log kitchen located approximately twenty feet from the house. In 1950 the house was renovated for use as a hunting lodge, and the interior plan of the house was altered. In 1970 the log kitchen was attached to the log house by a low single-story frame hyphen. Other additions, including a two-story frame wing and a single-story frame shed-roof wing, have been appended to the original log dwelling.

Angelica (Joseph Lawler House) (030-0240), *Orlean*, 1826; 1929. The land on which the Lawler house was built was originally leased to Nicholas Lawler in 1793 and was occupied by the Lawler family for seven generations. The existing house was built by Joseph Lawler in 1826 and added onto significantly in 1929. The original portion of the house consists of a one-and-a-half-story log building set upon a stone foundation and sheathed with weatherboarding. The interior features a hall-parlor plan with a boxed stair.

Edgeworth (030-0216), *Orlean*, 1828. Edgeworth, near Orlean, was the home of Lieutenant John Marshall, son of James Markham Marshall and known as "Navy John" because of his early naval career. Navy John purchased the ninety-acre tract of land on Thumb Run from Burgess Hitch who had been living in a pre-Revolutionary log dwelling on the site. The main house is a large stone dwelling. At its rear, now serving as the kitchen and study wing to the main house, is the late eighteenth-century log structure originally built as a hall-parlor-plan house. In 1828 "Navy John" added the two-story stone dwelling in front of the log building and connected them by a single-room hyphen. Wings were added to the principal block in the 1920s. A double-story porch that extends across the central three bays of the house replaced an earlier unassuming single-story porch that projected in front of the central entry door.

Thorpe House (030-0737), *Orlean*, 1830. Located off Route 647 near a branch of Carter's Run, the house known as the Thorpe house probably was built originally as a dependency to Eastwood, located nearby. The small and deteriorated building consists of a log wing, built ca. 1830, and a frame wing, added ca. 1900. The log section has a side-hall plan and stands one and a half stories tall. The two-story frame wing abuts the rear of the original log structure, giving the house an L-shaped plan today.

Holly Hill (Strother House, Orchard Grove) (030-0797), *Orlean*, ca. 1830. Holly Hill, the Strother house, or Orchard Grove, as this house is alternatively called, was built ca. 1830 by Hedgeman F. Strother on land he inherited from his father's estate. The oldest part of the house is the two-story, two-bay frame (possibly log) section with substantial stone end chimneys. Attached to the main house is a single-story stone wing which originally served as the detached kitchen. A large three-bay front porch was added to the house in the later nineteenth century, while further additions were made during the twentieth century. Despite the loss of surrounding outbuildings and the alterations to the original house, Holly Hill survives as an excellent example of a mid-nineteenth-century two-story, two-bay dwelling, which was at one time a common building form in the area.

Jett House (030-0825), *Orlean*, ca. 1830. Built by William Jett ca. 1830, the Jett house is a two-story log dwelling with stone end chimneys. A single-story frame addition abuts one end of the original section. The interior of the log house was completely remodeled in 1965, and all of the original trim was removed.

Leeds Manor (030-0219), *Orlean*, ca. 1830. According to local tradition, the main house at Leeds Manor—Lord Fairfax's personal estate—was built ca. 1740. As it currently stands, however, it appears to have been entirely rebuilt during the second quarter of the nineteenth century. The story follows that Lord Fairfax came to live on his remote Virginia estate in the mid-eighteenth century, having been disappointed in love in England. The estate was later acquired by John Marshall from Fairfax heirs and was deeded to his son James Keith Marshall, who in 1829 built a two-story stone house. In 1833 a single-story stone addition was built for the chief justice about twelve feet northwest of this house. Around 1850 the two buildings were joined together by a two-story entrance tower. A kitchen and other service rooms were added to the rear of the house ca. 1900.

Payne House (near Marshall) (030-0507), *Orlean*, ca. 1830. The Payne house was built ca. 1830 by Thomas Withers Payne at the head of Poorhouse Branch of South Run. Originally the house stood as a two-bay, hall-parlor log structure with a stone end chimney on each end. Shortly after its construction the house was enlarged by the addition of another log room with a loft above, abutting the end of the original house. The addition similarly included a stone end chimney, giving the house a total of three stone chimneys. The house stands in ruinous condition today but provides an excellent example of log construction in rural Virginia.

Riley House (030-0241), *Orlean*, ca. 1830. The original section of the Riley house is the one-and-a-half-story log structure with a steeply pitched roof and stone end chimneys. Unlike the one-room Riley cabin (030-0242) nearby, the interior of the Riley house features the slightly more private hall-parlor layout. In the mid-nineteenth century a two-story frame ell was added to the rear elevation of the log structure. Although still a fine example of a mid-nineteenth-century log house, the building stands in ruinous condition.

Westwood (030-0555), *Orlean,* ca. 1835. The house at Westwood was remodeled and rebuilt around 1979 but incorporated part of the original structure into the new building. The house was built ca. 1835 by Thomas C. Maddux, son of Thomas Maddux, former innkeeper in Warrenton, and consists of a two-story, two-bay stone section with a stone end chimney. In addition to incorporating the stone section into the new house, another stone chimney, which was built against a log addition to the original stone structure, was similarly retained, while the log construction itself was demolished. The two-story frame wings abutting the stone house were built during the 1979 remodeling.

County Poorhouse (030-0505), *Orlean,* 1840. Fauquier County's poorhouse was started in the mid-nineteenth century and continued to serve the indigent residents until the 1920s. The site currently consists of the poorhouse manager's residence and the only surviving pauper house. The latter building is a frame structure that measures 45 by 45 feet and was built ca. 1900. It was one of two similar poorhouses on the property and is said to have housed African Americans. These two structures are said to have replaced mid-nineteenth-century log buildings. The original section of the manager's house is the two-story, three-bay section with exterior end chimneys.

Adams-Gibson Farm (Fox Hollow) (030-0655), *Orlean,* ca. 1840. The Adams-Gibson house was built ca. 1840 on land belonging to Edward Carrington Marshall by Marshall's tenant, John F. Adams, who later bought the property. This one-and-a-half-story stone house with large inside end chimneys features a three-bay front elevation and a central-passage plan. The house is set upon a high basement that until recently retained its dirt floor.

Eastwood (Valley Dale Farm) (030-0709), *Orlean*, ca. 1840; ca. 1875. The existing house at Eastwood was built in the mid-nineteenth century on the site of the original eighteenth-century house, which was destroyed by fire in 1833. The rebuilt house was erected in two phases following the conflagration. The oldest section consists of a one-and-one-half-story frame wing with dormer windows, while the newer section, built ca. 1875, stands a full two stories tall and presents the typical three-bay elevation with end chimneys and central-passage plan. The late nineteenth-century addition was built to abut the end of the older section, giving the house its L-shaped footprint today. A single-story screened-in porch is located along the rear elevation of the older section of the house.

Grafton (030-0579), *Orlean*, ca. 1840; 1850; 1905. Originally built ca. 1840 as a simple two-story side-passage-plan house, Grafton was greatly enlarged in 1850 and then again in 1905. Tradition holds that Samuel Bayley, owner of the property during the Civil War, escaped from a Union search party at Grafton by dropping from a second-story window into a huge boxwood bush below. Although the boxwood no longer survives, the original section of the house does; it has a three-bay front elevation whose side-passage entry is protected by an elegant Greek Revival porch. In 1850 an addition was constructed at the rear of the house that practically doubled the size of the original structure. In 1905 the original section of the house was extended an additional three bays along one end. Although these additions have altered the original configuration and massing of the dwelling, many of the details were designed in sympathy to the existing Greek Revival stylistic tendencies.

Hirst Place (030-0876), *Orlean*, ca. 1840; 1880; 1970. The Hirst place was originally built ca. 1840 by Thomas Mason Hirst on land inherited from his father-in-law, Withers Payne, who was the original grantee of the land. The original two-story, three-bay stone structure was enlarged in 1880 by the addition of a frame wing at the rear. In 1970 the entire house was gutted. At this time the original plan was modified, and the double-story portico was added on the front elevation.

Mount Jett (Mount Marshall) (030-0819),
Orlean, ca. 1840. Located on a high hill across Dixon Valley from Cobbler Mountain stands Mount Jett, home of Marshall Jett in the nineteenth century. The two-story frame dwelling is representative of the mid-nineteenth-century rural vernacular architecture of Virginia.

Mountjoy Farm (030-0684), *Orlean,* ca. 1840; ca.
1890; ca. 1915. Built on Carter's Run near Marshall, the oldest part of Mountjoy Farm is the two-story stone section of the house, built ca. 1840. About 1890, a taller two-story wing was built perpendicular to the stone structure, doubling the size of the house. This wing features Victorian details such as the scroll-saw barge-board in the gable end and the bracketed wood cornice. Another wing, extending from the other end of the stone structure, was added ca. 1915.

Sands Log House (030-0875), *Orlean,* ca. 1840. This
log house, along with its associated buildings, is on the south side of Route 635, west of Route 730, in the middle of an open field. The domestic complex at one time included a meat house, shed, springhouse, and barn. The barn is all that remains of the auxiliary structures today.

Silver Spring Farm (030-0556), *Orlean,* ca. 1840.
Built by Thomas Thornton Withers ca. 1840, the small-scale house known as Silver Spring provides a good example of a mid-nineteenth-century hall-parlor house. Of frame construction, covered with stucco, it features two stone end chimneys and a steep catslide roof. A frame meat house with a pyramidal roof with a wood finial still survives behind the main residence.

German House (030-0506), *Orlean*, 1840–60. Located at the head of Poorhouse Branch of South Run, the German house survives as an intact and relatively unaltered example of a mid-nineteenth-century hall-parlor-plan house. Built between 1840 and 1860 and named for then-resident William German, it is of log construction and features massive stone end chimneys. The interior is divided into two rooms—the hall and the parlor—by an enclosed staircase at the center leading to the loft level. The center-stair plan is one of a few in the area. The lower wing attached to one end of the building serves as the kitchen and was added in the early to mid-twentieth century.

Payne House (030-0735), *Orlean*, 1840–50. This house is another home built by the Payne family on the large tract of land originally leased by William Payne of King George County ca. 1775. This portion of the land fell to Berryman Payne, who in the period 1840–50 built the present house on the site. Originally constructed as a typical hall-parlor-plan house, the dwelling was significantly expanded and added onto in both the nineteenth and twentieth centuries.

Vernon Mills (030-0799), *Orlean*, 1840–60. Built facing Thumb Run near ruins of the old mill, the house known as Vernon Mills is a well-executed example of the two-story, three-bay frame farmhouse that is representative of the mid- to late nineteenth-century vernacular buildings of Virginia. The mill on the property, now in ruins, was built for A. G. Smith before 1822 and continued to operate until 1938. The house at Vernon Mills served as a post office from 1873 to 1920 and is said to have been a general store at some point during its history.

Old Acres (030-0866), *Orlean*, 1850. Originally built as a tenant house by the Ambler family, Old Acres stood as a two-story, two-bay log dwelling covered with a stucco finish. Toward the end of the nineteenth century, the house was enlarged to become a three-bay, central-passage-plan dwelling. The house, along with a log barn and log corncrib on the property, survives as an example of a typical mid- to late nineteenth-century farm complex.

Cabin Branch (030-0651), *Orlean*, ca. 1850; 1940. Built ca. 1850, Cabin Branch was greatly enlarged and altered in 1940. The original house consists of a two-story frame structure with a center-hall plan. In 1940 a large frame addition extended the original east front, and a double-story portico with a balustrade was constructed across the new front elevation.

Rector House (030-0898), *Orlean*, 1850–80. Located across from Orlean Cemetery on Route 732, the Rector house stands as a two-story frame farmhouse with a well-proportioned two-story portico.

Francis Lawler House (030-0900), *Orlean*, ca. 1855. Francis Lawler built this house in 1855, having decided to remain on his family's land in Fauquier County while his brothers left for Indiana. The log house and its log outbuildings provide a good example of a mid-nineteenth-century vernacular farm complex.

Parr House (Bauserman Residence) (030-0730), *Orlean,* ca. 1860; 1880. Built by A. J. Parr ca. 1860, the original part of the house consists of the two-story front-gable section with an elegant Greek Revival porch. In 1880 the house was extended toward the rear, and the orientation of the house was changed. At this time the original part of the house was converted into a store; the front elevation in the gable end served as the primary entrance for store customers. The entrance to the living quarters to the house was moved to the south side of the now-expanded dwelling, making the long side the primary elevation of the dwelling.

Anderson-Rector House (030-0180), *Orlean,* 1860–80. The Anderson-Rector house, constructed in the period 1860–80, is a two-story frame I-house representative of the rural vernacular buildings of the region. In 1905–7 the Rector Store next to the house was constructed by Thomas Rector; these two buildings form the center of this small crossroads community.

Monterey (030-0764), *Orlean,* 1868. Built by William Hume in 1868, Monterey is representative of the two-story farmhouses of rural Virginia. The two-bay house was later enlarged by a rear wing featuring a large entrance porch. Across the driveway from the main dwelling stands a single-room log building with a stone end chimney. This building predates the main dwelling and undoubtedly was the kitchen dependency associated with an older, now-demolished house on the site.

Clarendon (030-0823), *Orlean,* ca. 1870 [destroyed]. Shortly after being surveyed in 1980, the house known as Clarendon and located off Route 647 burned down. It stood as an idiosyncratic farmhouse built with Second Empire–style design features, most notably the mansard roof.

Payne House (near Orlean) (030-0720), *Orlean,* ca. 1872. The Payne house, built ca. 1872, is a two-story, three-bay I-house with stone end chimneys. Although typical of the period and similar to other I-houses of rural Virginia, the Payne house bears a strong resemblance to the Russell house across the road and probably was built by Thomas A. Russell for his wife's brother, W. Wood Payne.

Russell House (030-0719), *Orlean,* ca. 1872. Erected ca. 1872, the Russell house was built by Thomas Alfred Russell, a Marylander, who joined the Confederate army and settled in Virginia after his marriage to Emily Jane Payne of Glensworth. The two-story, three-bay Russell house with stone end chimneys is representative of the rural Virginia farmhouse from this period. The property includes several domestic outbuildings and agricultural structures from the period including a springhouse, dairy, corncrib, and barn.

Riley Cabin (030-0242), *Orlean,* ca. 1875. The Riley cabin was built ca. 1875 in Leeds Manor by Wesley Riley and survives as a late example of a one-room log cabin. Although not built until the late nineteenth century, the cabin was constructed using early nineteenth-century building techniques and may have been inspired by the older Riley house (030-0241), located nearby and owned by the same family.

Priestly Farm (030-0245), *Orlean*, ca. 1879. Built near Vernon Mills by James Markham Marshall the younger, Priestly survives as a late example of the Greek Revival style in Fauquier County. Although built in the late nineteenth century at the height of the Victorian era, the house retains the temple-form massing and plan typical of the earlier Greek Revival style. Exterior details, including the 2/2-light windows and the rosette in the central gable, however, reveal the later date of construction. The triple-hung sash on the first floor were evidently inspired by those at Edgeworth, Marshall's boyhood home, and are reflective of an earlier period.

Glen Ara (030-0915), *Orlean*, 1883. Formerly an exuberant Italianate-style house, Glen Ara was designed by architect William B. Tuthill and built in 1883. The house, supposedly inspired by a Victorian pattern book with details taken from one of the Italian villas shown in Samuel Sloan's *The Model Architect,* featured a central stair tower, wraparound porches, and a hipped roof with dormer windows. The house has been completely altered by the removal, most notably, of the tower and porches and given a more regularized and Colonial Revival appearance.

Mountain View (The White House) (030-0827), *Orlean*, ca. 1890. This house, known alternatively as Mountain View and the White House, was originally built in the mid-nineteenth century and then rebuilt ca. 1890. The two-story, L-shaped house, with a centrally projecting gable, is characteristic of the late nineteenth-century domestic architecture of rural Virginia.

Walnut Hollow (030-0718), *Orlean,* 1890–1900. Located near Orlean, Walnut Hollow is a good example of the rural Queen Anne style of architecture. The two-story frame house with its L-shaped plan is typical of the late nineteenth-century vernacular domestic architecture of rural Virginia, while the bargeboard detailing, scalloped weatherboarding, fish-scale shingles, projecting polygonal bay, and corbeled chimney are characteristic of Queen Anne–style detailing.

Runnymede (Davis Place) (030-0824), *Orlean,* 1896. Built in 1896 by Willis Golder Davis the younger, Runnymede is a fine local example of the rural Queen Anne style of architecture. The house features the asymmetrical massing, irregular footprint, varied roofline, and decorative features characteristic of the style. The imposing dwelling is complete with a corner tower, a bracketed cornice, dormer windows, a porch with spindle columns and scroll-saw brackets, and fish-scale shingles on the tower and in the gable ends.

Henchman's Lea (030-0897), *Orlean,* ca. 1940. Henchman's Lea was built on land purchased from the Fairfax proprietary by John Puller Smith. In 1935 Albert Pope Hinckley bought the property from the heirs of Grace Parr Russell and built the two-story Georgian Revival–style house, designed by architect Henri de Heller ca. 1940, on the site. Executed in stone, the house is classical in plan, detailing, and massing and is notable for its elaborate interior detailing.

Marshall

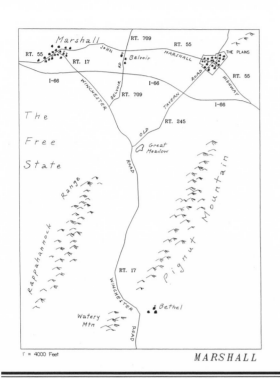

MARSHALL

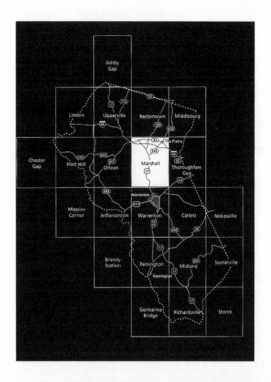

James Strother House (Molly's Folly) (030-0661), *Marshall*, 1780s(?); 1830–50. Though the Strother house has the overall form and massing of a late eighteenth-century structure and may possibly have been built by James Strother as early as the late 1780s, the house displays construction techniques that would date it more accurately to the second quarter of the nineteenth century and illustrates the enduring vernacular forms of the rural countryside. The house was later the home of Wilfred N. Utterback and descended to his daughter, Drucilla Russell. In 1965 Mary Ramey Cunningham purchased the house, which was located in the path of the proposed interstate highway I-66, and moved it to its current site on the western limits of Marshall. Thus its nickname, "Molly's Folly," was coined. At the time it was moved, the foundation was relaid, and the stone chimneys were rebuilt. A shed-roof wing was added to the rear of the house during the late nineteenth or early twentieth century.

Gordonsdale Cabin (030-0027), *Marshall,* ca. 1790. The Gordonsdale cabin, currently the guesthouse on the Gordonsdale estate, was built in the late eighteenth century on a 481-acre tract purchased in 1735 by the Reverend Alexander Scott and, after 1777, lived on by his nephew, the Reverend John Scott. A native of Scotland, the younger Scott was chaplain to the governor of Maryland, Sir Robert Eden; at the outbreak of the Revolution, Scott was thought to have loyalist sympathies and was forced to sell his Maryland real estate. He moved to Gordonsdale in Fauquier County. The Gordonsdale cabin, built ca. 1790, is an excellent example of a late eighteenth-century log dwelling, having a traditional hall-parlor plan. The one-and-a-half-story structure features the steeply pitched gable roof and massive stone end chimneys that characterize the domestic architecture of that period. Despite the addition of a lean-to and a front porch as well as the replacement of the original woodwork and trim, the house retains its late eighteenth-century form.

The Meadows (030-0529), *Marshall,* ca. 1800. Originally constructed ca. 1800, The Meadows was remodeled in 1973 to the designs of architect Albert P. Hinckley. The Meadows historically consisted of two principal parts. The oldest section, of which little remains today, was built on land owned by Major Joseph Blackwell, an officer in the Revolutionary War. This was a one-and-a-half-story, hall-parlor frame house. In 1846 the two-story, side-hall rubblestone addition was built to abut the original frame house. In 1973 a modern wing was added to the stone structure, and the interior was completely remodeled. The Bethel Academy, a military school of note in the late nineteenth century, was built on the property of The Meadows.

Meadowville (030-0831), *Marshall,* ca. 1800. The property known as Meadowville, located at the head of Broad Run, comprises two nineteenth-century houses. The original Meadowville, built ca. 1800, is a one-and-one-half-story stone dwelling which features two entry doors located side-by-side. This indicates that the house may originally have been built for two different families. The larger, more recent house was built in 1885 and was remodeled in 1950s into a Colonial Revival–style house.

Rock Valley (030-0525), *Marshall,* 1800–1840 [destroyed]. Originally a two-story, three-bay frame house with end chimneys, Rock Valley was extensively added onto and altered over the years. About 1840 a two-story, two-bay stone addition was built against the north end of the original frame structure, and sometime during the later nineteenth century a mansard roof replaced the original gable roof. Several outbuildings, including a stone meat house and springhouse from the original period of construction, as well as frame barns and sheds from a later date, surrounded the primary residence. Rock Valley burned down in 1984.

Duncan-Glascock House (030-0665), *Marshall,* 1810. Purchased by Charles Duncan in 1814, the Duncan-Glascock house and property remained in Duncan family hands throughout the succeeding centuries. The Glascock family who married into the Duncan family still owned the house at the time of the survey. The oldest section of the house is log and was built ca. 1810. Consisting of two rooms, the log structure is covered with a steeply pitched gable roof, and the log walls are clad with weatherboard siding. A rubblestone addition with a shed roof extends across the rear of the original house. The property, which also supports a stone springhouse, a log corncrib, and a sheep barn, is a fine example of an early to mid-nineteenth-century farm complex.

Grigsby House (030-0500), *Marshall,* 1810. According to local history, the Grigsby house was built as an overseer's house on property that supported a much grander mansion house, now destroyed. However, no architectural evidence supports this claim, and it seems likely that this house may well have been the primary house on the property. Built in two different sections at two different times, it consists of a three-bay stone section from ca. 1810 and a two-bay frame addition from ca. 1850. The original one-and-a-half-story stone section is raised upon a high stone foundation and built into the hillside. The frame addition, built atop a series of brick piers, is a full two stories but is the same height as the stone section. The house was being used for storage at the time of the survey and no longer retains its original interior finishings.

Humblestone (030-0490), *Marshall, 1810; 1912; 1927.*
Although the large and rambling Tudor-style house called Humblestone primarily dates from the twentieth century, it does incorporate a ca. 1810 house into its overall structure. This early nineteenth-century dwelling, a two-story stone building with stone end chimneys, serves as one room of the now extensive dwelling. In 1912 the original two-story house was significantly added onto and converted into a double-story living room of the enlarged L-shaped house. In 1927 a turreted entrance was added to the front, and a second wing was made, giving the house its present U-shaped footprint.

McSweeny House (030-0671), *Marshall, ca. 1810.*
This early nineteenth-century log house located on the north slope of Pignut Mountain was named the McSweeny house after the McSweeny family who owned the property in the mid-nineteenth century. The house is located near a graveyard containing Federal soldiers; local tradition holds that Mosby's raiders caught an advanced patrol of Federal troops, killed them, and moved on. The McSweenys are said to have buried them and built a rock wall around the graveyard.

Chelsea (030-0177), *Marshall, ca. 1815.* Located near Bethel, Chelsea was built on land purchased by Colonel William Rowland Smith in 1815. Originally a hall-parlor-plan house, Chelsea was extended in the later nineteenth century to become a central-passage-plan house with stone and brick end chimneys. William Smith, the son of the original owner, lived here from 1836 until 1886 and operated a sawmill, gristmill, and blacksmith shop on the farm.

Southern View (030-0663), *Marshall,* ca. 1815. The oldest part of Southern View was built by James Morgan ca. 1815 after he purchased more than 1,800 acres of Leeds Manor from the Marshall syndicate. This house probably was a one-and-a-half-story, hall-parlor house that was later raised to two stories. In the late 1870s or 1880s, a cross-gable wing was added to the original house, giving it the overall appearance of a typical late nineteenth-century farmhouse. Although in poor condition, two outbuildings, a smokehouse and a kitchen, survive from the original nineteenth-century domestic complex.

Greenmont (030-0289), *Marshall,* ca. 1820; 1880–90. Greenmont was originally constructed ca. 1820 by Senator Henry Peyton and later was "Victorianized" by the addition of a projecting polygonal bay, a bracketed wood cornice, and a wraparound porch. A log house from the ca. 1820 period still survives on the property.

Mountain View (Dondoric) (030-0575), *Marshall,* 1826. Originally built in 1826 and known as Mountain View, this property was owned by the locally renowned Horner family. Tradition holds that during the Civil War, Braxton Horner, wife of Richard B. Horner, was caught behind Union lines while in Philadelphia. Her diary is said to provide an account of her attempts to persuade Union soldiers and even President Lincoln to let her return to her Fauquier County home, Mountain View. Added onto and altered in different phases, Mountain View consists today of a two-story central block flanked by lower two-story wings with other additions projecting off these. The original section is the two-story central block that was at one time a central-passage-plan house.

Bright Prospect (030-0577), *Marshall*, ca. 1829 [demolished]. Bright Prospect was built ca. 1829 by Francis Whiting who bought the property from John Horner, whose family owned extensive land in the county. This quaint house on a residential estate, designed in a vernacular Greek Revival style, resembled a small-town law office or small government building more than it did a residence. The house was a one-and-a-half-story, one-room stone structure covered with a front-gable roof with return cornices in the gable end (see fig. 46). This diminutive temple-form residence provided a perfect example of how the Greek Revival style had permeated America's built environment during the 1830s and 1840s. The building, which fell into disrepair, was replaced by a new house on the site ca. 1999.

Glenville (030-0026), *Marshall*, ca. 1830. Glenville was built ca. 1830 by local builder William Sutton for James William Foster, who was given the property by his father, Isaac Foster of Whitewood. The house at Glenville is an elegant and stately example of Greek Revival–style architecture in Fauquier County and Virginia. The imposing dwelling is of stone construction and features, most prominently, an elegant Greek Revival porch across the central entry door. The porch is defined by pairs of wood columns that support a Doric entablature with alternating triglyphs surmounting a plain frieze. Local tradition has it that General Stonewall Jackson was a breakfast guest of the Fosters on his way to the Second Battle of Manassas during the Civil War. A bank barn on the property is said to have been built with restitution money given to Foster by the federal government for the demolition of a barn on his property by Union soldiers during the Civil War.

Road Island (030-0197), *Marshall,* ca. 1830. Built near Bethel ca. 1830, Road Island is named for its location on a tract of sixteen acres of land that is surrounded by roads on all sides. The land was part of a larger tract that was owned by Major Joseph Blackwell who left it to his daughter Agatha Blackwell Jeffries, the wife of Major Enoch Jeffries. The two-story, three-bay frame house was built by Jeffries family descendants on the stone foundations of an earlier building. A double-story portico dates from a later period. Local history has recorded that just after the Civil War, Colonel John S. Mosby lived at Road Island and practiced law in Warrenton.

Gordonsdale (030-0028), *Marshall,* 1830–40. Purchased in 1735 by the Reverend Alexander Scott, the Gordonsdale estate near The Plains was inherited by his nephew, the Reverend John Scott. In 1777 Scott moved to the estate from tidewater Maryland, where he had been banished for his loyalist sympathies. The log cottage on the property, called the Gordonsdale cabin, is said to have been built as early as 1777, but construction techniques indicate it was erected ca. 1790. The principal dwelling at Gordonsdale is an imposing two-story brick building designed in the Greek Revival style of architecture and built in the mid-nineteenth century. The cubelike building is articulated on the exterior by a refined front porch having Greek Revival details and by a double-story sleeping porch on the side elevation. In addition to its architecture, Gordonsdale is known for its magnificent box hedge, said to have been planted by John Scott's wife, Elizabeth Gordon Scott, first female resident of the estate, after whom Gordonsdale was named.

Wheatland (030-0501), *Marshall*, 1830–60. Built before to the Civil War, Wheatland was owned by John Baker and the Morgan family of Waveland and Clover Hill. The property was later owned by Marshall Lake, a productive cattle farmer who also held local political positions. In 1884 and 1885 Lake served as the supervisor of the Marshall district. The long, four-bay frame house is actually two two-bay houses joined together. The oldest of the two structures is the hall-parlor-plan section located at the north end. It is raised upon a high stone basement and features a large stone end chimney. In 1853 Marshall Lake extended the house by adding an identical two-story, two-bay, hall-parlor house to the south end of the existing structure. Today the house stands in deteriorating condition and is surrounded by a residential subdivision.

Clover Hill (030-0516), *Marshall*, 1833. Built on Carter's Run in 1833 by the locally prominent Morgan family, notable for their wealth and social prestige, Clover Hill was the site of many lavish entertainment scenes. The house, undoubtedly the result of a builder or architect's hand, is an elegant and well-proportioned dwelling designed in the Greek Revival style. Raised upon a high brick foundation with a molded water table, the house stands two stories tall and presents a pedimented gable end, three bays wide, as its front elevation. A single-story porch projecting in front of the central entry door features pairs of fluted Doric columns that support a Doric entablature and provide an impressive entry into the farmhouse. Typical of the Greek Revival period, the plan consists of a reception hall that runs the width of the house, behind which are two square parlor rooms, each with a fireplace against the back wall.

Waveland (030-0512), *Marshall, 1833.* Located near Marshall, the property on which Waveland stands was bought in 1806 by James Morgan, a wealthy and prominent Alexandria man who purchased several tracts of land in Fauquier County during the early nineteenth century. The present house at Waveland was built in 1833 by James Henry Loughborough and was later purchased by John Augustine Washington III, the last individual owner of Mount Vernon. Waveland, designed in a Greek Revival style, consists of a two-story brick structure that has a temple-form shape, with the entrance located in the gable-end elevation. In 1858 a six-bay wing was added to the rear of the house, with a long porch facing east. In 1880 verandas and bays were added to the house, but they have since been removed. Only the front entrance porch, with its turned posts and scroll-sawn brackets, remains from this period of modifications.

Ryan Cabin (Rappahannock Mountain Log House) (030-0228), *Marshall, ca. 1835.* The Ryan cabin was named for William Ryan, farm manager of the property who subsequently inherited the land and house from the owner, Lucy B. Jeffries, in 1897. The cabin, said to be the overseer's house on the farm, was originally a one-and-a-half-story log dwelling that was at one time covered with board-and-batten siding. The house was later raised to two full stories, and in 1975 a stone shed-roof wing was erected around the side and rear of the house, and the stone end chimney was rebuilt. At that time the interior was remodeled, and all of the original details were removed.

Lawler-Walker House (The Chimneys)

(030-0515), *Marshall, 1836.* The house now known as The Chimneys was constructed in two distinct phases by William Lawler. The original ca. 1836 part of the house includes the one-and-a-half-story stone building with a single room on the ground floor. A two-story twentieth-century frame section was added to the end of this modest dwelling, more than doubling the overall size of the house. An enclosed front porch and a rear lean-to were added to the house in the first decades of the twentieth century.

Summerfield (030-0489), *Marshall, 1837.* Built by Alfred Gaskins in 1837, the original part of Summerfield consists of a two-story, three-bay stone section. A two-story rear ell, also of stone, was constructed during the late nineteenth century. In 1936 a one-and-a-half-story stone wing was attached to the end of the original house to serve as a library space. The original stone kitchen is now attached to the main house by a covered passageway.

Adams Farm (030-0611), *Marshall, ca. 1840; 1920s.* This house, located off Route 628 and west of Alton Farm, probably was originally built as a tenant house to Alton Farm. The house was significantly altered in the 1920s, leaving only a Greek Revival–style mantel as a reminder of its historic past.

Mount Eccentric Farm (030-0288), *Marshall, ca. 1840.* According to local history, Mount Eccentric was built about 1740 by Captain Thomas Smith; however, the two-story brick house on the property today does not appear to predate the mid-nineteenth century. It is possible that the present house replaced a mid-eighteenth-century house or incorporated it into its structure, although this is not readily apparent. In either case, the property has long been associated with the locally prominent Smith family and is a local landmark. An early eighteenth-century kettle crane from the original kitchen on the site adorns the fireplace in the present library. The house, a two-story brick structure covered with a hipped roof with a central cupola, features details characteristic of the Italianate style of architecture. The stair located in the central entry hall leads to the cupola, which offers a spectacular panorama of the surrounding countryside.

West View (Chestnut Hill) (030-0528), *Marshall,* ca. 1840. Located on Trapp Branch of Broad Run, West View (Chestnut Hill) was built ca. 1840 by Henry Smith. He acquired the land on which West View was built on his twenty-first birthday from his parents, Colonel William Rowley Smith and Lucy Steptoe Blackwell Smith of Alton. The oldest part of the house is the hall-parlor frame section raised upon a high stone basement. In 1846 the house was enlarged by the addition of a room as well as the wraparound porch. In 1860 a small office was added off the 1846 addition. The present kitchen wing was not built until 1952. Also located on the property are a nineteenth-century schoolhouse, a log dairy, and a log servant/slave quarters.

Alton (030-0526), *Marshall,* ca. 1850. Although primarily a product of the mid-nineteenth century, the large two-and-a-half-story house at Alton is actually the result of two building phases. The original section is a one-and-a-half-story log structure erected ca. 1807 by William Rowley Smith (1781–1857), who grew up at Mount Eccentric and married Lucy Steptoe Blackwell. William Smith commanded a company of cavalry in the War of 1812 and served as a colonel in the Fauquier militia in 1815. He was also a member of the state legislature for three terms. Around 1850 a two-story center-hall-plan house was added to the original log structure, giving the house its mid-nineteenth-century appearance. The property also contains a slave cabin, a meat house, and an imposing bank barn that is now separated from the house and its outbuildings by a road.

Edgehill (030-0021), *Marshall,* ca. 1850. Located near Bethel, Edgehill was built on a tract of land in the decade after it was inherited by James Eustace Jeffries in 1840. The property consists of a large dwelling including its many additions, a stone kitchen, stone dairy, and log meat house, all from the mid-nineteenth century. The main section of the house, which is also the oldest part, is an impressive two-story stone structure having a central-passage plan. The house is known locally for its mural depicting the horn of plenty painted on the front pedimented gable. In July 1874 then owners Estha Jeffries and her daughter exchanged Edgehill, including 534 acres, with C. Columbus Bradley for a lot and house in Alexandria, Virginia. In 1875 Bradley erected a long frame wing that extends perpendicular to the rear of the house and contains the dining room, kitchen, and service rooms.

Beaconsfield Farm (030-0420), *Marshall,* 1870–90. Built in the latter half of the nineteenth century, the house at Beaconsfield Farm is a one-and-a-half-story frame structure. Originally a hall-parlor house, the building was later enlarged to incorporate a central passage. The frame house is covered with stucco and is set upon a stone foundation.

Cubbage House (030-0195), *Marshall,* 1870–90. Now known as the Cubbage house, this handsome two-story stone building is traditionally thought to have served as a saloon. The building, noteworthy for its meticulous stonework including corner quoining, flat-arched stone lintels, and stone sills, offers a single-cell interior plan with a second floor and an attic level above. A two-story frame addition abutting the old stone building, along with the shed-roof porch across the end elevation of the stone building, probably was built around the turn of the twentieth century.

Edenburn (030-0532), *Marshall,* 1870–80. Designed in a Victorian Gothic Revival style, Edenburn is a two-and-a-half-story frame dwelling covered with a cross-gable roof that is flanked at the ridge line by interior brick chimneys. Extending from the rear of the main house is a long and low two-story wing, one-half of which is of log construction, with the other half possibly of log and sheathed with board-and-batten walls. Either one or both sections of this wing probably predate the main house.

Sudley (030-0081), *Marshall*, 1870–90. Located near Marshall, Sudley was originally part of the large tract of land purchased by the Reverend Alexander Scott in 1735. The 1870s frame center-hall house replaced a ca. 1805 dwelling on the site known as Locust Grove that burned during the Civil War. Sudley has been significantly rebuilt and enlarged in several different building campaigns during the twentieth century. In 1945 architect Washington Reed designed a music room and sunporch addition to the house; later architect William Bowman remodeled the front of the house, adding a bay window and a two-story New Orleans–style cast-iron porch.

Enoch Smith House (030-0281), *Marshall*, ca. 1875. The Enoch Smith house is a two-story, side-hall house which stands in ruinous condition on the west slope of the Wildcat Mountain. The Smith house is named for its builder, Enoch Smith, who constructed it ca. 1875. Also located on the site is a two-story stone springhouse with an outside stair leading to the second floor. Inside, the springhouse features the typical arrangement of space for cooling perishable food and accumulating springwater.

The Moorings (030-0576), *Marshall*, 1875–76. The Moorings was built in 1875–76 by Dr. Frederick Cecil Horner, whose family owned Mountain View. Dr. Horner broke with his family during the Civil War when he supported the Union and later was banished from the family property at Mountain View. The Moorings was supposedly built using stone from Lawrence's Tavern, which had burned a few years earlier. Although built in a vernacular mode, the house features Italianate details such as the bracketed wood cornice, the window moldings, and 2/2-light, double-hung window sash. A large rear wing was added to the house in 1963.

Clifton (030-0018), *Marshall*, 1889. At one time owned by Major Joseph Blackwell, an officer in the Revolutionary War, Clifton has been enlarged and improved upon since its original construction The oldest building on the property is a one-and-a-half-story log structure that was built as a dwelling but later was converted into a kitchen. The main house, primarily a late nineteenth-century building which may incorporate parts of an eighteenth- or nineteenth-century house into its structure, consists of a two-story frame building with brick nogging. The house has an L-shaped footprint with legs of equal length. The two wings are covered with a cross-gable roof and present features of the Victorian Gothic style of architecture: a steeply pitched end gable has a projecting bay superimposed by windows with stylized pedimented moldings.

Barrymore (030-0502), *Marshall*, 1890; 1962. The principal residence at Barrymore was built by Henry de Butts Norris in 1890 after a fire destroyed an older house on the property. The 1890 house, however, was completely remodeled in the twentieth century, leaving little of its original configuration, massing, or details intact. Despite the modern appearance of the primary residence, several other resources on the property attest to its historic roots. A small frame house, probably built as an overseer's house, dates from ca. 1800, while a magnificent stone barn (*shown*), built at the time of the rebuilding of Barrymore in 1890, stands in excellent condition. The barn, a tall, two-and-a-half-story structure with a full basement, is built into the hillside and supports a cross-gable roof with Victorian details. Ornate wooden brackets decorate the cornice line, and fish-scale shingles laid out in a floral pattern ornament the roof itself. The large barn-door openings are articulated by stone arches, while the windows are surmounted by flat stone lintels.

Bud Carter House (030-0513), *Marshall*, ca. 1890. Located off Route 719 in the fertile Carter Run valley is the Bud Carter house. Built ca. 1890, the house is a tall, two-story stone building set upon a raised stone foundation. Its height and projecting stone gable on the front elevation make this house a distinctive and noteworthy landmark.

Contest (Shady Valley Farm) (030-0286), *Marshall, 1892.* The property commonly known as Shady Valley Farm and historically as Contest is located on the site of a late eighteenth- or early nineteenth-century house that was destroyed by fire toward the end of the nineteenth century. Following the fire, this two-story, three-bay frame house was built, on the exterior in a manner characteristic of the farmhouses of the period but featuring such interior embellishments as painted and grained doors. Of particular note is the pressed metal ceiling—a feature commonly found in commercial architecture from 1890 to 1920 but less often seen in residential construction.

Belvoir (030-0080), *Marshall, 1914.* Located on the site of a mid-nineteenth-century dwelling called Rock Spring and possibly incorporating part of it into the current structure, Belvoir was built in 1914 by Mr. and Mrs. Fairfax Harrison. Mr. Harrison, a president of the Southern Railway, named the property Belvoir to honor the William Fairfax house in Fairfax County which is no longer standing. He built his own personal railroad station on the property, so that he could easily commute to work in Washington, D.C. Designed by Washington, D.C., architect Waddy B. Wood, the large and assuming Belvoir displays building massing and details, such as the central block with a pedimented front porch and the arched entry and window surrounds, that are characteristic of the Classical Revival style of the early to mid-twentieth century.

Scarborough (030-0632), *Marshall, 1915.* Located on top of Wildcat Mountain, Scarborough was built in 1915 by Truman Stowe Vance, a wealthy orchardist. The large two-story stone house was designed in the early twentieth-century Colonial Revival style. Its most distinguishing architectural feature is the porte cochere built against the end of the house to accommodate the owner's Model T Ford. Vance lost the property following the collapse of the orchard business, and the house fell to ruins. It was bought by Russell M. Arundel in 1940 and was remodeled at that time.

Airlie House (030-0205), *Marshall*, 1925. Airlie House, designed in 1925 by architect W. H. Irwin Fleming, was built upon the foundations of a 1906 house that burned down in 1924. Designed in the Classical Revival style that was popular for country estates in Fauquier in that period, Airlie House consists of a slightly projecting central pavilion flanked by end wings. The central pavilion is delineated by fluted pilasters and supports a pedimented gable with large dentils ornamenting the cornice and raking cornice.

Harkaway Farm (030-0487), *Marshall*, 1932. Located on Watery Mountain near Bethel, Harkaway Farm was designed and built in 1932 by Henri de Heller, a Swiss architect, for his own use. The house has a definite Swiss chalet appearance to it and features wide shingled gables and large expanses of glass. Also on the property is a mid-nineteenth-century tenant house that was significantly remodeled during the twentieth century.

Arborvitae (030-0531), *Marshall*, 1938. Located between Warrenton and New Baltimore, Arborvitae was built in 1938 after a fire destroyed an earlier 1880 house on the property. The house, designed by architect W. H. Irwin Fleming, recalls mid-nineteenth-century English country architecture on the exterior, while the interior exhibits a variety of architectural and decorative styles from Gothic Revival to Greek Revival to Art Deco. The outbuildings, moved to their present sites from more remote locations on the farm, date from the 1880s.

Flint Hill (Eshton, Rawlingsdale) (030-0662), *Marshall*, 1945 (with ca. 1795 and 1835 sections). Flint Hill was originally constructed ca. 1795 as a single-cell stone house by Benjamin Rust who rented the property from owner George Washington. In 1832 a two-story, side-hall frame wing was added to the stone section, while the original house was used as a dining room, connected by a covered passage to a detached kitchen, since removed. During the Civil War the property then known as Rawlingsdale for its owner, John Will Rawlings, was at the heart of Mosby's Confederacy. In 1945 Thomas Tileston Waterman, architect and architectural historian, remodeled the historic core by changing its orientation and redesigning the north wall and added onto it with one-and-a-half-story wings and connecting hyphens. Although aspects of the historic structure survive, Flint Hill is primarily a product of the twentieth century.

Whitehall (030-0542), *Marshall*, 1947. Whitehall, near New Baltimore, was built primarily in 1947 to the designs of New York architect William Lawrence Bottomley. Two log rooms forming a core of the large two-story frame structure remain from an earlier house on the site, as does another frame section of the building. The house was completely rebuilt and redesigned in 1947. The new house includes such interior detailing as a fully paneled library.

Thoroughfare Gap

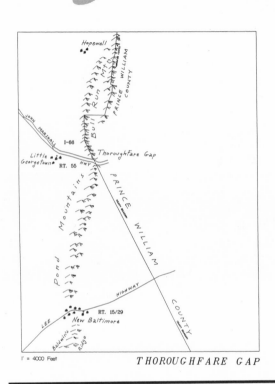

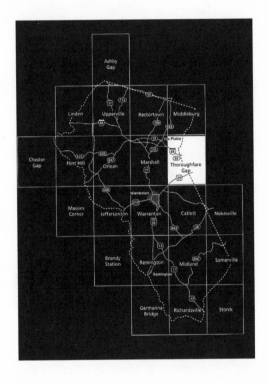

THOROUGHFARE GAP

Snow Hill (030-0887), *Thoroughfare Gap,* ca. 1790; late 19th century. According to local tradition, the land on which Snow Hill stands once belonged to William Kirk, a pirate, who was murdered in 1780. Following his death, Kirk's widow married David McNish who presumably built the original part of Snow Hill when he acquired title to the property. The original house, the rear wing of the existing house, is a one-and-a-half-story frame dwelling with a narrow gable dormer and a stone end chimney. A late nineteenth-century two-story frame section was added to the original house. The entire structure survives in a ruinous condition.

Mountain End (030-0683), *Thoroughfare Gap, ca.*
1798. This house, Mountain End, and another house
called Mountain View (030-0673) and located nearby,
were originally built ca. 1798 by two brothers, Nimrod
and Charles Martin. The brothers built nearly identical two-story stone houses set upon high stone base-
ments. The two houses have been altered somewhat
over the years: the interior floor plan at Mountain End
was altered during the Civil War–era, and a basement
porch was built during the twentieth century. Local
tradition holds that Mountain End served as an inn before the Civil War.

Mountain View (030-0673), *Thoroughfare Gap, ca.*
1798. Mountain View and the house called Mountain
End (030-0683), located nearby, were originally built
ca. 1798 by two brothers, Nimrod and Charles Martin.
At Mountain View dormer windows and a side porch
from the twentieth century embellish the two-story
stone structure set upon a high foundation.

Afton Farm (030-0519), *Thoroughfare Gap, ca. 1800;*
mid-19th century. Although Afton appears from the
exterior to be a mid-nineteenth-century central-
passage-plan I-house featuring a three-bay front elevation and two stone and brick end chimneys, interior
details reveal that the building was enlarged from an
early nineteenth-century one-and-a-half-story, single-
cell house. These details, including the mantels, windows, and doors, are Federal-period elements from
around 1800.

Evergreen (030-0890), *Thoroughfare Gap, ca. 1800; ca.*
1900. Originally built about 1800 by General Thomas
Hunton, the main residence at Evergreen was rebuilt
around 1900. At Hunton's death in 1828, the buildings
on the property were worth $5,000. It is a locally held
tradition that George Washington's will was kept in
the wine cellar of Evergreen during the Civil War.

Fairview (030-0550), *Thoroughfare Gap*, 1810; ca. 1915. Located near present New Baltimore, Fairview survives as an elegant example of a Federal house in Fauquier County. The house was built by William Hunton of Lancaster County who moved to Fauquier shortly after the Revolution, and it remained in Hunton family hands until 1927. William Hunton is probably most well known locally for having established, in 1822, the village of New Baltimore on twenty-five acres of land that he owned. Fairview is an imposing two-story, five-bay brick building raised upon a high stone foundation. The plan, typical of the Federal style, features a central passage with two rooms to either side on each floor. Details on the exterior, such as the jack-arched lintels above the windows, and interior details, including the mantels, molded baseboards, chair rails, and cornices, are all elegant examples of Federal-period design and craftsmanship. The house remains intact to its original design, save for a brick kitchen wing added ca. 1915.

Meadowview (030-0672), *Thoroughfare Gap*, 1810. Located on Route 601, near The Plains, the house called Meadowview is sited on land that has been owned by the Howdershell family since the land was granted to John Howdershell by Lord Fairfax in 1747. The original part of Meadowview was a small one-and-one-half-story stone house with a single room on each floor. In the late nineteenth century, a two-story frame addition was made to the stone house, and the upper floor was raised to a full two stories. In an effort to join the two construction phases visually, a front porch was built across the full width of the front elevation. The stone section of the house is painted, as is the frame section, making it further blend into the later construction.

Hunton House Kitchen (Lone Star Farm) (030-0275), *Thoroughfare Gap*, ca. 1820. Only the kitchen and a springhouse remain on this property near Thoroughfare Gap; the original mansion burned ca. 1910. The kitchen is an impressively sturdy one-and-a-half-story stone structure with a large stone end chimney and a gable roof. Simply fitted, the interior trim and enclosed corner stair are original and in good condition.

Mount Hope (030-0778), *Thoroughfare Gap,* ca. 1820.
In 1801 Samuel Porter Jr. bought 434 ½ acres for £1,300.
According to insurance records, by 1820 the property
held $1,000 worth of buildings. By 1850 the present
house, log meat house, and large barn stood on the
site.

Acorn Farm Cabin (030-0782), *Thoroughfare Gap,*
1820–50; 1870. Built 1820–50, the Acorn Farm cabin is a
one-and-a-half-story log structure clad with vertical
board siding and covered with a steeply pitched gable
roof. Original twin entrances and an interior partition
indicate that the dwelling probably was built as slave
quarters for two individual families. The house was altered ca. 1870 to become a single-family farmhouse:
the two entrances were blocked up, and a single entrance was cut into the log structure.

Ball's Inn (Wadsworth House) (030-0160),
Thoroughfare Gap, 1820–55. This brick building in the
village of New Baltimore was built in the first part of
the nineteenth century as an inn by John Hampton.
On December 21, 1822, the Virginia legislature passed
an act incorporating the town of New Baltimore. In
1824 the trustees of the town met at this tavern, and in
1825 General Lafayette was entertained here. Andrew
Jackson also stopped at the inn en route from the Her-
mitage to Washington. Following its use as an inn, the
building was used as a saddlery, schoolhouse, store,
and residence. In 1855 the original inn was greatly enlarged to include the two-story brick building with the
four-bay front elevation designed with late Federal details. Only the rear wing of the present building was
standing before this addition. The front entry porch is
a twentieth-century addition.

Cedar Hill (030-0779), *Thoroughfare Gap*, ca. 1822; 1855. Originally built by William Hampton Jr., the house at Cedar Hill consists of two principal sections. The oldest section, built ca. 1822, is a two-and-a-half-story brick building with a gable roof. In 1855 then-owner Henry Mars Lewis built a two-story stone addition to the north end of the house. According to local tradition, Lewis had the stone quarried from Thoroughfare Gap, the brick fired on the site, the wood cut on the property, and the nails forged by local blacksmiths. A large porch was built across the entire length of the front elevation, unifying the house and its additions.

Hopewell (030-0523), *Thoroughfare Gap*, 1830–50. Built ca. 1830–50, the house called Hopewell is a simple two-story frame dwelling with a stone end chimney on either end of the gable roof. Although the front elevation has a typical three-bay-wide appearance, the first-floor door and the second-floor window above it are located off-center. This asymmetrical treatment is due to the fact that a central stair hall with two rooms to either side is fitted with a flight of stairs directly on center. The door, therefore, opens off-center to the side of the stairs. A two-story rear wing was added to the house, probably in the late nineteenth or early twentieth century.

Beulah (Kalorama) (030-0068), *Thoroughfare Gap*, 1837; 1885; ca. 1910 [destroyed]. Originally called Kalorama, Beulah is located west of The Plains and was built by Sylvester Welch Jr. in 1837. The house was sold in 1868 and renamed Beulah by the then-owner, Captain Drayton Meade. The name is not the only aspect of change about the house: the building, originally a two-story, central-passage-plan house, has since been added onto several times to become a large, irregularly massed dwelling with a variety of rooflines. The largest alteration occurred in 1885 when a two-story frame addition was built along the southeast elevation to include an extensive entry hall flanked by two large rooms with projecting bays. Subsequent additions, such as the front entry porch, occurred around 1910. Since the time of the survey, Beulah has burned down.

East View (Fauquier Farm) (030-0276), Thoroughfare Gap, ca. 1840.

East View is one of several houses built by the Hunton family in this area of Fauquier County. Although it has been altered and added onto over the years, East View was originally built ca. 1840 for William G. Hunton on land he inherited from his father, William Hunton, the patriarch and builder of Fairview (030-0550), who is best known as the founder of New Baltimore. The house stands today with the original two-story frame building with end chimneys flanked by lower frame wings that were added during the early to mid-twentieth century. The central block is set upon a raised stone foundation and presents the typical three-bay, central-passage-plan configuration of Virginia domestic architecture of the mid-nineteenth century.

Evergreen Cabin (New Mown Hay Farm) (030-0231), Thoroughfare Gap, ca. 1840.

New Mown Hay Farm is located on a parcel of land which at one time belonged to the larger Evergreen tract owned by the Hunton family. The house is an excellent local example of a one-and-a-half-story, single-room log cabin raised upon a high stone basement. In addition to its stone foundation, the log cabin features an impressive stone chimney. The interior of the building retains some of its original detailing including the ceiling of beaded boards and the corner box stair leading to the attic loft level. An addition on the east side of the building dates from the turn of the twentieth century.

Springfield Farm (030-0908), Thoroughfare Gap, ca. 1840.

Originally built ca. 1840, Springfield has been significantly altered and added onto over the years. The original section of the house is the two-story frame house covered with a low-hipped roof. This main block has been surrounded by one- and two-story wings; the entire house stands in ruinous condition.

Roland (030-0075), *Thoroughfare Gap*, 1840–50; 1940s. Built on the western slope of the Bull Run Mountains by Thomas Henderson in the mid-nineteenth century, Roland survives as an excellent example of a late Federal I-house. The two-story, five-bay frame house has the same form and massing of the typical vernacular farmhouse but features details such as the cornice with dentils, pedimented front porch, and longer first-floor window treatment that are generally associated with the formal Federal style of architecture. The house was significantly altered in the 1940s, at which time the modest and original interior details were replaced by much grander and older elements than the house itself. The dining room and kitchen wing also was added to the house at that time.

Avenel (030-0003), *Thoroughfare Gap*, 1842; 1901. Located near The Plains, the original Avenel was built in 1824 by James Bradshaw Beverley, a Washington lawyer whose D.C. residence later became Dumbarton Oaks. Now demolished, the original Avenel was a two-story, center-hall house of wood frame construction. In 1842 Beverley's son Robert Beverley built a one-story stone wing which stands as the oldest part of the house today. In 1901, at Robert Beverley's death, a two-story frame building connected to the stone wing replaced the original 1824 house. Some of the interior woodwork from the 1824 house can be found in the 1901 addition. Tradition holds that Robert E. Lee visited Avenel when a young man, and later, during the Civil War, the general and several of his staff stayed at Avenel.

Bayley House (030-0521), *Thoroughfare Gap*, ca. 1850. Built on land that was originally part of the Gaylemont estate, the Bayley house is a mid-nineteenth-century log structure clad with board and batten. The modest-sized hall-parlor-plan house was built by Sampson Bayley who owned several hundred acres in Fauquier at that time.

Kinloch (030-0077), *Thoroughfare Gap, 1933.* Erected in 1933, the house at Kinloch was built on the site of two earlier houses. The first house, built ca. 1813, burned down before 1823. Following the fire, Thomas Turner IV and his wife, Elizabeth Carter Randolph Turner, who came to Fauquier from King George County, built the second house on the site. The Turner family occupied the house for almost a century. During the Turner ownership Robert E. Lee spent much of his boyhood at Kinloch with Thomas Turner, his relative and guardian. Tradition holds that Lee became so attached to the horse he rode at Kinloch, named Fancy Traveller, that when he became commander in chief of the Confederate army, he named his horse Traveller after his Kinloch horse. Lee's wife and daughters are said to have sought refuge at Kinloch when it was no longer safe for them to remain at Arlington House. After a hundred years of Turner ownership, the property was sold in 1931 to Russell Grace, who pulled the house down, except for one section of one wing, and built the existing house in its place. The present house has been remodeled since its construction in 1933.

Massies Corner

1" = 4000 Feet

MASSIES CORNER

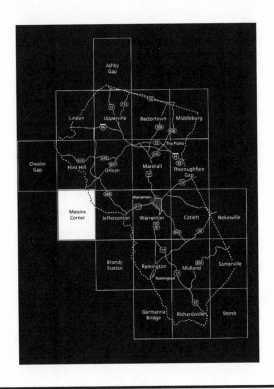

Hopper-Collins House (Marshall-Gore Log House) (030-0721), *Massies Corner*, ca. 1800. Named for the two earliest owners of the tract of land near the mouth of Thumb Run on which this log dwelling was built, the Hopper-Collins house appears to have been erected around the turn of the nineteenth century. The single-story log structure has a steeply pitched gable roof with a single dormer window on the rear elevation and two stone end chimneys. The interior is divided into two rooms with a corner box stair leading to the loft level. Despite its deteriorating condition, the Hopper-Collins house provides an excellent example of an early log dwelling in Fauquier County.

Jeffersonton

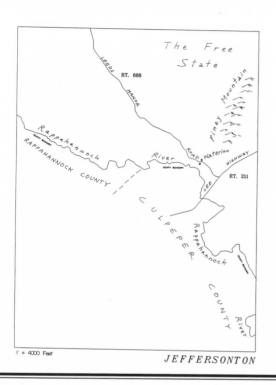

JEFFERSONTON

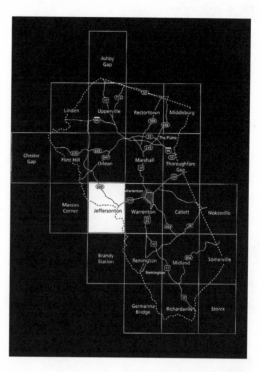

Asa Hume House (030-0367), *Jeffersonton*, ca. 1810.
The Asa Hume house was built ca. 1810 on a tract of
land just below the village of Orlean. Built by Robert
Hume but occupied by Asa Hume, the one-and-a-half-
story frame structure is a tiny, one-room dwelling that
has been little altered over the years. The single-room
house with its steeply pitched roof and stone end
chimney is a rare survivor of what was at one time a
common dwelling form. The log addition at the rear,
also from the nineteenth century, detracts little from
the original shape and form of the house.

Jacob Hume House (030-0376), *Jeffersonton*, ca. 1810. The Jacob Hume house was built ca. 1810 by Robert Hume on a tract of land taken in the name of his three sons in the Free State. This was a mountainous section of the county whose residents avoided paying rents and taxes until John Marshall's title to the land was confirmed in 1833. All three sons left Fauquier County, so the land was then acquired by Jacob Hume, the next in line, who lived in the house until his death in 1873. The Jacob Hume house consists of two principal parts: a one-and-a-half-story log structure with a stone end chimney built ca. 1810 and a slightly taller frame wing, added to the log structure by the mid-nineteenth century. A front porch which extends across the entire front elevation was built about the same time the frame wing was added. The house has been used in recent years as a barn.

Marshall-Smith Place (030-0361), *Jeffersonton*, ca. 1810. Originally built ca. 1810 on land leased from the Fairfax proprietary, the Marshall-Smith place is a one-room log structure with a box stair and stone chimney to which a larger frame house was added ca. 1830. The land, leased by William Corder, apparently reverted back to the Marshall family and descended to Marshall Smith who sold it in 1920. Though in ruinous condition, the house contains evidence that the original builder referred to pattern books while constructing the dwelling, as evidenced by the door and window trim.

Snowden (Hart-Stinson House) (030-0340), *Jeffersonton*, ca. 1820. Originally constructed ca. 1820 as a two-story, two-bay structure, the Hart-Stinson house or Snowden was later enlarged to become a three-bay, central-passage-plan house. The house was remodeled in 1978.

Sutphin House (030-0374), *Jeffersonton*, 1830–50. Located off Route 681, the Sutphin house was built in at least two phases in the mid-nineteenth century and includes two large two-story attached frame wings placed at perpendicular angles to one another. Several outbuildings, including a dairy house, smokehouse, and log house, are all contemporary to the main house and form a cohesive farm complex that is typical of the era.

Blackwell House (030-0355), *Jeffersonton*, ca. 1840. The Blackwell house is a one-and-a-half-story frame dwelling built ca. 1840 and later enlarged. Several log structures at the rear of the house indicate that it was at one time a viable domestic complex.

Ashby Cabin (030-0371), *Jeffersonton*, ca. 1850. The Ashby cabin, located in Leeds Manor, is a quaint one-room log dwelling covered with weatherboard siding. The house sits upon a low stone foundation and features a side-gable roof and a large stone end chimney. A shed addition from 1910 has been removed, while the shed-roof porch addition that extends across the front elevation remains intact. The Ashby cabin is a fine example of the one-room log house that was a common house form in Fauquier County in the nineteenth century.

Jackson House (030-0378), *Jeffersonton*, ca. 1850. The oldest section of the Jackson house, built ca. 1850, is the log-bodied rear wing. Around 1890 the two-bay, side-passage-plan house was added to the smaller log structure, and a spacious staircase was built in the hall.

Needwood (030-0392), *Jeffersonton*, ca. 1850. The original part of Needwood is the one-and-a-half-story section and is said to have been built as an overseer's house on the estate of Jaquelin Ambler Marshall. Built ca. 1850, the house was enlarged ca. 1890 by the addition of the two-story section. Both parts of the house are of frame construction, stuccoed, and both sections feature a stone end chimney. In 1965 the house was renovated, a kitchen addition was extended, and dormer windows were added on the original part of the house.

Woodland Croft (030-0393), *Jeffersonton*, ca. 1850. Now called Woodland Croft, this two-story stone house was built ca. 1850 near Carter's Run. The house may have served as a miller's house, as several mills were located along Carter's Run during the nineteenth century. The house currently stands in good condition and provides a good example of a two-story, two-bay house that was typical of Fauquier County vernacular architecture in the nineteenth century.

Morgan-Wingfield House (Morgan House) (030-0356), *Jeffersonton*, ca. 1853. Now part of Cliff Mills subdivision, the Morgan-Wingfield house was originally built ca. 1853 by John J. Wingfield who at that time owned several tracts of land in Fauquier County. The small, three-room house was enlarged during the late nineteenth century and again in the 1920s.

J. E. Ashby House (Willow Ford) (030-0372), *Jeffersonton*, 1865. The J. E. Ashby house was so named because the first record of the dwelling's occupancy was traced to Joseph E. Ashby in 1865. At that time the dwelling consisted of a one-and-a-half-story frame structure with a hall-parlor plan. In 1870 the small house was doubled in size by the addition of a shed-roof wing that extends across the rear elevation of the house and a long wing that projects perpendicularly from it. In 1920 the house was further enlarged by the addition of a kitchen wing.

Sanker House (030-0389), *Jeffersonton,* 1865. The Sanker house, built ca. 1865, is a two-story, two-bay house set upon a dry-laid stone foundation. This house form, though once prevalent in rural Virginia, is no longer a commonly found dwelling type.

Smoot House (030-0390), *Jeffersonton,* ca. 1865. The Smoot house, built ca. 1865, is a two-story frame dwelling set upon a dry-laid rubblestone foundation and featuring a stone end chimney. Like the Sanker house, the Smoot house represents a once-prevalent but now uncommon house form in rural Virginia.

Strother-Hart Farm (Parkinson Home–Malwin Hill) (030-0352), *Jeffersonton,* ca. 1870. The Strother-Hart house or Parkinson home–Malwin Hill was built on land owned by the Hart family in the nineteenth century. The two-story, three-bay frame I-house is a typical vernacular Virginia farmhouse.

Cliff Mills Farm (030-0370), *Jeffersonton*, 1870–80. The primary residence at Cliff Mills Farm is a large two-story building with stone first-floor walls and a frame upper structure. The first-floor stone walls were built using stone taken from an eighteenth-century structure, possibly a mill, as attested to by a stone with the date 1789 inscribed on it. The stone portion most likely was rebuilt at the same time that the upper story was erected, sometime during the mid- to late nineteenth century based upon the Italianate brackets. The property was at one time home to a mill and a store, built and operated in the first part of the twentieth century. The mill burned in 1923; the store remains, but in ruins.

Fishback-Beale House (Waterloo Tract Farm) (030-0353), *Jeffersonton*, 1880–90. Originally located on the 700-acre Waterloo Tract Farm, the Fishback-Beale house was erected in the late nineteenth century on the site of the older Martin Brook house, which apparently washed away in a flood.

Hart-Smith House (030-0341), *Jeffersonton*, ca. 1890. Although a portion of the main house on this property may date from the mid- to late nineteenth century, it was significantly altered in the 1950s and retains little of its original massing or detail. A late nineteenth-century barn with board-and-batten walls, however, survives on the farm property.

Brooks House (030-0409), *Jeffersonton*, 1891. Located on Route 688, the Brooks house was originally built in 1891 and was significantly enlarged in two later campaigns, in 1907 and 1913. The original house is a log structure with a side-passage plan. A rear kitchen addition was made to the house in 1907, while a large frame addition on the west side practically doubled the original building's size. The entire house was clad with stucco to give it a more uniform appearance.

Brown-Moore House (030-0375), *Jeffersonton*, ca. 1900. The Brown-Moore house was built ca. 1900 in the tradition of the typical Virginia farmhouse. It has an L-shaped plan, a three-bay symmetrical facade, and exterior end chimneys. The interior trim and mantels appear to be from a pattern book.

Canterbury Tenant House (030-0347), *Jeffersonton*, ca. 1900. Located on the Canterbury property, the Canterbury tenant house is a typical late nineteenth-century farmhouse of frame construction.

Hiner House (030-0354), *Jeffersonton*, ca. 1900. The Hiner house was built ca. 1900 and is a typical turn-of-the-century vernacular farmhouse. The house has been stripped of its porch, which may originally have given the house a more decorative character.

Curtis House (030-0377), *Jeffersonton*, 1900–1915. Built on land near Orlean that was originally leased to Jacob Hume by Alexander Mason Curtis, the Curtis house was designed in a vernacular Queen Anne style of architecture. Characteristic of the exuberant architectural style, the house features an irregular plan and roofline along with asymmetrical massing with whimsical projecting bays, gables, and a wraparound porch. The wraparound porch is supported by spindle columns with decorative knee brackets—a typical Queen Anne–style detail.

George Reid House (030-0360), *Jeffersonton*, ca. 1920. The George Reid house was built ca. 1920. It is currently located in a residential subdivision and stands as the oldest building in the development.

Canterbury (030-0345), *Jeffersonton*, 1930. The grand three-story Georgian Revival house known as Canterbury is located on a site that was originally part of a tract of land granted to Isaac Settle in 1742. Designed in 1930 by Russell Walcott and Robert Work of Chicago for owner Albert Pierce, Canterbury was selected by the American Institute of Architects to appear in the French publication *L'Illustration* as one of the best examples of Georgian Revival houses. The house consists of a tall and imposing central block flanked by symmetrical two-story wings and projecting pavilions. The interior is in keeping with Georgian Revival–style architecture on a grand scale and includes a cantilevered circular stair with Adamesque details.

Prospect Hill (030-0926), *Jeffersonton*, 1934. The original Prospect Hill was built in 1811 by Chief Justice John Marshall for his son Dr. Jaquelin Ambler Marshall. In 1933 the house burned down, and a new mansion was built on its site the following year. This Prospect Hill was designed in a flamboyant Jacobean Revival style by architect Thomas Franzioli. Although the house recalls English prototypes that inspired such Virginia houses as Bacon's Castle, Prospect Hill was designed without regard to local Fauquier County building traditions of the eighteenth and nineteenth centuries.

Mulberry Hill Farm (030-0357), *Jeffersonton, 1947.*
The main house at Mulberry Hill Farm was completely rebuilt in 1947 but apparently retains some of its original nineteenth-century log walls. Local tradition holds that the property, originally a 660-acre tract of land, was divided into eighteen plots that were given to freed slaves.

Warrenton

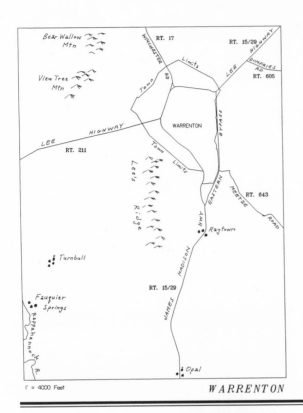

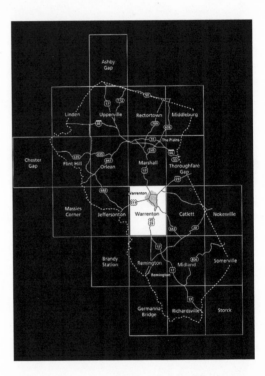

1' = 4000 Feet

North Wales (030-0093), *Warrenton, 1773–81; 1914.*
Built 1773–81, North Wales was erected on land granted in 1718 to Captain John Hooe of Barnsfield on the
Potomac and his brother Rhys Hooe. Upon his death
in 1763, Captain Hooe bequeathed his share of the
land to his daughter Ann, who married William Alla-
son, a prosperous merchant. In 1773 the Allasons began
construction of North Wales, possibly to the designs
of master builder John Ariss. The house was designed
in a Georgian manner and features all of the form,
massing, and details characteristic of the style, including the five-bay facade, the pairs of end chimneys and
the central-hall, double-pile plan. North Wales was significantly enlarged by the flanking wings in 1914 and
was again altered in the mid-twentieth century. Despite these modern additions and alterations, North
Wales survives as an important example of Georgian
domestic architecture in Fauquier County.

Settle Cottage (Canterbury Cottage) (030-0346), *Warrenton,* ca. 1780. Settle Cottage or Canterbury Cottage was the house of George Settle whose father, Isaac, received a land grant from Lord Fairfax in 1742. George Settle is thought to have built the house by 1780 and named it Settledown. The one-and-a-half-story frame structure is set upon a stone foundation and is covered with a steeply pitched gable roof with exterior end chimneys. A one-story wing addition connects the house to a former dairy or springhouse.

Hooewood (Ashley) (030-0497), *Warrenton,* 1780–90. In 1865 Henry Ashton gave his daughter Eileen this house along with 150 acres located on the eastern portion of his farm and in front of the main residence of Ashley. Hooewood remained in the family until the 1930s when Helen Whitney Gibson purchased the property and eventually gave it to the state as a state forest called Whitney State Forest. Built between 1780 and 1790 and contemporary with the dwelling called North Wales, Hooewood is a diminutive stone house with one frame end wall having a typical hall-parlor plan. The narrow, two-bay structure is set upon a high foundation and is covered with a gable roof pierced with a single dormer window located on center. The exterior stone walls have refined stone jack arches over the doors and window openings; the interior door openings feature six-paneled wood doors with matching soffits and side panels. The frame end wall is clad with weatherboard siding.

Loretto (Edmonium) (030-0035), *Warrenton, 1790; 1895; ca. 1900.* Loretto is located on a site which was originally part of the land patented by Richard Henry Lee, a signer of the Declaration of Independence, from the royal grant of Thomas Fairfax, sixth Baron Fairfax of Cameron. The first house on the site, called Edmonium, was built before the Revolutionary War by the Edmonds family who had purchased the land from Lee in 1759. In the late eighteenth century, following a fire which destroyed this first house, Captain Elias Edmonds built another house on the site. This house was a two-story, three-bay brick house with walls laid in Flemish bond. Later a two-story frame addition was made to the rear of the house, converting the dwelling from a single-pile plan to a double-pile plan. In 1895 this rear addition was demolished and re-laid in brick. Around 1900 the roof was raised to a steeply pitched hipped roof, and two dormers were added. Shortly after this addition, the distyle Ionic portico was erected, giving the house its Classical Revival appearance. Although Loretto retains only traces of its Flemish bond brick walls from the 1790 construction period and is in no way a pure representation of the house from that period, it provides important insight into the evolution of a Fauquier estate. In 1820 the house passed into the Foote family through marriage. Legend has it that Richard Foote buried silver in the yard and died before revealing its location. Local tradition also claims that a lady in gray can be seen walking the property at midnight with a candle in her hands. The property's name was changed to Loretto following the Civil War when it was sold to Colonel John Scott. Scott's wife, a Roman Catholic, presumably took the name from the Irish order of nuns or from the source of their name, a small central Italian town with a celebrated shrine to the Virgin Mary, known there as "Our Lady of Loreto."

Mount View (Glenaman, Morehead House) (030-0548), *Warrenton*, ca. 1790; 1900. Although it has been greatly altered, Mount View probably was built as early as ca. 1790 by either Charles or Turner Morehead. Each of the two oldest sections of the house is one and a half stories in height. The two wings form an L-shape in plan and share a cross-gable roof buttressed by brick end chimneys. The original modest farmhouse was enlarged and altered about 1900 and includes a wing the size of the original building. A one-and-a-half-story, one-room stone structure behind the house originally served as the kitchen dependency.

Porter Place (030-0351), *Warrenton*, ca. 1790. Built by Samuel Porter at the end of the eighteenth century, the Porter house is an excellent surviving example of a stone hall-parlor house in the county. The Porter family was locally prominent in the eighteenth and nineteenth centuries, with extensive landholdings in Fauquier, particularly west of Warrenton on the banks of the Rappahannock River. The newly restored and charming house features a steeply pitched gable roof with inside end chimneys and solid stone lintels above the window and door openings. The interior remains intact and includes the original doors, sills, chair rails, and corner stair leading to the loft level. A lean-to addition was built at the southwest corner of the house in the twentieth century.

Blackwell Farm (030-0421), *Warrenton*, 1810s. Though the house at Blackwell Farm is a modest early nineteenth-century log structure with twentieth-century alterations, the property has been owned by prominent Fauquier County families since the eighteenth century, including the Edmonds, the Jeffries, and the Blackwell families.

Chilly Bleak (030-0569), *Warrenton,* ca. 1820; ca. 1840. Legend holds that Chilly Bleak was built ca. 1700, but no architectural evidence for this date exists. Instead, the long and narrow stone house appears to have been built in two phases during the mid-nineteenth century. The original part of the house, constructed ca. 1820, is three bays wide and was altered from a hall-parlor plan to a central passage plan ca. 1840 when the single-room stone addition was made to the north end of the house. The addition continues the denticulated cornice line of the old section and is braced on the end by a stone end chimney that repeats the south end chimney. Later additions of frame abut the stone house.

Granville (030-0396), *Warrenton,* ca. 1820. Originally the home of Daniel Payne, Granville consists of two houses joined together. Daniel Payne (1784–1860) was the son of an English immigrant, William Payne, who came to Falmouth, Virginia, from his homeland. Daniel Payne married Elizabeth Hooe Winter in 1805; their children grew to be prominent Fauquier County citizens.

Woodbourne (030-0322), *Warrenton,* ca. 1820; 1925. Built ca. 1820 by Mrs. Charles Marshall, the stone house known as Woodbourne sits upon a slight hill and presents an elegant example of a Greek Revival house. The two-and-a-half-story stone structure, said to have been built by a local builder named Clarkson, proudly stands atop a stone basement overlooking its domain. The front elevation, located in the gable end, features a steeply pitched enclosed pediment pierced by a round window opening and a central entry door surrounded by sidelights and a fanlight. In 1925 the house was significantly enlarged at the rear, more than doubling the original size of the house. The original builder, Clarkson, is also credited with having built the similar Greek Revival–style houses of Oakwood (030-0083) and Bellevue (030-0493).

Ball-Shumate House (030-0464), *Warrenton,*
1820–40; 1920. The Ball-Shumate house is located on a
tract of land that was granted to John Smith by Lord
Fairfax on September 25, 1760, for "40 shillings sterling
yearly." The grant stipulated that Smith build one
"good and sufficient dwelling house" and plant "150
good apple trees at 50' distance in regular order." This
original house probably was destroyed in the mid-
nineteenth century and replaced by the present house
on the property. This house is a two-story, three-bay I-
house covered with a side-gable roof and featuring
one brick and one stone end chimney. The interior
woodwork reflects a transition from the Federal to the
Greek Revival style. The house has been added onto
over the years, including a kitchen wing that replaced
the separate kitchen building in 1920. Tucked off
Route 29, the Ball-Shumate house managed to survive
the road's widening as well as new construction.

Harkaway Tenant House (030-0488), *Warren-*
ton, 1820–40. Set among a group of domestic outbuildings and located at a distance from the main house,
the Harkaway Farm tenant house is a one-and-a-half-
story log structure clad with stucco. The steep roof
pitch and general configuration of the house make it
likely to have been built between 1820 and 1840; however, the interior was completely remodeled during
the twentieth century, leaving none of the original
materials intact.

Bellevue (030-0493), *Warrenton, ca. 1830.* In 1819 Colonel William Payne purchased the Bellevue tract of land, and between 1820 and 1830 he had the local builder Clarkson erect this elegant Greek Revival house for his daughter Marion Morson Payne Clarkson and her husband, Dr. Henry Martin Clarkson. Dr. Clarkson, no relation to the builder, was the grandson of Colonel Martin Pickett. The Clarksons only occupied the house until 1841 when they moved to Missouri. Similar to Oakwood (030-0083) and Woodbourne (030-0322), which were also built by Clarkson, Bellevue is a two-story, temple-form brick house with the familiar three-room plan. The house is located at the end of a long drive and presents its elegant three-bay gable end to the road. The pediment, formed by the enclosed gable end, features a lunette window that was a typical feature of the period. The central door is a later Colonial Revival addition, as is much of the interior detailing. Despite these alterations, Bellevue provides a fine example of the Greek Revival style in Fauquier County.

Licking Run Farm (Bell Haven) (030-0474), *Warrenton, ca. 1830; 1960s.* Constructed on the site of an older eighteenth-century dwelling, the main house at Licking Run Farm was built by George Nelson about 1830. The two-story, five-bay brick house provides a good example of Fauquier's Federal dwellings. The two side wings, the double-story porch, and the engaged entry surround are additions from the 1960s.

Locust Grove Farm (near Hurleyville) (030-0432), *Warrenton, ca. 1830; 1875.* Built ca. 1830 on a large tract of land inherited by Dr. John Gillison Beale, this two-story log dwelling known as Locust Grove possibly was built as an overseer's house. The rather modest structure was later converted into a central-hall house by the addition of a two-story wing to the northeast. In 1875 the house was again enlarged by the addition of a long rear wing. At the end of this wing was a schoolhouse, which now serves as the kitchen. Other alterations, including the front porch and the weatherboard siding, have occurred over the years.

Poehlmann Log House (030-0383), *Warrenton*, ca. 1830; ca. 1840. Originally a one-room log structure built ca. 1830, the Poehlman house was expanded ca. 1840 by the addition of a frame wing. Because of the abundance of Civil War relics located in the area, including bullet molds and bullets, local tradition claims that Civil War armies camped out near the house.

Rosedale (Bronough Farm) (030-0413), *Warrenton*, ca. 1830. Rosedale Farm was at one time known as Bronough Farm, after its mid-nineteenth-century owner, John J. Bronough. In 1875 the 274-acre property was purchased by Robert Mott, who then gave 27½ acres of the property to his daughter and son-in-law and renamed his tract Rosedale. In 1888 Frederick A. B. Portman, a well-known sportsman who was the first whipper-in of the Warrenton Hunt and later became its master, purchased the Rosedale property. The original section of the dwelling at Rosedale is the small one-and-a-half-story, one-room log building that was typical of the vernacular domestic architecture of Fauquier County in the mid-nineteenth century. The log house was added onto over the years, but little remains of these additions. Ruins of numerous buildings surround the house; the entire property is in a ruinous state.

Hunting Ridge (030-0321), *Warrenton,* ca. 1840; 1930; 1948. Significantly remodeled in 1930 and added onto again in 1948, Hunting Ridge incorporates a ca. 1840 two-story, center-hall house into its construction. Hunting Ridge was originally built for Elizabeth Hutton on her marriage to Henry S. Halley Jr. She died in 1869 and is buried on the property near the guesthouse. In 1930 Colonel Frederick Stuart Greene had the house completely remodeled, doubled in size and covered with stucco. At this time the front entrance was altered, the front porch was added, and the interior was completely redone. In 1948 the west wing of the house was added.

Oakwood (030-0083), *Warrenton*, ca. 1840; 1925. Once part of a huge land grant given to Colonel Martin Pickett for his services in the American Revolution, the Greek Revival–style house at Oakwood was built ca. 1840 in proximity to the original hall-parlor house on the property. The house later belonged to Lincoln's personal physician, Dr. Robert King Stone, and in 1922 the property was the site of the first Gold Cup Steeplechase. The main house, designed in an elegant Greek Revival style, was built by a local builder named Clarkson, who is also credited with the construction of Bellevue (030-0493) and Woodbourne (030-0322). The primary elevation is located in the gable end with the gable enclosed to form a pediment. The central entry door opens onto a wide transverse stair hall, behind which open two large 20-foot-square parlors. In 1925 wings were added to either side of the main block. The stables and farm buildings, built at the same time as the main house, are still standing, as is a historic garden with boxwood hedges, fountains, and statuary. Oakwood offers magnificent views of the mountains and survives as one of the finest examples of Greek Revival–style architecture in Fauquier.

Ivy Hill (030-0403), *Warrenton*, 1840–60 [destroyed]. Originally constructed as a hall-parlor-plan house, Ivy Hill was enlarged in the mid-nineteenth century to a two-story, central-passage-plan house. Only the site of Ivy Hill survives.

The Grove (030-0339), *Warrenton*, 1847; 1920s. The Grove, originally a tract of land owned by John Chapman, was inherited by Georgianna Alexander Blight in 1846 from her brother, Dr. Alexander Chapman. In 1847 she and her husband, Samuel Blight, constructed the present house on the property, valued at $8,000 in 1870 at the time of Samuel Blight's death. Georgianna Blight was forced to sell the property to pay the couple's debts, and in 1871 Richard Cooper bought it and named it The Grove. The Cooper family lived at The Grove until 1919 when William Henry Pool purchased the property and greatly enlarged the house. It survives as an imposing two-and-one-half-story brick house with pairs of massive brick end chimneys. The interior was originally laid out with a transverse-hall plan typical of the Greek Revival period but was converted to a central-passage, double-pile plan in the 1920s when Pool remodeled the house.

Watery Mountain Cabin (Hesperides Cabin) (030-0399), *Warrenton, 1848*. This one-and-a-half-story log cabin, known as the Watery Mountain cabin, was built in 1848 on the Watery Mountain estate of George Fitzhugh. The two single-door openings into two separate rooms indicate that the house may have accommodated two families and served as servant/slave quarters on the Fitzhugh estate. A frame wing was added to the rear of the house sometime in the late nineteenth century.

Appleton Cottage (Fauquier Springs Cottage) (030-0335), *Warrenton, 1850*. The Appleton cottage, located on the tract of land that was once part of the Fauquier White Sulphur Springs Hotel, may have once accommodated guests who came to "take the waters." The cottage is a two-story log structure with a central stone chimney. Two individual entry doors that originally provided access to the interior indicate that the cottage was most likely originally designed to accommodate two separate parties or guests who were visiting the springs. The rear wing and the two porches were added ca. 1930.

Lewis Shumate House (Foxmoor Farm) (030-0478), *Warrenton, 1870*. The Shumate house was built in 1870 by Lewis Shumate and remained in Shumate family hands until 1930. The house has been significantly altered and added onto during the twentieth century and retains little of its original massing or details.

Winmill-Nelson House (030-0381), *Warrenton, 1870; 1930s*. The Winmill-Nelson house is a typical mid-nineteenth-century I-house. It was enlarged and renovated in the 1930s.

Log House in Turnbull (030-0348), *Warrenton,* ca. 1870. Tradition holds that this ca. 1870 log house was built by freed slaves of Samuel Porter, who owned a large farm adjacent to this land.

Magbie Hill (030-0312), *Warrenton,* ca. 1870; 1898; 1927. Built ca. 1870, the building at Magbie Hill was originally a one-and-a-half-story dwelling with board-and-batten and weatherboard siding. In 1898 the house was raised to two stories, and in 1927 it was clad with stucco. The property also includes a board-and-batten barn, root cellar, and icehouse.

Caton-McClanahan House (McClanahan House) (030-0326), *Warrenton,* 1880–1900. Built 1880–1900, the Caton-McClanahan house is a good example of the late Victorian farmhouse. The L-shaped plan, projecting polygonal bay window, rounded shingles, finely decorated barge boards and brackets, and other millwork are all typical Victorian characteristics and embellishments.

McClanahan House (030-0349), *Warrenton,* 1880–1900. Built 1880–1900, the McClanahan house is a typical late nineteenth-century farmhouse. It is L-shaped in plan, of frame construction, and features a three-bay front elevation with a central entry.

Carter House (030-0384), *Warrenton*, ca. 1890. In deteriorating condition, the Carter house on Route 678 was originally constructed as a one-room, one-and-a-half-story house. In 1890 a two-story I-house was built, incorporating the massive chimney of the original building into the new structure.

Little Ashland (030-0344), *Warrenton*, ca. 1890. Historically part of Ashland (030-0005), the property designated Little Ashland today includes a contemporary (1972) primary residence and a ca. 1890 tenant house. The tenant house, of frame construction, is representative of the late nineteenth-century vernacular domestic buildings of rural Virginia.

R. Noland House in Rayton (030-0466), *Warrenton*, 1890–1900. The R. Noland house is located in the small community of Rayton, an African-American settlement that emerged as former slaves established themselves as freedmen following the Civil War. The house itself appears to have been built in the mid- to late nineteenth century as a two-bay, side-passage dwelling and later extended to three bays in length.

Tantivy (030-0323), *Warrenton*, ca. 1900. Built ca. 1900, the main house at Tantivy is a typical turn-of-the-century rural dwelling form with a center-hall plan and a regular five-bay facade. Flourishes of Victorian detail, such as the bracketed cornice, still linger in this twentieth-century farmhouse.

Mary McClanahan House (030-0325), *Warrenton, 1900–1910.* The Mary McClanahan house was built in 1900–1910 and is nearly identical in form and detail to Manor Lane Farm (030-0338). The same builder may have constructed these two-story frame I-houses with projecting central gables, or they may have been built from the same pattern book.

Leeton Hill (030-0299), *Warrenton, 1902.* Leeton Hill was built in 1902 by I. J. R. Murling, who purchased the land the previous year from the East Virginia Mineral and Warrenton Improvement Company. Prior to that, the land belonged to Governor William Smith.

Orchard Cottage (Maple Hill) (030-0315), *Warrenton, 1903; ca. 1945.* Named for the extensive orchard that once stood on the property, Orchard Cottage was originally built in 1903 as a four-room, one-story cottage. Around 1945 the roof was raised, and dormer windows were added, giving the building its present appearance. A barn used as an apple storage building still stands on the property.

Manor Lane Farm (Carter Farm) (030-0338), *Warrenton*, 1906. The main house at the old Carter farm, or Manor Lane Farm, was built in 1906 on the site of an older house that burned down. The present house is almost identical to the nearby Mary McClanahan house (030-0325). These two-story frame I-houses with projecting central gables may have been built by the same builder or from the same pattern book.

Elway Hall (030-0317), *Warrenton*, 1908. Constructed in 1908, the present house at Elway Hall was built for General Baldwin Day Spilman, a prominent resident of Warrenton. Before Spilman's ownership of the property, famed pianist Thomas Greene "Blind Tom" Bethune lived on the property after he received his freedom from slavery in 1865. Unlike the modest house of "Blind Tom" that undoubtedly occupied the site during his residency, the Elway Hall of Spilman is a rambling stone house designed in an eclectic style that has the feel of an English manor house. While the exterior presents an irregular and somewhat medieval appearance, the interior abounds in eclectic details such as a grand staircase with a Chinese motif and a number of mantels ranging in style from Tudor to Colonial Revival.

Hutton House (030-0311), *Warrenton*, 1908. The imposing Hutton house was built near the head of Licking Run in 1908 by J. Sidney Hutton on land that had belonged to the Hutton family for many years. Square in plan, the two-and-a-half-story house has a center-hall, double-parlor plan. The boxlike house is covered with a steeply pitched hipped roof with hipped dormers on all four elevations and a balustrade above. A single-story front porch with a balustrade is supported by pairs of wood columns. The house burned in part in 1976 and has since been remodeled to its original condition.

Odd Angles Farm (030-0302), *Warrenton, 1911*. Located near Warrenton, Odd Angles Farm was built in 1911 by Thomas F. Bartenstein, Fauquier County clerk from 1918 to 1958. The grounds around the two-story frame house contain objects from old Warrenton, including a stoop from the original clerk's office, curbstones from the original Main Street, and an entrance slab from the clerk's vault. In 1924 a single-bay addition was added, converting it from a side-passage to a central-passage house. At the same time the gable roof was altered to become a steeply pitched hipped roof, and a front porch was built to extend across the entire front elevation.

Lee's Ridge House (030-0305), *Warrenton, 1912*. Lee's Ridge House, located on Lee's Ridge Road, is a two-story frame house constructed in 1912. Mrs. George Lawrence, former owner and horticulturist, planted extensively on the property when she owned it.

Wyndham (Walker House) (030-0303), *Warrenton, 1912*. Wyndham was built by Maurice Pilson in 1912 on land that was originally part of Waverly. Pilson, an inventor, was forced to sell Wyndham when two items that he had invented fell out of usefulness. The house, which consists of a two-story central block flanked by single-story wings, was designed in a Colonial Revival style that was popular in the area during the first quarter of the twentieth century.

Black Rock (030-0301), *Warrenton, 1913; 1938*. Originally part of the Waverly property, this house, located south of Warrenton, was designed in 1913 for D. Harcourt Lees by architect Samuel Appleton. Lees reputedly named the property Black Rock for a place in Ireland. The two-and-a-half-story frame structure, set upon a stone foundation, was designed in the Georgian Revival style of architecture. The house has a side-passage plan with interior details executed by the Appleton Brothers, who operated a carpentry shop in Warrenton. A single-story wing was added to the west side of the house in 1938.

Waverly (Morborne) (near Warrenton) (030-0337), *Warrenton*, 1920. Waverly, located near Warrenton, was originally part of the tract of land granted to Thomas Lee in 1718 and inherited by Charles Lee of Leeton Forest farmhouse. The property, at one time known as Morborne, was constructed in the mid-nineteenth century. The house was significantly enlarged and altered in the 1920s. A single stone room survives from the mid-nineteenth century and forms one room of the substantial house today. The rest of the house was designed in the 1920s in the English country-house tradition. Several outbuildings and agricultural buildings located on the property are all designed in an eclectic English farm manner with stone and imitation half-timbering.

Leeton Forest Farmhouse (030-0309), *Warrenton*, 1921. The original Leeton Forest farmhouse on this site was built by Charles Lee, attorney general of the United States, 1795–1801. Although the original house survived several fires and was rebuilt several times, it finally succumbed to a large conflagration in 1921. Following this incendiary destruction, the current house was built on the site of the older houses.

Ridgelea (030-0084), *Warrenton*, 1921. Located southwest of Warrenton, Ridgelea was built in 1921 for Richard Barrett, who found the site while foxhunting. Ridgelea was designed by Waddy Butler Wood, a Washington, D.C., architect, in a Georgian Revival style that takes advantage of a commanding view. The house is a large two-story stone structure with a double-story portico recessed within the central bays. The end elevations feature paired brick chimneys, flat stone lintels, and a Roman arch window—all of which appear as a true and accurate representation of Georgian design. The house took two years to construct and was built of local stone by local craftsmen. The Warrenton Hunt was stabled at Ridgelea from the 1920s until 1979.

Hopefield (030-0085), *Warrenton, 1923–24.* Located on the site of an older house, and perhaps using part of that house in its structure, the existing house called Hopefield was built in 1923–24. Designed in a twentieth-century Federal Revival style by architect W. H. Irwin Fleming, the house features massing and architectural details that recall the early nineteenth-century Federal style of architecture. The imposing two-story, five-bay house has the typical Federal form, including the pairs of end chimneys and the pedimented dormer windows. The projecting pedimented front porch and the door and window treatments are similarly typical of the Federal period.

Clovelly (The Cedars, Cedar Grove) (030-0318), *Warrenton, 1924.* Historically known as The Cedars or Cedar Grove, this house, now called Clovelly, is located on a tract of land that was patented in 1727 by John and Peter Kemper, members of one of the first German families to settle in Fauquier at the German settlement of Germantown in 1724. The present house incorporates part of an eighteenth-century building on the site but is primarily the result of a major rebuilding effort in 1920. Well-known country-house architect William Lawrence Bottomley was responsible for the Colonial Revival–style Clovelly, with its architectural details taken from well-known colonial Virginia buildings. The front entrance door, for instance, has an engaged pedimented surround adapted from Westover, while a Mount Vernon–type portico extends across the east elevation. Equally prominent at Clovelly are the stables in which an outstanding collection of coaches and other horse-drawn vehicles is housed.

Dakota (030-0300), *Warrenton, 1925.* Located on the site of a late nineteenth-century dwelling, Dakota was designed by architect William Lawrence Bottomley in 1925. The two-story brick house is executed in a Colonial Revival style and features a hipped roof and brick end chimneys. The brick is said to be from the old Clerk's Office in Warrenton. The exterior has an austere five-bay front elevation with decoration reserved primarily for the central entry door. This door is flanked by engaged Ionic columns supporting a pediment that surmounts a fanlight and by round window openings. Although recalling colonial-era massing and details, the building's proportions and execution clearly identify it as a mid-twentieth-century revival.

Fenton (030-0402), *Warrenton*, 1925. Located on land once owned by the Fitzhugh family, Fenton was built in 1925 to replace an early nineteenth-century frame dwelling on the site which burned in 1925, having just undergone complete remodeling. The present house, designed by architect W. H. Irwin Fleming, is a refined stone structure that sits upon extensive lawns and takes full advantage of its fabulous site.

Emory Place (Sunset Hills) (030-0307), *Warrenton*, 1926–30. The house called the Emory place on Lee's Ridge Road actually consists of a house, a barn, and a stable all united into one. The three structures were combined in 1926–30 according to designs prepared by the Washington, D.C., architectural firm of Waddy Wood.

Hodgkin House (030-0382), *Warrenton*, ca. 1928. The Hodgkin house was built in the late 1920s. The house, with its half-timbered end wall and arched stone entry, recalls English Tudor houses and is a good local expression of the popular twentieth-century Tudor Revival style.

Leeton Forest (030-0308), *Warrenton*, 1929. Located on land that was part of Thomas Lee's 4,200-acre grant of 1718, Leeton Forest was designed and built by Washington, D.C., architect Waddy Butler Wood for himself in 1929. Directly inspired by the architecture of Thomas Jefferson, the characteristic detail of Leeton Forest, like so many of the houses designed and inspired by Jefferson before it, is the impressive temple-front portico that projects from the front entrance. The house is built with reused materials from buildings in Washington, D.C., and the surrounding area.

Farrar-Gray House (030-0306), *Warrenton, 1930s.* The Farrar-Gray house was originally part of the large tract of land owned by Charles Lee, U.S. attorney general from 1795 to 1801. The two-story frame house was erected in the 1930s for Ned Farrar to the designs of Washington, D.C., architect Eimer Cappelman. The house was designed in a Colonial Revival style characteristic of this period of house design in Fauquier County.

Broadview (030-0401), *Warrenton, 1930–32.* Perched atop a hill overlooking Warrenton, Broadview was the site of the Virginia Gold Cup Race from 1935 to 1984. The property once belonged to the locally venerable Blackwell family who have been residents of Fauquier County since the eighteenth century. The present house on the site was built in 1930–32 in the Georgian Revival style that was favored by Fauquier County's elite at that time. The two-story, double-pile stone house features a central-passage Georgian plan but combines architectural details from a variety of styles and periods. The exterior, for instance, presents Georgian massing and Greek Revival details, such as the lunette fanlight above the entry door and return cornices in the gable ends, as well as the dormer windows. The interior is Adamesque in detail with Greek and Egyptian decorative motifs.

The Oaks (Innis Hill) (030-0320), *Warrenton, 1932.* The original house on the site was called Innis Hill and was owned by the Honorable John Murray Forbes, a Warrenton attorney. Local tradition contends that Federal troops burned this first house during the Civil War, and that another house was built in its place. That house stood until 1931, when the Reverend Paul D. Bowden, rector of Saint James Episcopal Church, Warrenton, and his wife tore it down and replaced it with the present house, changing the name to The Oaks. This new house is a two-story brick structure designed in a Georgian Revival style. Elaborate exterior and interior details, such as the front porch, which is derived from the Temple of the Winds, are based upon plates from historic pattern books. Two small log outbuildings from the mid-nineteenth century survive as remnants of the earlier farm complex on the property.

Ashlawn (Holtzclaw House) (030-0941), *Warrenton, 1935.* The original late eighteenth-century house at Ashlawn was almost entirely remodeled and added onto in 1935 to the designs of architect William Lawrence Bottomley. The original house was a single-story, one-room building with a large end chimney. In 1840 a central-passage house was built onto it, and in 1889 the Holzclaw family enlarged the entire structure. In 1935 the house was remodeled and added onto by the Carhart family of New York who used it as a hunting lodge. This 1935 house, designed in a Georgian Revival style, consists of a large central block of stone, 40 feet square, covered with a hipped roof and flanked by single-story wings.

Sunnyside (030-0422), *Warrenton, 1936.* Sunnyside is located on the site of a substantial house from ca. 1800 that was gutted by fire sometime before 1936. In 1936 Dorothy Neyhart had the present house at Sunnyside built to the designs of architect Thomas A. Franzioli. The house was designed in the English manor house style that was popular in Fauquier County during the 1930s.

Hickory Hollow (030-0310), *Warrenton, 1937.* Hickory Hollow was part of the "wood lot" of the estate of Henry S. Halley Jr. that he divided among his children. The house, built in 1937, was altered in later years.

Saint Leonard's (030-0304), *Warrenton,* 1940. The original house on this site became the home of John Barton Payne, secretary of the Interior under President Wilson, president of the American Red Cross in 1921, and benefactor of the Virginia Museum of Fine Arts in Richmond. After Payne's death in 1935, the original house was replaced in 1940 by the substantial stone dwelling currently occupying the site. The newly built house, presented in a northern European vernacular tradition of architecture, was designed by Edis Van der Gracht, a Dutch architect known most notably for his design of the library at Princeton University.

Whiffletree Farm (030-0319), *Warrenton,* 1940. Located on the site of a tenant house of Clovelly (Cedar Grove), the main house at Whiffletree Farm was built in 1940 by Robert and Viola Winmill, a well-known couple in foxhunting circles. The present house on the site is a rambling structure with a series of wings and connected outbuildings, all designed in a Colonial Revival style. Included among the farm buildings is a large carriage house–stable which at one time housed a superb collection of horse-drawn carriages.

Catlett

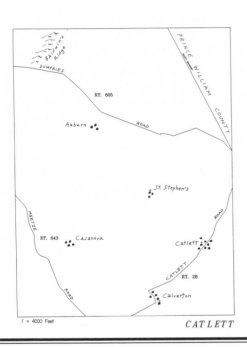

CATLETT

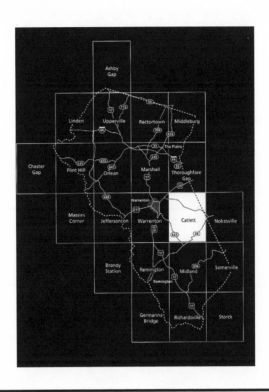

Grapewood (030-0517), *Catlett,* 1780–1800. The intriguing and idiosyncratic house at Grapewood was built on property that was originally owned by descendants of Robert "King" Carter and was sold in 1776 to Travers Nash. Designed in a vernacular mode, the house at Grapewood is an excellent and rare example of late colonial domestic architecture in Virginia that is characterized, in particular, by the gambrel roof with shed-roof dormers and the central-passage plan. The house has been added onto over the years but still retains its original massing and general configuration.

Heale-Weaver Farm (030-0889), *Catlett,*
1780–1800. The Heale-Weaver house, built in the last
quarter of the eighteenth century, provides an excellent example of a traditional Virginia farmhouse from
that period. The one-and-a-half-story frame structure
is defined on the exterior by its steeply pitched gable
roof and stone end chimneys and on the interior by its
three-room plan. The center hall is entered through a
centrally placed door. The parlor opens off the east
side of the hall, while two rooms, served by corner
fireplaces, open off the west side of the hall. In addition to its generally unaltered configuration, the
Heale-Weaver house illustrates Federal-period interior
trim and details.

Weston (030-0058), *Catlett,* 1780–1800; 1840–60. Off
Route 747 near Casanova stands Weston, a farmhouse
built in several different phases from the late eighteenth century until the late nineteenth century. The
original part, said to have been built by Giles Fitzhugh
ca. 1754, was more likely built between 1780 and 1800
by another Fitzhugh family member. This section of
the house consists of the small one-and-a-half-story
frame building that is characteristic of the vernacular
building of the period. Additions made to the house
between the mid- and late nineteenth century reflect
the Gothic cottage influence of A. J. Downing and include the dormer windows with scalloped gable ends
and a two-story frame wing to the house, similarly
with scalloped bargeboard in the gable ends and
around the dormers. Another one-and-a-half-story
wing further extended the overall length of the house.
Weston provides a good example of the evolution of
the vernacular house in Fauquier County from a small
hall-parlor house to a rambling domestic complex
with several wings of various dates. Weston was
named after Weston in England, a house built by Walter Nourse, ancestor of the mid-nineteenth-century
owner of the Fauquier Weston, Charles Joseph
Nourse Jr. Weston is a Virginia Historic Landmark and
is listed on the National Register of Historic Places.

Mount Sterling (030-0439), *Catlett,* ca. 1790. Mount Sterling is located off Route 605 in a heavily developed part of the county. The house was named by Younger Johnson, who bought the tract of land in 1820. Though he owned Mount Sterling, Johnson lived in King George County, Virginia. The original part of the house is the rear section consisting of a modest two-story structure with two rooms on each floor separated by a central chimney. In 1890 the house was significantly enlarged, giving it its current appearance.

Elmwood (Mount Hibla) (030-0477), *Catlett,* ca. 1810. Elmwood is located on part of the tract of land called Pageland that Robert Carter gave his son-in-law Mann Page in 1724. The land was eventually sold to William Fitzhugh who built the first house on the site ca. 1810. When that house burned down ten years later, another house was built just south of it; this house lasted 100 years until in 1920 it, too, burned down. No attempt was made to rebuild the house; however, one of the frame dependencies, probably the kitchen from the ca. 1810 estate, was refurbished and converted into the house presently known as Elmwood. In 1937 the two-story, single-pile house was remodeled so that it now includes several features of the Colonial Revival style.

Locust Grove Farm (Misty Farm) (030-0265), *Catlett,* 1810–40. Originally built in the first part of the nineteenth century, Locust Grove has been greatly added onto and renovated over the years. The original house is the two-story, side-hall frame house set upon a low stone basement. This central block was extended in the 1880s by single-story wings to either side. The entire house was renovated in the mid-twentieth century, leaving little of the original interior intact.

Dudley Fitzhugh House (The Weed Patch, etc.) (030-0458), *Catlett*, 1822. Located near Saint Stephen's Church, the Fitzhugh house was built in 1822 by Dudley Fitzhugh on his share of the estate of his father, William Fitzhugh. The simple one-and-a-half-story, three-bay frame house stands with its original configuration intact. It is covered with a steeply pitched gable roof and features massive end chimneys of stone. Despite some alterations, including paired windows on either side of the central entry door as opposed to single window openings, the house provides an excellent example of a vernacular central-passage-plan house. Like other members of the Fitzhugh family, Dudley Fitzhugh fell into great debt and was forced to sell his land in the mid-nineteenth century. The property changed ownership several times during the late nineteenth and twentieth centuries and has been known by several names including The Weed Patch, the Mansion House, and the old Glaettle place.

Stanley House (030-0473), *Catlett*, ca. 1830; ca. 1890; 1970. This large two-story house was originally built ca. 1830 as a small log structure and later was expanded ca. 1890 to its present three-bay configuration. In 1970 the house was completely renovated, and portions of the original building were removed.

John Martin House (030-0870), *Catlett*, ca. 1834. This house was built ca. 1834 by a descendant of the Martins of Germantown, John Martin, who purchased the property at public auction in 1827. The property was inherited by his son, George W. Martin, who served as a soldier in the Confederate army during the Civil War. Local history recounts that after being shot and wounded by a Union prisoner, George Martin returned fire, killing his attacker. The Martin house, a one-and-a-half-story frame structure set upon a stone foundation, is representative of the vernacular architectural traditions of Fauquier County.

Nicholson Log House (030-0475), *Catlett,* ca. 1840. Located near the Prince William County line, the Nicholson house was built ca. 1840, most likely by Samuel Weaver. The log walls were once covered with board-and-batten siding, and a stone chimney once stood on the south side of the house. In the mid-nineteenth century a single-story frame addition was built across the rear, and a porch stretched across the front elevation.

Vivian (Old Catlett House, Silver Brook Farm) (030-0254), *Catlett,* ca. 1840; 1870s. Vivian was originally built ca. 1840 by Samuel Catlett, descendant of the Catlett family who had occupied the land since before the Revolution. The house was begun as a typical Greek Revival–style dwelling with the entrance located in the gable end. In 1854 Samuel Catlett's son, Samuel Gibson Catlett, inherited the property. In the 1870s he added decorative details to the house to render it more stylishly Victorian.

Green Acres (William Smith House) (030-0268), *Catlett,* 1850–70. The house known as Green Acres, or the William Smith house, was originally located on a larger tract of land. The house probably was constructed in the third quarter of the nineteenth century as a tenant house to the larger main residence on the property. The two-door facade and the large central chimney suggest that two separate families occupied the house.

Mountjoy House (030-0437), *Catlett*, 1850–90. Standing in deteriorating condition, the Mountjoy house is a mid-nineteenth-century two-bay frame structure. The house is set upon a raised sandstone foundation and features a massive stone end chimney.

Prospect Acres (030-0267), *Catlett*, 1855. The house known as Prospect Acres was built on a tract of land inherited by the Catlett family, after whom the community of Catlett was named. The house, which was constructed in 1855, withstood the ravages of the Civil War and is alleged to be the oldest building in Catlett. Alterations in the 1910s and 1950s significantly enlarged the house from a one-room log structure to a four-room frame dwelling.

Spring Hill Farm (030-0441), *Catlett*, 1856. The property known as Spring Hill Farm includes a primary residence and a small log structure approximately fifty yards away from the dwelling. The log building was built by Dadridge Pitt Chicester ca. 1810; the main house dates from several decades later. Built by Robert R. Tompkins in 1856, the main house consists of a large two-story frame structure with subsequent additions. In 1970 the main house was renovated, and the interior was completely remodeled.

Melrose Castle Farm (030-0070), *Catlett*, 1857–58.
Melrose Castle, built between in 1857–58 for Dr. James
Murray, was designed in a castellated mode of the
Gothic Revival style by Edmund George Lind of Baltimore, Maryland, and constructed by local builder
George Washington Holtzclaw. The house presents a
fortified medieval appearance, with a central tower
and crenellated roofline. Dr. Murray, who settled in
Baltimore from his homeland of Scotland, commissioned the construction of the house and named it after Melrose Abbey in Scotland, which he claimed as an
ancestral home. During the Civil War, Federal troops
occupied the house. A threatening message, inscribed
by a lieutenant in the Indiana Volunteers, remains leg-
ible on the interior of a closet door: "Dear Sir, I think
you would have saved the destruction of your beautiful house by remaining at it. I am much pained to see
so fine a place destroyed. Yet I presume you think it
none of my business either. My desire is that all good
citizens shall enjoy their homes, of course, you do not
fall under the above either." Despite these foreboding
words, Melrose was not destroyed and is still standing
today. In addition to its architectural significance, Melrose provided mystery writer Mary Roberts Rinehart
the inspiration for her thriller *The Circular Staircase*.
Melrose is a Virginia Historic Landmark and is listed
on the National Register of Historic Places.

Shumate House (030-0273), *Catlett*, ca. 1860. The
Shumate house is located on land that was owned by
Captain Tilman Weaver at the time of his death in
1809. Although a house may have existed on this site
from the early nineteenth century, the present house
on the property was built ca. 1860. The Shumate
house features the typical two-story, three-bay massing of the vernacular farmhouse but incorporates details such as the bracketed cornice, the 2/2-light windows, and the corbeled brick chimney that are
associated with the Italianate style of architecture—an
architectural aesthetic from the period that was becoming popular in both urban and rural settings.

Longwood (030-0457), *Catlett,* ca. 1868. Longwood is located on the site of an older house owned by the Fitzhugh family that burned down during the Civil War. The existing house was built ca. 1868 for Howson Hooe by local builder H. P. Waite, who was responsible for the construction of several houses in the area. Longwood is a large two-story frame building that may have incorporated parts of the old house into its structure. Although the house is built in a vernacular mode, it does feature certain elements of a more academic Greek Revival style, including the entry located in the gable end of the house.

Montevideo (Marlen Farm, Bastable Farm) (030-0453), *Catlett,* 1869. Built in 1869, Montevideo is a substantial two-and-a-half-story frame house that has the scale and detail typical of a grand Victorian house. Originally located on a 1,916-acre tract of land known as Woodstock Farm, Montevideo was built as a summerhouse by Gilbert M. Bastable, from Baltimore, Maryland. The house features the somewhat restrained and regularized plan and massing of earlier pre-Victorian architectural styles, while exterior details such as the bracketed cornice, corbeled chimney caps, polygonal bay, and mansard roof and interior architectural details such as the ornate turned stair exhibit strong Victorian influences.

Woodstock (030-0454), *Catlett,* 1870–90. Built in the period 1870–90 by Gilbert M. Bastable, Woodstock features the symmetry and regularity associated with the typical late nineteenth-century vernacular farmhouse, but it also enjoys the whimsical details of the more exuberant Queen Anne style. The boxlike massing of the two-story frame dwelling is offset by the picturesqueness of the projecting bays and gables, dormer windows, and wraparound porch—all features commonly found on Queen Anne–style houses.

Pageland (030-0438), *Catlett*, 1880. Although this house is built on the land granted to Mann Page that is known as Pageland, it is not associated with the locally prominent Page family. This typical two-story frame farmhouse was built in the late nineteenth century and originally featured an L-shaped plan common for the period. Since its construction, the house was been enlarged over the years, but it still retains its original late nineteenth-century interior details.

Taylor House (030-0433), *Catlett*, ca. 1880. This one-and-a-half-story frame dwelling is set upon stone footings and is constructed with hand-hewn beams and studs. An enclosed winder stair provides the only access to the half-story sleeping quarters. A springhouse is located behind the house.

Seven Oaks (030-0476), *Catlett*, 1880–1910. The house known as Seven Oaks is principally a product of the late nineteenth to early twentieth century, although it may incorporate parts of an earlier house into its structure, such as the stone and brick end chimneys. The two-story, three-bay frame house features the typical scale and massing of the rural Virginia farmhouse from this period.

Saint Stephen's Farm (030-0456), *Catlett*, 1883. Originally built in the late nineteenth century on land adjacent to Saint Stephen's Church, this house has been known as Saint Stephen's Farm since the time of its construction. This simple two-story I-house has undergone substantial later additions. In the mid-twentieth century a two-story frame wing, similar in size and shape to the original house, was built, and the two structures were joined by a connecting wing which extends almost 30 feet between the two sections. The exterior was remodeled with shingles, diamond-paned windows, and pedimented door, while the interior features eclectic details of Victorian charm.

Birdwood (030-0255), *Catlett*, 1902. Designed in a Classical Revival style of architecture, the large and imposing Birdwood was built in 1902 to reflect a historical style of architecture associated with the Old South. The two-story frame house consists of a large block with a projecting double-story portico.

Nokesville

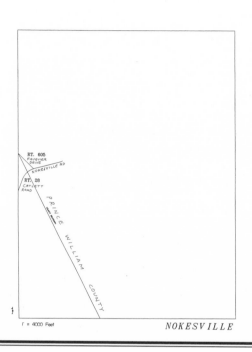

NOKESVILLE

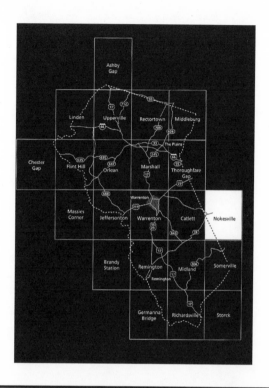

Teneriffe (030-0270), *Nokesville*, 1800–1840. Teneriffe is the site of one of the oldest mills to be established in Fauquier County and also one of the last to operate in approximately the same location on Cedar Run near Catlett. The first known mill on the site dated to 1762 and lasted over 100 years before it was torn down about 1896. At that time the stone from the old mill was used as a foundation for the mill that still stands, which was in operation until 1952. The house on the site is a two-story, three-bay stone structure. Several additions, including the frame wings, double-story porch, dormer windows, and window and door surrounds, give the house its mid-twentieth-century Colonial Revival appearance. Teneriffe supposedly was built by an old sea captain who named the property after the Teneriffe Islands where he was once shipwrecked. Cactus, said to have been imported from these islands, thrives on the rocky terrain of the farm that overlooks Cedar Run.

Douglas Residence (030-0266), *Nokesville, ca. 1867.*
The Douglas house, constructed ca. 1867 in Catlett,
was one of several houses built along the railroad line
that went through Catlett.

Brandy Station

Γ = 4000 Feet

BRANDY STATION

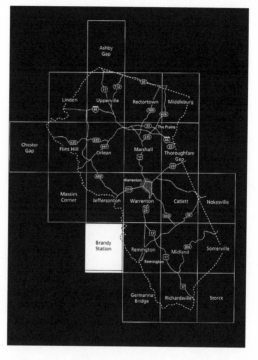

Remington

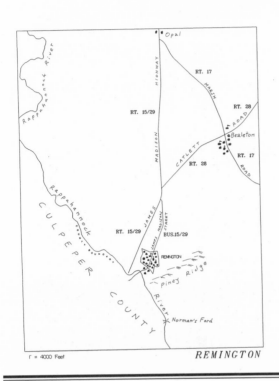

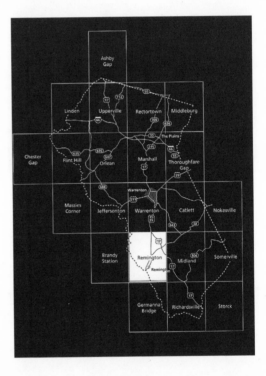

Chippewa (030-0426), *Remington,* ca. 1760 [destroyed]. Abandoned and in ruinous condition at the time of its survey, Chippewa had the distinction of being one of the oldest houses in Fauquier County. Probably originally built by the Bronough family as early as 1760, the house was later owned by Alexander F. Rose who endowed the property with the name Rose's Chippewa Farm. Subsequent owners later shortened the name to Chippewa. Chippewa provided an excellent example of an eighteenth-century vernacular house form. The original one-and-a-half-story frame house had a hall-parlor plan but was extended ca. 1800 by an additional room. Both the original section of the house and its addition were covered by a sagging gable roof with catslide additions supported by the front porch. Three narrow dormers projected from the roof, while a brick chimney, laid in Flemish bond, buttressed one end elevation.

Greenview (030-0427), *Remington*, ca. 1765 [demolished]. Built for Hancock Lee about 1765, the house at Greenview originally consisted of a frame structure with brick nogging that was built around a massive central chimney. This large chimney formerly had three immense fireplaces, each with a separate flue, and highly ornate Georgian mantels. During the 1930s the owners of Greenview sold the fireplace mantels to the Colonial Williamsburg Foundation for use in the restoration of the colonial town. As historian Thomas Waterman noted in his *Mansions of Virginia*, Greenview's mantels were erected in the east dependency of the rebuilt Governor's Palace *(shown)*, and they can be seen there today. The house had been significantly enlarged and altered over the years but at the time of the survey still retained its original stone basement that apparently served as a kitchen. The basement had a large fireplace with an iron bar which once held kitchen utensils. Since the survey, Greenview has burned down.

Waverley (030-0891), *Remington*, ca. 1787; 1890. Built by the Chapman family ca. 1787, Waverley stands on land granted to Samuel Skinner in 1742. Waverley was originally a central-hall-plan house, but its interior partitions have been altered. The flat-fronted exterior rises two stories above a stone foundation and features original 9/6 and 9/9 windows and one original end chimney laid in Flemish bond. In 1890 the house was significantly enlarged by an addition. Apparently a dirt road located north of the house was once lined with forty slave cabins.

Cornwell House (Old Cornwell Place) (030-0428), *Remington*, 1800–1820. This house, known as the Cornwell house and located off Route 651, was originally built in the early nineteenth century but was extensively altered during the twentieth century. The original part of the house is log and is enveloped by a turn-of-the-century frame structure, giving it the appearance of a typical frame farmhouse from the late nineteenth century.

Winter's Retreat (Fisher House) (030-0425), *Remington*, 1815; ca. 1890.

The house at Winter's Retreat was built in 1815 on land near Botha by then-owner Robert Fisher. The name Winter's Retreat was given to the property because it was the site of a winter encampment of the Union army during the Civil War. The one-and-a-half-story frame house, set upon a raised brick foundation, remains in a remarkably unaltered state. The house plan features a central passage with nearly square rooms flanking either side and a kitchen located in the basement level. The interior woodwork is carved with a vernacular interpretation of classical ornamentation including sunbursts and scrolls. A rear wing and a porch were added ca. 1890. A summer kitchen and traces of other outbuildings are found due north of the house.

Water Dale (Riverview) (030-0154), *Remington*, ca. 1820.

The house known as Water Dale was originally built ca. 1820 near Norman's Ford on the Rappahannock River. Norman's Ford, named for Isaac Norman who owned land on the Culpeper shore of the river, served a ferry crossing established by Charles Carter of Cleve in 1736. The Carolina Road, which crossed the Rappahannock at Norman's Ford, carried heavy traffic across Carter lands and prompted Charles Carter's son Landon Carter to begin the layout of a river-port town on the Fauquier side of the river in order to make a profit off the traveling settlers. In 1785 the Virginia General Assembly laid off fifty acres of Landon Carter's land at Norman's Ford into lots of half acres with streets that were to become the town of Carolandville. In 1787 Carter built a toll bridge across the river. The Carolina Road, however, did not survive as a favored route, and the town never became a reality. Water Dale was built on the site of the paper town. The building was originally a one-and-a-half-story hall-parlor house that was extended and raised to a full two stories during the nineteenth century to become the long two-story frame house that it is today.

Wellington (030-0772), *Remington,* ca. 1820. The house known as Wellington is located on the Rappahannock River at Norman's Ford on the site of the eighteenth-century platted town of Carolandville. Like Water Dale, Wellington was built ca. 1820 on the site of the proposed river port. During the Civil War, soldiers camped at Wellington. The house is nearly square in plan and features a cross-gable roof with gables on all four elevations.

Merry Hill (030-0158), *Remington,* ca. 1830–40; 1900. The house at Merry Hill was built in two separate phases. The original house, constructed in the early to mid-nineteenth century, was a small one-and-one-half-story frame building. Around 1900 a larger two-story frame building was built in front of the old dwelling, now a rear wing. Both the original house and the larger addition are representative of the type of dwellings found in the region from this period.

Edgewood (030-0634), *Remington,* 1840; 1890; 1950s. Behind its 1950s stone veneer, Edgewood survives as a ca. 1840 house with features expressive of the Greek Revival style. The dwelling, probably built by Dr. John Gillison Beale for his daughter Mary Beale, is a typical two-story, three-bay house with a chimney at either end. The most remarkable feature of the house is its elegant tetrastyle pedimented porch that decorates what was once the front elevation. In 1890 the orientation of the house was altered with an addition that abuts the original building and includes a new front porch.

Robinson House (030-0469), *Remington*, ca. 1850; ca. 1875. In 1867 this house and thirty-two acres were allotted to Jesse B. Robinson's widow from the estate of Samuel Robinson following a chancery suit. The property remained in Robinson family hands until 1952. Today the house consists of two sections: the original one-and-a-half-story frame section built before the Civil War (currently the rear wing of the house) and the ca. 1875 addition (currently the front of the house). This front section with its paired projecting bays, central gable, and scroll-sawn front porch is architecturally striking.

MacDonald House (030-0461), *Remington*, ca. 1880. The MacDonald house is an unassuming nineteenth-century house notable mainly for its proximity to Greenview, the eighteenth-century residence of Hancock Lee. The MacDonald house consists of several sections, of which the two-bay section with the stone end chimney is the oldest. The later additions, made after its construction ca. 1880, give the dwelling its identifiable telescopic form.

Meadfield (030-0460), *Remington*, ca. 1880. Meadfield is located off Route 660 on the site of a late eighteenth-century manor house. In 1783 Meadfield was the main house for more than 1,000 acres of land owned by Billy "Buckleg" Beale. The present three-bay, two-story house on the site was built ca. 1880.

Lee's Mill Farm (030-0462), *Remington, 1880–1900.* At least one part of this house on Lee's Mill Farm may have originally been built as a miller's house for Hancock Lee's eighteenth-century mill that was located nearby on the Rappahannock River. In overall form and detail, the existing dwelling appears to date from the late nineteenth century, but it features an end chimney that may well have been part of an eighteenth-century house. This chimney has tiled weatherings, an architectural feature generally not found after the eighteenth century in Virginia.

Grassdale (030-0935), *Remington, 1920.* The present Grassdale house, an imposing American foursquare residence, was built on the site of an older house which burned in 1920. The first Grassdale was the home of Dr. Nathaniel Vandewall Clopton, who married Sarah Susan Grant Skinker.

Midland

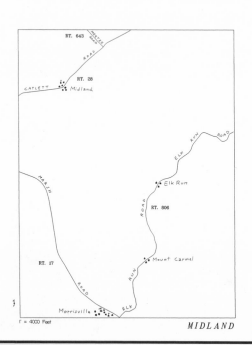

MIDLAND

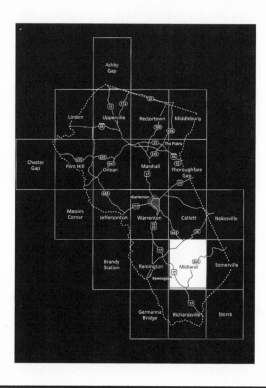

Greenvilla (030-0847), *Midland*, 1775. Located near Somerville, three miles from the Stafford County border, Greenvilla stands in ruinous condition as one of Fauquier County's oldest residences. The two-story frame house with its all-encompassing saltbox roof and end chimneys was built ca. 1775 by the Honorable Joseph Blackwell Sr., Fauquier's first sheriff, for his son Samuel Blackwell. Although deteriorating, the house survives in a relatively unaltered state and retains its original center-hall, three-room plan.

Cowne's Place (030-0886), *Midland,* ca. 1780; ca.
1910. Cowne's Place was built ca. 1780 on land granted
to John Rust. The original core of the house consists
of a hall-parlor plan; later additions made ca. 1910 include the kitchen wing to the east and a parlor and
stair hall to the south, as well as an L-shaped entrance
porch. Particularly noteworthy is the interior, which
retains its original woodwork, including a Federal-
style mantel in the living room (*detail shown*), as well
as the original paint in some areas. Cowne's Place was
named for its owner in 1900.

Clarence Lomax House (Furr Cabin) (030-
0041), *Midland,* 1780–1820. Located near Elk Run, this
log house is known locally as the Clarence Lomax
house for the property's owner in the early twentieth
century. Although in physical decline, the house survives as a good example of a log hall-parlor house
from the late eighteenth or early nineteenth century.

Beale House (Herd Farm) (030-0725), *Midland,*
ca. 1820. Located on land that was owned by John
Gordon Beale, the Beale house was built ca. 1820,
most likely for an overseer of the farm. Asymmetrical
in elevation, the three-bay I-house with stone chimneys was originally built as a log hall-parlor-plan house
that was expanded in several phases to its present configuration.

Bennett-Peters House (Belvederia) (030-0879), *Midland*, ca. 1820. Located on the site of an earlier log house, the Bennett-Peters house grew from its humble origins to a large and rambling dwelling after a series of several additions. Because the log section was torn down in 1906, the oldest surviving section of the house is the three-bay, side-passage-plan section of ca. 1820. This house was subsequently enlarged in two phases including the addition of a two-story frame wing, built ca. 1840, and a two-story projecting polygonal bay, built ca. 1910. The property on which the house stands is traditionally noted as having been the site of a building that served as the meeting place of the first Fauquier County Court in 1759.

Fletcher-Graves House (030-0043), *Midland*, 1820–40. Although the Fletcher-Graves house appears to be a single frame structure built at one time as an I-house form, the house actually consists of two separate parts. The oldest section was built in the early to mid-nineteenth century as a one-and-a-half-story log building with a stone chimney and a hall-parlor plan. In the same half century, the house was raised to a full two stories and extended by the addition of a two-story frame wing. This addition created the three-bay, central-passage-plan house that now stands in ruinous condition.

Bernard and Sally George Farm (Inglewood) (030-0872), *Midland*, ca. 1825. Built by 1825, the original two-room, one-and-a-half-story section of the house was greatly enlarged in 1933–40, and the whole was covered with a stone veneer in 1959.

Kane House (Windy Hill Farm) (030-0760),

Midland, ca. 1830. Located about one mile south of Elk Run Church, the Kane house was built ca. 1830. Local tradition holds that the Kane house served as a hospital during the Civil War. A hole in the south portion of the east facade is thought to have been made by a cannonball during the war. The two-story, side-passage-plan house is set upon a stone foundation and originally featured inside stone end chimneys that have since been removed. A single-story addition was made to the house ca. 1940 and is set back from the main house.

Morgansburg (030-0151), *Midland,* ca. 1830 [de-

stroyed]. Once the landmark of a crossroads village and post office, the Federal-era house known as Morgansburg was dismantled around 1980. The house, including its Federal mantels (*detail shown*) and interior woodwork, was taken down in anticipation of development on the site. The salvaged remains of the house are in private hands.

Boteler-Peters House (030-0849), *Midland,* ca. 1837.

The Boteler-Peters house was built ca. 1837 by William Henry Boteler. The two-story frame structure, set upon a stone foundation and covered with a side-gable roof, features a five-bay front elevation and inside end chimneys. A double-story porch recalling Mount Vernon extends across the front elevation.

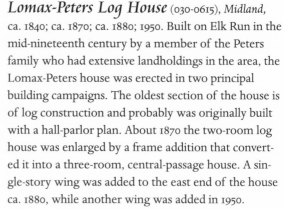

Lomax-Peters Log House (030-0615), *Midland,* ca. 1840; ca. 1870; ca. 1880; 1950. Built on Elk Run in the mid-nineteenth century by a member of the Peters family who had extensive landholdings in the area, the Lomax-Peters house was erected in two principal building campaigns. The oldest section of the house is of log construction and probably was originally built with a hall-parlor plan. About 1870 the two-room log house was enlarged by a frame addition that converted it into a three-room, central-passage house. A single-story wing was added to the east end of the house ca. 1880, while another wing was added in 1950.

Robert Flournoy Farm (030-0850), *Midland,* ca. 1850. The Flournoy farm originally consisted of 1,200 acres and included a large brick house which was burned during the Civil War. The two surviving antebellum log and frame houses (*one shown*) on the property are reported to be slave quarters.

Reed-Hansborough House (030-0096), *Midland,* ca. 1850; ca. 1880. Probably built by the Reed family in the mid-nineteenth century, the Reed-Hansborough house was been in the Hansborough family since at least 1880. At that time the mid-nineteenth-century frame building, which stood next to the Reed Inn and served as a store and dwelling combined, was enlarged and Victorianized by the addition of fish-scale shingles in the gable end and pedimented window surrounds. The house stands in dilapidated condition today.

Sulphur Springs (030-0616), *Midland,* ca. 1850. Although not built until the mid-nineteenth century, the original part of Sulphur Springs exhibits characteristics of dwellings built in the late eighteenth century. The small one-and-a-half-story, side-hall-plan house was enlarged in the late nineteenth century. The house stands in ruinous condition today.

Payne House (Elk Run) (030-0051), *Midland,* ca. 1878. The Payne house, built ca. 1878, is located on the site of an older house that burned down during the Civil War. The present house is built in a vernacular Victorian mode that was typical of rural Virginia architecture in the late nineteenth century. The three-bay house features brick end chimneys, a central projecting gable, and a front porch with scroll-saw details. The two-story rear ell burned down in 1970 and was rebuilt.

Old Chapman Place (030-0877), *Midland,* 1920. Though in deteriorating condition, the old Chapman place provides a good example of the two-story, two-bay house that was once a common dwelling form in rural Virginia. The house was originally built in the mid-nineteenth century but was completely rebuilt ca. 1920.

Somerville

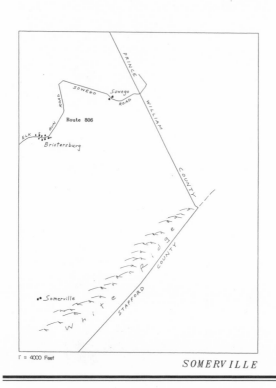

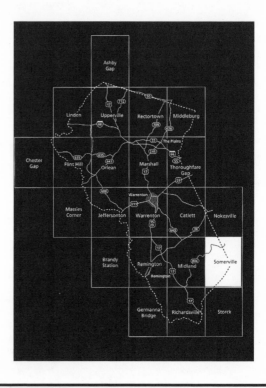

SOMERVILLE

Crosby-Waller House (030-0584), *Somerville*, ca. 1790. Located on land granted to George Crosby in the early 1700s, the Crosby-Waller house was built ca. 1790 and was sold in 1813 to tenant Lewis Waller. The frame house consists of two sections, including a one-and-a-half-story main block with stone end chimneys and a one-story frame addition from the later nineteenth century. The main block, which has been altered over the years and currently stands in deteriorating condition, has original and intact eighteenth-century construction details such as handmade nails, beaded interior and exterior siding, a steeply pitched roof, and a corner box stair.

Henry Peters House (Peters-Eskridge Property)

(030-0587), *Somerville, ca. 1830.* The Peters-Eskridge property is nestled within a group of mature trees near the intersection of Routes 806 and 609. The property includes ruins of an early nineteenth-century log house, an early to mid-nineteenth-century frame house, and a cemetery. The frame house, including the interior corner winder stair, still stands, though it is in ruinous condition and is completely overtaken by growth.

Bird House

(030-0761), *Somerville, 1830–50.* Traditionally known as the old Bird place, the house located on Town Run is a small side-passage log structure from the mid-nineteenth century. The log walls at one time were covered with board-and-batten siding that is still intact under the current weatherboard cladding.

Old Pearson House (Gravelly Ridge)

(030-0138), *Somerville, 1830–50; late 19th century.* Gravelly Ridge, or the old Pearson house, located near Somerville, was built in various stages during the nineteenth century. Construction techniques of the house date the main structure to the mid-nineteenth century. However, significant changes made to the house in the late nineteenth century, such as the addition of the central gable and the rebuilt end chimneys, give the house the look and feel of a typical late nineteenth-century farmhouse. Tradition holds that Gravelly Ridge was built by a slave carpenter who was killed during the construction of another house in the area.

Woodside (near Bristersburg) (030-0153),
Somerville, 1830–50. At Woodside the original two-story frame house with its two stone and brick end chimneys was built in the mid-nineteenth century by James Payne. The one-and-a-half-story wing attached to one end of the two-story structure features two stone end chimneys and probably dates from the pre–Civil War era.

Bumbrey House (Warren-Bumbrey Place)
(030-0585), *Somerville*, ca. 1840; 1910. Standing in deteriorating condition, the Bumbrey house is located off Route 609. The original section of the house was built ca. 1840 of log; in 1910 a rear frame addition was made, doubling the size of the house.

French Tenant House (030-0762), *Somerville*, ca.
1850. This small two-door board-and-batten house probably was built as a tenant house to the French property ca. 1850. The old French place, located nearby off Route 616, is a modern house built upon the foundations of an older structure.

Mauzey-George House (030-0612), *Somerville*, ca. 1870. Although this house was primarily constructed ca. 1870 and altered during the twentieth century, it incorporates aspects of an earlier ca. 1800 house on the site. In particular, a large stone chimney that serves two corner fireplaces survives as a remnant of the original dwelling on the site.

Brenton (Sowego) (030-0905), *Somerville, 1920s*. Rebuilt in the 1920s, this two-and-a-half-story, five-bay I-house retains large stone and brick end chimneys that were part of a nineteenth-century house on the site. The house features several Colonial Revival–style elements of the early twentieth century such as the symmetrical facade, projecting porch, and dormer windows.

Germanna Bridge

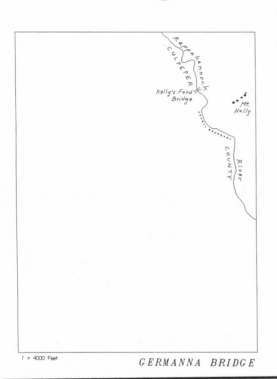

GERMANNA BRIDGE

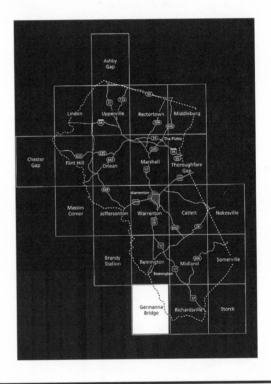

Hogue Cabin (030-0770), *Germanna Bridge*, ca. 1800–1820. The Hogue cabin is located on property that was owned by the Hogue family in the early nineteenth century. The house is a one-room log cabin with a rubblestone end chimney and a small frame addition to one side. The log structure has been substantially altered and is no longer clad with weatherboard siding.

Stevens-Maddux House (030-0938), *Germanna Bridge*, ca. 1820. Originally built as a two-story frame house ca. 1820, the Stevens-Maddux house was later added onto and faced with a brick veneer. The Federal-style woodwork and interior detailing survive intact.

Chestnut Lawn (030-0088), *Germanna Bridge*, 1832. Finished in 1832, the two-story stone house called Chestnut Lawn near Remington was built for Captain James Payne who hired a group of artisan slaves to erect his dwelling. The slaves were also responsible for the construction of the church at Goldvein, located nearby. An inscription found in one of the large stones at the top of the house reads "HAN 1832" and un-doubtedly was inscribed by Hannibal, the head slave in charge of construction. Chestnut Lawn is so named because it was sited in a grove of some of the largest chestnut trees in America, which were killed in the blight of 1910–30. Purchased in 1947 by Mr. and Mrs. John Wilkins Jr., Chestnut Lawn was restored with the help of Warrenton historian Randolph Carter.

Hogue House (030-0771), *Germanna Bridge*, ca. 1840; 1930s. The Hogue house, located near Kelly's Ford, provides a good example of the additive evolution that a small farmhouse typically undergoes. Reputed to date originally from ca. 1800, the oldest part actually appears to be from the mid-nineteenth century. The house was renovated in the 1930s.

Richardsville

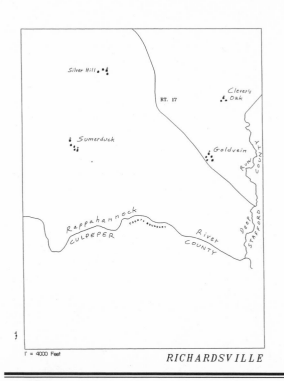

RICHARDSVILLE

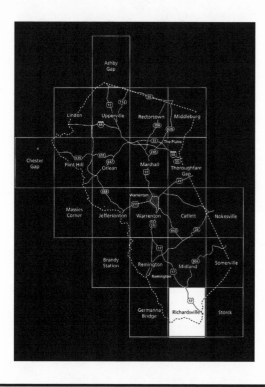

Spring Farm (030-0152), *Richardsville*, ca. 1770; ca. 1810. Located near the Stafford County line, the main house at Spring Farm was built in several different construction campaigns. The oldest part of the house is a one-and-a-half-story, two-room structure covered with a steeply pitched gambrel roof that was built by Thomas Skinker. Skinker, a wealthy and philanthropic landowner in Fauquier, Prince William, and Stafford Counties, either purchased or acquired the property from his father sometime before 1759 and built the house ca. 1770. At Skinker's death in 1802, his nephew William Skinker inherited his Fauquier County lands, including Spring Farm. About 1810 a one-and-a-half-story frame wing with a gable roof was appended to the original structure at a perpendicular angle. Throughout the nineteenth century several additions, including shed-roof extensions and open and closed porches, were built against both sections of the house. Spring Farm provides an excellent example of the evolution of the late eighteenth-century farmhouse.

Keith House (030-0588), *Richardsville*, 1780–1800. The Keith house was built on part of a tract of 1,146 acres purchased in 1779 by Captain Thomas R. Keith from the estate of Charles Carter of Cleve. The original house, built 1780–1800, is a two-story frame house with a hall-parlor plan and a chimney laid in Flemish bond. A log section was added to the house in the early nineteenth century. The entire complex stands in ruinous condition today.

Locust Grove (near Goldvein) (030-0589), *Richardsville*, 1802–10; 1847. Built on part of a tract of 1,146 acres of land, Locust Grove was begun by 1802 by Captain Thomas R. Keith. At Keith's death in 1810, construction on the house continued, and it was, in fact, enlarged as a dower for Keith's widow. This house consisted of a two-story structure with two rooms on each floor. In 1836 the house was partly destroyed by fire. Repairs, completed by 1847, include the stair-hall extension to the original house as well as the addition of the north wing. The south wing was added to the house in the early twentieth century.

Embrey House (030-0880), *Richardsville*, 1820–40. The land on which the Embrey house stands was granted to the first Robert Embrey in 1761. The house, however, probably was built by Robert Embrey's son, Robert Embrey Jr., between 1820 and 1840. The Embrey house, which includes its original front porch, remains as one of the few pure hall-parlor-plan houses from this period located in Fauquier County. A two-story frame addition from the early twentieth century to the right rear of the house is the only major addition.

Milburn (030-0218), *Richardsville*, ca. 1890. The property known as Milburn provides a good example of a late nineteenth-century farm complex in Fauquier County. The main dwelling on the farm is a typical farmhouse with Victorian embellishments such as a gable front and a porch supported by turned posts. A cohesive group of historic domestic outbuildings and agricultural buildings is located in close proximity to the house.

Storck

1' = 4000 Feet

STORCK

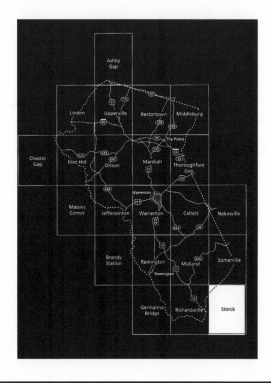

Green Branch (030-0848), *Storck,* 1760–90. Built in the period 1760–90, Green Branch is one of a few remaining eighteenth-century houses in Fauquier County. The one-and-a-half-story frame structure features a hall-parlor plan, a tall and steeply pitched gable roof, and a single stone end chimney. All of these features are typical of vernacular Virginian domestic buildings of the period and provide an excellent early example of this house type. The single end chimney serves corner fireplaces in the two rooms, while a boxed stair accesses the loft level above. A shed-roof bedroom wing and an enclosed porch have been added onto the small house but do not significantly detract from its historic character.

Ensor House (Mason Place) (030-0486), *Storck,* ca. 1790. The Ensor house was built ca. 1790 on land purchased by George Ensor from John Tayloe of Mount Airy in Richmond County. In ruinous condition at the time of its survey, this one-and-a-half-story log dwelling clad with board-and-batten siding features a typical hall-parlor plan and a massive stone and brick end chimney. The house is notable for its unusually heavy construction—10-inch-by-12-inch logs rest on a 12-inch log sill.

Appendixes
Property Indexes

A. Property Index by Date of Construction

Note: Alternative property names are set in italics.

Name of Resource	Date	USGS Quad Name	VDHR file no.	Page
Rose Hill	1750–70	Upperville	030-0073	62
Chippewa	ca. 1760	Remington	030-0426	210
Yew Hill *Watt's Ordinary*	ca. 1760	Upperville	030-0060	63
Green Branch	1760–90	Storck	030-0848	230
Hollow, The	1765	Upperville	030-0803	64
Greenview	ca. 1765	Remington	030-0427	211
Spring Farm	ca. 1770; ca. 1810	Richardsville	030-0152	228
Oak Hill	ca. 1773; 1819	Upperville	030-0044	64
North Wales	1773–81; 1914	Warrenton	030-0093	176
Greenvilla	1775	Midland	030-0847	216
Cowne's Place	ca. 1780; ca. 1910	Midland	030-0886	217
Lynn House	ca. 1780	Rectortown	030-0603	86
Settle Cottage *Canterbury Cottage*	ca. 1780	Warrenton	030-0346	177
Strother, James, House *Molly's Folly*	1780s(?); 1830–50	Marshall	030-0661	141
Chinn, Charles, House	1780–1840	Rectortown	030-0780	87
Grapewood	1780–1800	Catlett	030-0517	197
Heale-Weaver Farm	1780–1800	Catlett	030-0889	198
Hooewood *Ashley*	1780–90	Warrenton	030-0497-	177
Keith House	1780–1800	Richardsville	030-0588	229
Lomax, Clarence, House *Furr Cabin*	1780–1820	Midland	030-0041	217

Name of Resource	Date	USGS Quad Name	VDHR file no.	Page
Weston	1780–1800; 1840–60	Catlett	030-0058	198
Fields House *Pearle House*	1785; 1840	Rectortown	030-0774	87
Waverley	ca. 1787; 1890	Remington	030-0891	211
Loretto *Edmonium*	1790; 1895; ca. 1900	Warrenton	030-0035	178
Barbee's Tavern	ca. 1790	Flint Hill	030-0685	119
Crosby-Waller House	ca. 1790	Somerville	030-0584	222
Ensor House *Mason Place*	ca. 1790	Storck	030-0486	231
Gordonsdale Cabin	ca. 1790	Marshall	030-0027	142
Mount Sterling	ca. 1790	Catlett	030-0439	199
Mount View *Glenaman, Morehead House*	ca. 1790; 1900	Warrenton	030-0548	179
Porter Place	ca. 1790	Warrenton	030-0351	179
Snow Hill	ca. 1790	Thoroughfare Gap	030-0887	158
Waverley	ca. 1790; ca. 1830 1940s	Middleburg	030-0226	111
Hatherage	1790–1810	Middleburg	030-0629	112
Maidstone Ordinary *Floweree Tavern*	1790–1810	Rectortown	030-0036	88
Mill House *Chinn's Mill*	1790–1820; 1924–29	Rectortown	030-0650	88
Aspen Dale	ca. 1795; 1907	Upperville	030-0007	65
Mountain End	ca. 1798	Thoroughfare Gap	030-0683	159
Mountain View	ca. 1798	Thoroughfare Gap	030-0673	159
Green Dale	1800; 1820; 1920	Rectortown	030-0741	89
Afton Farm	ca. 1800; mid-19th cen.	Thoroughfare Gap	030-0519	159
Evergreen	ca. 1800; ca. 1900	Thoroughfare Gap	030-0890	159
Hopper-Collins House *Marshall-Gore Log House*	ca. 1800	Massies Corner	030-0721	166
Jeffries House *Glenmore Tenant House*	ca. 1800	Rectortown	030-0568	89
Locust Grove *Triplett House*	ca. 1800	Upperville	030-0838	65
Mann House *Lake Place*	ca. 1800	Rectortown	030-0833	89
Meadows, The	ca. 1800	Marshall	030-0529	142

Name of Resource	Date	USGS Quad Name	VDHR file no.	Page
Meadowville	ca. 1800	Marshall	030-0831	142
Millford Mills *Woolf's Mill*	ca. 1800	Rectortown	030-0713	90
Mount Independence	ca. 1800; ca. 1825; ca. 1890	Upperville	030-0674	65
Shirland Hall	ca. 1800; 1833	Rectortown	030-0706	90
Cornwell House *Old Cornwell Place*	1800–1820	Remington	030-0428	211
Glenmore Cabin	1800–1810	Rectortown	030-0593	90
Rock Valley	1800–1840	Marshall	030-0525	143
Teneriffe	1800–1840	Nokesville	030-0270	207
Western View	1800–1810	Rectortown	030-0571	91
Hogue Cabin	ca. 1800–1820	Germanna Bridge	030-0770	226
Rosemont *Orange Hill*	1801; 1848; 1935; 1977	Rectortown	030-0652	91
Locust Grove, near Goldvein	1802–10; 1847	Richardsville	030-0589	229
Montrose	ca. 1805; 1822; 1870	Rectortown	030-0518	91
Springfield	ca. 1805	Middleburg	030-0810	112
Ball House *Eric Sevareid House*	1807	Orlean	030-0243	125
Greystone *Rock Hill*	1807	Middleburg	030-0079	112
Brenton	1810	Rectortown	030-0636	91
Duncan-Glascock House	1810	Marshall	030-0665	143
Fairview	1810; ca. 1915	Thoroughfare Gap	030-0550	160
Grigsby House	1810	Marshall	030-0500	143
Humblestone	1810; 1912; 1927	Marshall	030-0490	144
Hunterleigh *Moreland, Turner House*	1810; 1850	Orlean	030-0658	126
Meadowview	1810	Thoroughfare Gap	030-0672	160
Mount Defiance	1810	Rectortown	030-0775	92
Aspen Hill	ca. 1810	Rectortown	030-0755	92
Bollingbrook *Waterloo*	ca. 1810; ca. 1854	Upperville	030-0010	66
Edmonds House *Yerby, Simper's Mill*	ca. 1810; ca. 1870	Upperville	030-0246	67
Elmwood *Mount Hibla*	ca. 1810	Catlett	030-0477	199

Name of Resource	Date	USGS Quad Name	VDHR file no.	Page
Fountain Hill	ca. 1810; 1973	Upperville	030-0896	67
Gibraltar	ca. 1810; ca. 1890	Upperville	030-0092	67
Glen Ora	ca. 1810; ca. 1930	Middleburg	030-0078	112
Hume, Asa, House	ca. 1810	Jeffersonton	030-0367	167
Hume, Jacob, House	ca. 1810	Jeffersonton	030-0376	168
Laurence House	ca. 1810	Linden	030-0748	58
Marshall-Smith Place	ca. 1810	Jeffersonton	030-0361	168
McSweeny House	ca. 1810	Marshall	030-0671	144
Mount Pleasant _The Meadows_	ca. 1810; 1840; 1890	Upperville	030-0567	68
Mountain View _Stribling House_	ca. 1810; ca. 1850	Linden	030-0132	59
Murray House	ca. 1810; 1840–50; ca. 1851	Rectortown	030-0767	92
Oakwood	ca. 1810	Upperville	030-0837	68
Porter Log House _Weaver Cabin_	ca. 1810	Rectortown	030-0639	93
Redman House	ca. 1810	Middleburg	030-0547	113
Rumsey House _Bishop-Glascock House, Smith House_	ca. 1810	Rectortown	030-0668	93
Blackwell Farm	1810s	Warrenton	030-0421	179
Crain House _Middleton_	1810–40	Rectortown	030-0744	93
Glenmore	1810–20	Rectortown	030-0025	94
Kelvedon	1810–50	Rectortown	030-0034	94
Locust Grove Farm _Misty Farm_	1810–40	Catlett	030-0265	199
Peake House	1810–40	Middleburg	030-0599	113
Pleasant Vale	1810–20	Upperville	030-0680	68
Orlean Farm	1812; ca. 1850	Orlean	030-0086	126
Belle Grove _Settle_	ca. 1812; ca. 1830; 1970s	Upperville	030-0008	69
Rutledge	ca. 1812; 1856	Upperville	030-0514	69
Waverly _Turner Adams House_	ca. 1812; 1851	Upperville	030-0057	69
Palmerstone	1813; 1850; 1881; 1930	Rectortown	030-0601	94
Owen House	1815; 1850	Rectortown	030-0667	95

Name of Resource	Date	USGS Quad Name	VDHR file no.	Page
Winter's Retreat *Fisher House*	1815; ca. 1890	Remington	030-0425	212
Chelsea	ca. 1815	Marshall	030-0177	144
Southern View	ca. 1815	Marshall	030-0663	145
Atoka	1816; 1930s; 1976	Rectortown	030-0704	95
Fieldmont *Fruit Farm*	1817	Middleburg	030-0630	113
Delacarlia *Walnut Grove*	1818	Rectortown	030-0387	95
Whitewood	ca. 1818	Rectortown	030-0561	96
Morven	ca. 1819; 1835; 1950	Orlean	030-0864	127
Shacklett, George W., House *Myers House*	ca. 1819; ca. 1830	Orlean	030-0657	127
Armistead-Glascock House	1820	Rectortown	030-0700	96
Cobbler Mountain *Mont Blanc*	1820	Orlean	030-0653	128
Anderson Farm	ca. 1820	Rectortown	030-0606	96
Baird House	ca. 1820; ca. 1880	Upperville	030-0675	70
Balthorpe House *Marly*	ca. 1820	Rectortown	030-0769	97
Beale House *Herd Farm*	ca. 1820	Midland	030-0725	217
Bennett-Peters House *Belvederia*	ca. 1820	Midland	030-0879	218
Bleak House	ca. 1820; 1853	Orlean	030-0191	128
Chilly Bleak	ca. 1820; ca. 1840	Warrenton	030-0569	180
Fiery Run Miller's House	ca. 1820	Flint Hill	030-0758	120
Glanville	ca. 1820; ca. 1900	Orlean	030-0210	128
Greenmont	ca. 1820; 1880–90	Marshall	030-0289	145
Granville	ca. 1820	Warrenton	030-0396	180
Halfway Farm *Haines House*	ca. 1820	Middleburg	030-0359	114
Hunton House Kitchen *Lone Star Farm*	ca. 1820	Thoroughfare Gap	030-0275	160
Manor Farm	ca. 1820; 1950; 1970	Orlean	030-0649	129
Montana	ca. 1820; ca. 1890	Upperville	030-0883	70
Mount Hope	ca. 1820	Thoroughfare Gap	030-0778	161

Name of Resource	Date	USGS Quad Name	VDHR file no.	Page
Mountain View Log Building *Red Oak Farm Log House*	ca. 1820	Linden	030-0863	59
Snowden *Hart-Stinson House*	ca. 1820	Jeffersonton	030-0340	168
Stevens-Maddux House	ca. 1820	Germanna Bridge	030-0938	227
Valley View *Gibson House, Linden Goose Creek Farm, The Anchorage, Belle Meade Farm*	ca. 1820; 1938	Linden	030-0836	59
Water Dale *Riverview*	ca. 1820	Remington	030-0154	212
Wellington	ca. 1820	Remington	030-0772	213
Woodbourne	ca. 1820; 1925	Warrenton	030-0322	180
Acorn Farm Cabin	1820–50; 1870	Thoroughfare Gap	030-0782	161
Ball's Inn *Wadsworth House*	1820–55	Thoroughfare Gap	030-0160	161
Ball-Shumate House	1820–40; 1920	Warrenton	030-0464	181
Creel House	1820–60	Middleburg	030-0600	114
Crossroads Farm *Rector House*	1820–30	Rectortown	030-0705	97
Embrey House	1820–40	Richardsville	030-0880	229
Fletcher-Graves House	1820–40	Midland	030-0043	218
Grasslands	1820–50	Rectortown	030-0781	97
Harkaway Tenant House	1820–40	Warrenton	030-0488	181
Mount Airy Farm *Morf, Robert House*	1820–60	Rectortown	030-0209	98
Pleasant Valley	1820–40	Rectortown	030-0024	98
Fitzhugh, Dudley, House *The Weed Patch, etc.*	1822	Catlett	030-0458	200
Wolf's Crag	1822	Upperville	030-0097	70
Cedar Hill	ca. 1822; 1855	Thoroughfare Gap	030-0779	162
Hale House	1825; 1974	Rectortown	030-0773	98
George, Bernard and Sally, Farm, *Inglewood*	ca. 1825	Midland	030-0872	218
Montmorency	ca. 1825; 1946	Upperville	030-0039	71
Angelica *Joseph Lawler House*	1826; 1929	Orlean	030-0240	129
Boxwood *Gen. William "Billy" Mitchell House*	1826; 1925	Middleburg	030-0091	115
Mountain View *Dondoric*	1826	Marshall	030-0575	145

Name of Resource	Date	USGS Quad Name	VDHR file no.	Page
Elmore	1826–27	Linden	030-0751	59
Locust Grove *Lake House, Polk-a-Dot Farm*	1827; ca.1840; 1937	Rectortown	030-0740	99
Edgeworth	1828	Orlean	030-0216	129
Bright Prospect	ca. 1829	Marshall	030-0577	146
Carrington	1830	Upperville	030-0017	71
Stoneleigh	1830	Rectortown	030-0904	99
Thorpe House	1830	Orlean	030-0737	130
Bellevue	ca. 1830	Warrenton	030-0493	182
Canaan	ca. 1830	Flint Hill	030-0873	120
Glenville	ca. 1830	Marshall	030-0026	146
Holly Hill *Strother House, Orchard Grove*	ca. 1830	Orlean	030-0797	130
Jett House	ca. 1830	Orlean	030-0825	130
Kane House *Windy Hill Farm*	ca. 1830	Midland	030-0760	219
La Grange	ca. 1830	Ashby Gap	030-0200	57
Leeds Manor	ca. 1830	Orlean	030-0219	131
Licking Run Farm *Bell Haven*	ca. 1830; 1960s	Warrenton	030-0474	182
Locust Grove Farm, near Hurleyville	ca. 1830; 1875	Warrenton	030-0432	182
Morgansburg	ca. 1830	Midland	030-0151	219
Payne House, near Marshall	ca. 1830	Orlean	030-0507	131
Peters, Henry, House *Peters-Eskridge Property*	ca. 1830	Somerville	030-0587	223
Poehlmann Log House	ca. 1830; ca. 1840	Warrenton	030-0383	183
Riley House	ca. 1830	Orlean	030-0241	131
Road Island	ca. 1830	Marshall	030-0197	147
Rosedale *Bronough Farm*	ca. 1830	Warrenton	030-0413	183
Stanley House	ca. 1830; ca. 1890; 1970	Catlett	030-0473	200
Avoka *Ovoka*	1830–40	Upperville	030-0048	72
Bird House	1830–50	Somerville	030-0761	223
Byrnley	1830–40	Rectortown	030-0013	99
Colvin House	1830–60	Upperville	030-0763	72

Name of Resource	Date	USGS Quad Name	VDHR file no.	Page
Gordonsdale	1830–40	Marshall	030-0028	147
Hopewell	1830–50	Thoroughfare Gap	030-0523	162
Old Pearson House *Gravelly Ridge*	1830–50; late 19th century	Somerville	030-0138	223
Sutphin House	1830–50	Jeffersonton	030-0374	168
Tannery Farm *Tan Yard Farm*	1830–50	Rectortown	030-0660	100
Wheatland	1830–60	Marshall	030-0501	148
Woodside, near Bristersburg	1830–50	Somerville	030-0153	224
Merry Hill	ca. 1830–40; 1900	Remington	030-0158	213
Ashland	1831	Upperville	030-0006	72
Puller House	ca. 1831	Rectortown	030-0609	100
Chestnut Lawn	1832	Germanna Bridge	030-0088	227
Eastern View *Salem House*	1832; 1880s	Rectortown	030-0715	100
Clover Hill	1833	Marshall	030-0516	148
Hitt-Halley Place	1833	Rectortown	030-0800	101
Waveland	1833	Marshall	030-0512	149
Martin, John, House	ca. 1834	Catlett	030-0870	200
Ryan Cabin *Rappahannock Mountain Log House*	ca. 1835	Marshall	030-0228	149
Sky Meadows *Mount Bleak*	ca. 1835	Upperville	030-0283	73
West View	ca. 1835; 1910	Rectortown	030-0893	101
Westwood	ca. 1835	Orlean	030-0555	132
Lawler-Walker House *The Chimneys*	1836	Marshall	030-0515	149
Belle Grove *Armistead, Woodside*	ca. 1836; ca. 1870	Upperville	030-0791	73
Beulah *Kalorama*	1837; 1885; ca. 1910	Thoroughfare Gap	030-0068	162
Grove, The *Woodlawn*	1837; ca. 1960	Upperville	030-0053	74
Summerfield	1837	Marshall	030-0489	150
Boteler-Peters House	ca. 1837	Midland	030-0849	219
Ashleigh	1840	Upperville	030-0005	74
Benvenue *Kincheloe House*	1840	Rectortown	030-0635	101

Name of Resource	Date	USGS Quad Name	VDHR file no.	Page
Seaton Farm	ca. 1840	Upperville	030-0049	75
Silver Spring Farm	ca. 1840	Orlean	030-0556	134
Springfield Farm	ca. 1840	Thoroughfare Gap	030-0908	163
Toll House	ca. 1840	Middleburg	030-0624	116
Vivian *Old Catlett House, Silver Brook Farm*	ca. 1840; 1870s	Catlett	030-0254	201
West View *Chestnut Hill*	ca. 1840	Marshall	030-0528	151
Western View *Castle of Hope*	ca. 1840	Upperville	030-0253	75
Wine, Marshall, House	ca. 1840	Upperville	030-0817	76
Courtney *Buena Vista*	1840–50	Upperville	030-0796	76
Dell, The	1840–60	Flint Hill	030-0917	121
Fairfield	1840–50	Flint Hill	030-0696	121
Garrison House	1840–60; 1979	Middleburg	030-0596	116
German House	1840–60	Orlean	030-0506	135
Hill, The	1840–60; 1941	Upperville	030-0054	77
Holland's Mill	1840–70	Upperville	030-0801	77
Ivy Hill	1840–60	Warrenton	030-0403	184
Kirkpatrick House	1840–60	Middleburg	030-0598	116
Payne House	1840–50	Orlean	030-0735	135
Roland	1840–50; 1940s	Thoroughfare Gap	030-0075	164
Spring Valley Farm	1840–50	Upperville	030-0679	77
Vernon Mills	1840–60	Orlean	030-0799	135
Avenel	1842; 1901	Thoroughfare Gap	030-0003	164
Littleton Tanyard House	ca. 1842	Linden	030-0747	60
Littleton-Saffell House	ca. 1842	Linden	030-0746	60
Grove, The	1847; 1920s	Warrenton	030-0339	184
Watery Mountain Cabin *Hesperides Cabin*	1848	Warrenton	030-0399	185
Appleton Cottage *Fauquier Springs Cottage*	1850	Warrenton	030-0335	185
Hartland	1850	Linden	030-0840	60
Jeffries House	1850	Upperville	030-0759	78
Kinross *Reid Place*	1850; 1964	Rectortown	030-0753	103

Name of Resource	Date	USGS Quad Name	VDHR file no.	Page
Prospect Acres	1855	Catlett	030-0267	202
Lawler, Francis, House	ca. 1855	Orlean	030-0900	136
Spring Hill Farm	1856	Catlett	030-0441	202
Downing, John, Farm *Cold Hill*	1857	Flint Hill	030-0687	122
Elmwood *Elmington*	1857	Upperville	030-0717	81
Western View *Denton*	1857	Rectortown	030-0570	105
Melrose Castle Farm	1857–58	Catlett	030-0070	203
Farmington *Whitewood*	1858; ca. 1940	Rectortown	030-0573	105
Bendermeer	ca. 1860; ca. 1890	Upperville	030-0282	81
Parr House *Bauserman Residence*	ca. 1860; 1880	Orlean	030-0730	137
Shumate House	ca. 1860	Catlett	030-0273	203
Anderson-Rector House	1860–80	Orlean	030-0180	137
Ashby, J. E., House *Willow Ford*	1865	Jeffersonton	030-0372	170
Sanker House	1865	Jeffersonton	030-0389	171
Smoot House	ca. 1865	Jeffersonton	030-0390	171
Anderson-Green House	ca. 1867	Flint Hill	030-0280	123
Douglas Residence	ca. 1867	Nokesville	030-0266	208
Rockburn	ca. 1867	Rectortown	030-0214	106
Monterey	1868	Orlean	030-0764	137
McCarty Home *Old Switchboard House*	ca. 1868	Upperville	030-0252	81
Longwood	ca. 1868	Catlett	030-0457	204
Cloverland	1869	Rectortown	030-0862	106
Montevideo *Marlen Farm, Bastable Farm*	1869	Catlett	030-0453	204
Gaskins Log House	1870	Upperville	030-0788	81
Shumate, Lewis, House *Foxmoor Farm*	1870	Warrenton	030-0478	185
Winmill-Nelson House	1870; 1930s	Warrenton	030-0381	185
Clarendon	ca. 1870	Orlean	030-0823	137
Heathfield *Beaulieu*	ca. 1870; 1950s	Rectortown	030-0892	106

Name of Resource	Date	USGS Quad Name	VDHR file no.	Page
Log House in Turnbull	ca. 1870	Warrenton	030-0348	186
Magbie Hill	ca. 1870; 1898; 1927	Warrenton	030-0312	186
Mauzey-George House	ca. 1870	Somerville	030-0612	225
Strother-Hart Farm *Parkinson Home–Malwin Hill*	ca. 1870	Jeffersonton	030-0352	171
Utterback-Foster House *Turnby*	ca. 1870; 1950s	Rectortown	030-0608	107
Beaconsfield Farm	1870–90	Marshall	030-0420	152
Clairemont	1870–80	Flint Hill	030-0726	123
Cliff Mills Farm	1870–80	Jeffersonton	030-0370	172
Clifton	1870–90	Linden	030-0923	61
Cubbage House	1870–90	Marshall	030-0195	152
Edenburn	1870–80	Marshall	030-0532	152
Sudley	1870–90	Marshall	030-0081	153
Woodstock	1870–90	Catlett	030-0454	204
Payne House, near Orlean	ca. 1872	Orlean	030-0720	138
Russell House	ca. 1872	Orlean	030-0719	138
Sumption-Shacklett House *Shacklett-Hatcher Property*	1874	Upperville	030-0536	82
Riley Cabin	ca. 1875	Orlean	030-0242	138
Rose Bank *Rosebanks*	ca. 1875	Upperville	030-0101	82
Smith, Enoch, House	ca. 1875	Marshall	030-0281	153
Moorings, The	1875–76	Marshall	030-0576	153
Houynhym Farm *David Carper House*	1877	Flint Hill	030-0278	123
Payne House *Elk Run*	ca. 1878	Midland	030-0051	221
Priestly Farm	ca. 1879	Orlean	030-0245	139
Pageland	1880	Catlett	030-0438	205
MacDonald House	ca. 1880	Remington	030-0461	214
Meadfield	ca. 1880	Remington	030-0460	214
Taylor House	ca. 1880	Catlett	030-0433	205
Caton-McClanahan House *McClanahan House*	1880–1900	Warrenton	030-0326	186
Cove, The, Tenant House	1880–1910	Flint Hill	030-0756	124
Fishback-Beale House *Waterloo Tract Farm*	1880–90	Jeffersonton	030-0353	172

Name of Resource	Date	USGS Quad Name	VDHR file no.	Page
Herringdon House	1880–1900	Rectortown	030-0562	107
Lee's Mill Farm	1880–1900	Remington	030-0462	215
McClanahan House	1880–1900	Warrenton	030-0349	186
Seven Oaks	1880–1910	Catlett	030-0476	205
Glen Ara	1883	Orlean	030-0915	139
Maizemoor	1883; 1945	Rectortown	030-0669	107
Saint Stephen's Farm	1883	Catlett	030-0456	206
Cove, The	1885	Flint Hill	030-0757	124
Fairview	1888	Rectortown	030-0754	108
Clifton	1889	Marshall	030-0018	154
Triplett House	ca. 1889	Linden	030-0105	61
Barrymore	1890; 1962	Marshall	030-0502	154
Bergen	1890	Upperville	030-0942	82
Greenland Farm *Belmont*	1890	Upperville	030-0250	83
Carter House	ca. 1890	Warrenton	030-0384	187
Carter, Bud, House	ca. 1890	Marshall	030-0513	154
Fallingbrook *Heronwood*	ca. 1890; 1956; 1988	Upperville	030-0881	83
Hart-Smith House	ca. 1890	Jeffersonton	030-0341	172
Little Ashland	ca. 1890	Warrenton	030-0344	187
Milburn	ca. 1890	Richardsville	030-0218	229
Mountain View *The White House*	ca. 1890	Orlean	030-0827	139
Ridgeville	ca. 1890	Upperville	030-0882	83
Noland, R., House in Rayton	1890–1900	Warrenton	030-0466	187
Walnut Hollow	1890–1900	Orlean	030-0718	140
Brooks House	1891	Jeffersonton	030-0409	172
Contest *Shady Valley Farm*	1892	Marshall	030-0286	155
Runnymede *Davis Place*	1896	Orlean	030-0824	140
Brown-Moore House	ca. 1900	Jeffersonton	030-0375	173
Canterbury Tenant House	ca. 1900	Jeffersonton	030-0347	173
Hiner House	ca. 1900	Jeffersonton	030-0354	173
Ivanhoe	ca. 1900	Upperville	030-0789	84

Name of Resource	Date	USGS Quad Name	VDHR file no.	Page
Airlie House	1925	Marshall	030-0205	156
Dakota	1925	Warrenton	030-0300	192
Fenton	1925	Warrenton	030-0402	193
Emory Place *Sunset Hills*	1926–30	Warrenton	030-0307	193
Hodgkin House	ca. 1928	Warrenton	030-0382	193
Leeton Forest	1929	Warrenton	030-0308	193
Canterbury	1930	Jeffersonton	030-0345	174
Farrar-Gray House	1930s	Warrenton	030-0306	194
Broadview	1930–32	Warrenton	030-0401	194
Tirvelda Farm *High Meadows*	1931	Middleburg	030-0626	117
Ardarra	1932	Rectortown	030-0742	108
Cloverland	1932	Rectortown	030-0768	109
Harkaway Farm	1932	Marshall	030-0487	156
Oaks, The *Innis Hill*	1932	Warrenton	030-0320	194
Kinloch	1933	Thoroughfare Gap	030-0077	165
Locust Hill, near Middleburg	1934; 1979	Rectortown	030-0752	109
Prospect Hill	1934	Jeffersonton	030-0926	174
Ashlawn *Holtzclaw Farm, Ashland*	1935	Warrenton	030-0941	195
Blue Ridge Farm	1935	Upperville	030-0894	85
Sunnyside	1936	Warrenton	030-0422	195
Hickory Hollow	1937	Warrenton	030-0310	195
Arborvitae	1938	Marshall	030-0531	156
Little Cotland	1940	Rectortown	030-0743	109
Saint Leonard's	1940	Warrenton	030-0304	196
Whiffletree Farm	1940	Warrenton	030-0319	196
Henchman's Lea	ca. 1940	Orlean	030-0897	140
Flint Hill *Eshton, Rawlingsdale*	1945	Marshall	030-0662	157
Mulberry Hill Farm	1947	Jeffersonton	030-0357	175
Whitehall	1947	Marshall	030-0542	157
Over-the-Grass	1950	Rectortown	030-0620	110
Highbury	1950–70	Middleburg	030-0642	117

B. Property Index
by Primary Name

Note: Alternative property names are set in italics.

Name of Resource	Date	USGS Quad Name	VDHR File no.	Page
Ashlawn *Holtzclaw House*	1935	Warrenton	030-0941	195
Ashleigh	1840	Upperville	030-0005	74
Aspen Dale	ca. 1795; 1907	Upperville	030-0007	65
Aspen Hill	ca. 1810	Rectortown	030-0755	92
Atoka	1816; 1930s; 1976	Rectortown	030-0704	95
Avenel	1842; 1901	Thoroughfare Gap	030-0003	164
Avoka *Ovoka*	1830–40	Upperville	030-0048	72
Baird House	ca. 1820; ca. 1880	Upperville	030-0675	70
Ball House *Eric Sevareid House*	1807	Orlean	030-0243	125
Ball's Inn *Wadsworth House*	1820–55	Thoroughfare Gap	030-0160	161
Ball-Shumate House	1820–40; 1920	Warrenton	030-0464	181
Balthorpe House *Marly*	ca. 1820	Rectortown	030-0769	97
Barbee's Tavern	ca. 1790	Flint Hill	030-0685	119
Barrymore	1890; 1962	Marshall	030-0502	154
Bayley House	ca. 1850	Thoroughfare Gap	030-0521	164
Beaconsfield Farm	1870–90	Marshall	030-0420	152
Beale House *Herd Farm*	ca. 1820	Midland	030-0725	217
Belle Grove *Settle*	ca. 1812; ca. 1830; 1970s	Upperville	030-0008	69
Belle Grove *Armistead, Woodside*	ca. 1836; ca. 1870	Upperville	030-0791	73
Bellevue	ca. 1830	Warrenton	030-0493	182
Belvoir	1914	Marshall	030-0080	155
Bendermeer	ca. 1860; ca. 1890	Upperville	030-0282	81
Bennett-Peters House *Belvederia*	ca. 1820	Midland	030-0879	218
Benvenue *Kincheloe House*	1840	Rectortown	030-0635	101
Bergen	1890	Upperville	030-0942	82
Beulah *Kalorama*	1837; 1885; ca. 1910	Thoroughfare Gap	030-0068	162
Bird House	1830–50	Somerville	030-0761	223

Name of Resource	Date	USGS Quad Name	VDHR File no.	Page
Chilly Bleak	ca. 1820; ca. 1840	Warrenton	030-0569	180
Chinn, Charles, House	1780–1840	Rectortown	030-0780	87
Chippewa	ca. 1760	Remington	030-0426	210
Clairemont	1870–80	Flint Hill	030-0726	123
Clarendon	ca. 1870	Orlean	030-0823	137
Cleaveland	1850–70	Flint Hill	030-0874	122
Cliff Mills Farm	1870–80	Jeffersonton	030-0370	172
Clifton	1870–90	Linden	030-0923	61
Clifton	1889	Marshall	030-0018	154
Clovelly *The Cedars, Cedar Grove*	1924	Warrenton	030-0318	192
Clover Hill	1833	Marshall	030-0516	148
Cloverland	1869	Rectortown	030-0862	106
Cloverland	1932	Rectortown	030-0768	109
Cobbler Mountain *Mont Blanc*	1820	Orlean	030-0653	128
Colvin House	1830–60	Upperville	030-0763	72
Contest *Shady Valley Farm*	1892	Marshall	030-0286	155
Cornwell House *Old Cornwell Place*	1800–1820	Remington	030-0428	211
County Poorhouse	1840	Orlean	030-0505	132
Courtney *Buena Vista*	1840–50	Upperville	030-0796	76
Cove, The	1885	Flint Hill	030-0757	124
Cove, The, Tenant House	1880–1910	Flint Hill	030-0756	124
Cowne's Place	ca. 1780; ca. 1910	Midland	030-0886	217
Crain House *Stonehedge*	1919	Middleburg	030-0809	117
Craine House *Middleton*	1810–40	Rectortown	030-0744	93
Creel House	1820–60	Middleburg	030-0600	114
Crosby-Waller House	ca. 1790	Somerville	030-0584	222
Crossroads Farm *Rector House*	1820–30	Rectortown	030-0705	97
Cubbage House	1870–90	Marshall	030-0195	152
Curtis House	1900–1915	Jeffersonton	030-0377	173

Name of Resource	Date	USGS Quad Name	VDHR File no.	Page
Heathfield *Beaulieu*	ca. 1870; 1950s	Rectortown	030-0892	106
Henchman's Lea	ca. 1940	Orlean	030-0897	140
Herringdon House	1880–1900	Rectortown	030-0562	107
Hickory Hollow	1937	Warrenton	030-0310	195
High Acre	1920–30	Middleburg	030-0645	117
Highbury	1950–70	Middleburg	030-0642	117
Highfield	ca. 1850; ca. 1925	Upperville	030-0247	78
Hill Farmhouse	ca. 1850	Upperville	030-0790	79
Hill, The	1840–60; 1941	Upperville	030-0054	77
Hiner House	ca. 1900	Jeffersonton	030-0354	173
Hirst Place	ca. 1840; 1880; 1970	Orlean	030-0876	133
Hitt-Halley Place	1833	Rectortown	030-0800	101
Hodgkin House	ca. 1928	Warrenton	030-0382	193
Hogue Cabin	ca. 1800–1820	Germanna Bridge	030-0770	226
Hogue House	ca. 1840; 1930s	Germanna Bridge	030-0771	227
Holland's Mill	1840–70	Upperville	030-0801	77
Hollow, The	1765	Upperville	030-0803	64
Holly Hill *Strother House, Orchard Grove*	ca. 1830	Orlean	030-0797	130
Hooewood *Ashley*	1780–90	Warrenton	030-0497	177
Hopefield	1923–24	Warrenton	030-0085	192
Hopewell	1830–50	Thoroughfare Gap	030-0523	162
Hopper-Collins House *Marshall-Gore Log House*	ca. 1800	Massies Corner	030-0721	166
Houynhym Farm *David Carper House*	1877	Flint Hill	030-0278	123
Humblestone	1810; 1912; 1927	Marshall	030-0490	144
Hume, Asa, House	ca. 1810	Jeffersonton	030-0367	167
Hume, Jacob, House	ca. 1810	Jeffersonton	030-0376	168
Hunterleigh *Moreland, Turner House*	1810; 1850	Orlean	030-0658	126
Hunting Ridge	ca. 1840; 1930; 1948	Warrenton	030-0321	183
Hunton House Kitchen *Lone Star Farm*	ca. 1820	Thoroughfare Gap	030-0275	160
Hutton House	1908	Warrenton	030-0311	189

Name of Resource	Date	USGS Quad Name	VDHR File no.	Page
Locust Grove Farm *Misty Farm*	1810–40	Catlett	030-0265	199
Locust Grove Farm, near Hurleyville	ca. 1830; 1875	Warrenton	030-0432	182
Locust Grove, near Goldvein	1802–10; 1847	Richardsville	030-0589	229
Locust Hill, near Middleburg	1934; 1979	Rectortown	030-0752	109
Locust Hill, south of Rectortown	1850–80	Rectortown	030-0860	104
Log House in Turnbull	ca. 1870	Warrenton	030-0348	186
Lomax, Clarence, House *Furr Cabin*	1780–1820	Midland	030-0041	217
Lomax-Peters Log House	ca. 1840; ca. 1870; ca. 1880; 1950	Midland	030-0615	220
Longwood	ca. 1868	Catlett	030-0457	204
Loretto *Edmonium*	1790; 1895; ca. 1900	Warrenton	030-0035	178
Lynn House	ca. 1780	Rectortown	030-0603	86
MacDonald House	ca. 1880	Remington	030-0461	214
Magbie Hill	ca. 1870; 1898; 1927	Warrenton	030-0312	186
Maidstone Ordinary *Floweree Tavern*	1790–1810	Rectortown	030-0036	88
Maizemoor	1883; 1945	Rectortown	030-0669	107
Mann House *Lake Place*	ca. 1800	Rectortown	030-0833	89
Manor Farm	ca. 1820; 1950; 1970	Orlean	030-0649	129
Manor Lane Farm *Carter Farm*	1906	Warrenton	030-0338	189
Marshall-Smith Place	ca. 1810	Jeffersonton	030-0361	168
Martin, John, House	ca. 1834	Catlett	030-0870	200
Mauzey-George House	ca. 1870	Somerville	030-0612	225
McCarty Home *Old Switchboard House*	ca. 1868	Upperville	030-0252	81
McClanahan House	1880–1900	Warrenton	030-0349	186
McClanahan, Mary, House	1900–1910	Warrenton	030-0325	188
McSweeny House	ca. 1810	Marshall	030-0671	144
Meadfield	ca. 1880	Remington	030-0460	214
Meadows, The	ca. 1800	Marshall	030-0529	142

Name of Resource	Date	USGS Quad Name	VDHR File no.	Page
Meadowview	1810	Thoroughfare Gap	030-0672	160
Meadowville	ca. 1800	Marshall	030-0831	142
Melrose Castle Farm	1857–58	Catlett	030-0070	203
Merry Hill	ca. 1830–40; 1900	Remington	030-0158	213
Milburn	ca. 1890	Richardsville	030-0218	229
Mill House *Chinn's Mill*	1790–1820; 1924–29	Rectortown	030-0650	88
Millford Mills *Woolf's Mill*	ca. 1800	Rectortown	030-0713	90
Montana	ca. 1820; ca. 1890	Upperville	030-0883	70
Monterey	1868	Orlean	030-0764	137
Montmorency	ca. 1825; 1946	Upperville	030-0039	71
Montrose	ca. 1805; 1822; 1870	Rectortown	030-0518	91
Moorings, The	1875–76	Marshall	030-0576	153
Morgansburg	ca. 1830	Midland	030-0151	219
Morgan-Wingfield House *Morgan House*	ca. 1853	Jeffersonton	030-0356	170
Morven	ca. 1819; 1835; 1950	Orlean	030-0864	127
Mount Airy	1911	Upperville	030-0042	84
Mount Airy Farm *Robert Morf House*	1820–60	Rectortown	030-0209	98
Mount Defiance	1810; 1930	Rectortown	030-0775	92
Mount Eccentric Farm	ca. 1840	Marshall	030-0288	150
Mount Hope	ca. 1820	Thoroughfare Gap	030-0778	161
Mount Independence	ca. 1800; ca. 1825; ca. 1890	Upperville	030-0674	65
Mount Jett *Mount Marshall*	ca. 1840	Orlean	030-0819	134
Mount Pleasant *The Meadows*	ca. 1810; 1840; 1890	Upperville	030-0567	68
Mount Seclusion	ca. 1840	Rectortown	030-0859	103
Mount Sterling	ca. 1790	Catlett	030-0439	199
Mount View *Glenaman, Morehead House*	ca. 1790; 1900	Warrenton	030-0548	179
Mount Welby Farm	ca. 1850	Flint Hill	030-0183	122
Mountain End	ca. 1798	Thoroughfare Gap	030-0683	159
Mountain View	ca. 1798	Thoroughfare Gap	030-0673	159

Name of Resource	Date	USGS Quad Name	VDHR File no.	Page
Mountain View *Stribling House*	ca. 1810; ca. 1850	Linden	030-0132	59
Mountain View *Dondoric*	1826	Marshall	030-0575	145
Mountain View *The White House*	ca. 1890	Orlean	030-0827	139
Mountain View Log Building *Red Oak Farm Log House*	ca. 1820	Linden	030-0863	59
Mountevideo *Marlen Farm, Bastable Farm*	1869	Catlett	030-0453	204
Mountjoy Farm	ca. 1840; ca. 1890; ca. 1915	Orlean	030-0684	134
Mountjoy House	1850–90	Catlett	030-0437	202
Mulberry Hill Farm	1947	Jeffersonton	030-0357	175
Murray House	ca. 1810; 1840–50; ca. 1851	Rectortown	030-0767	92
Needwood	ca. 1850	Jeffersonton	030-0392	170
Nicholson Log House	ca. 1840	Catlett	030-0475	201
Noland, R., House in Rayton	1890–1900	Warrenton	030-0466	187
North Wales	1773–81; 1914	Warrenton	030-0093	176
Oak Hill	ca. 1773; 1819	Upperville	030-0044	64
Oakley	1853–57	Rectortown	030-0046	104
Oaks, The *Innis Hill*	1932	Warrenton	030-0320	194
Oakwood	ca. 1810	Upperville	030-0837	68
Oakwood	ca. 1840; 1925	Warrenton	030-0083	184
Odd Angles Farm	1911	Warrenton	030-0302	190
Old Acres	1850	Orlean	030-0866	136
Old Chapman Place	1920	Midland	030-0877	221
Old Pearson House *Gravelly Ridge*	1830–50; late 19th cen.	Somerville	030-0138	223
Orchard Cottage *Maple Hill*	1903; ca. 1945	Warrenton	030-0315	188
Orlean Farm	1812; ca. 1850	Orlean	030-0086	126
Over-the-Grass	1950	Rectortown	030-0620	110
Owen House	1815; 1850	Rectortown	030-0667	95
Pageland	1880	Catlett	030-0438	205
Palmerstone	1813; 1850; 1881; 1930	Rectortown	030-0601	94

Name of Resource	Date	USGS Quad Name	VDHR File no.	Page
Parr House *Bauserman Residence*	ca. 1860; 1880	Orlean	030-0730	137
Payne House	1840–50	Orlean	030-0735	135
Payne House *Elk Run*	ca. 1878	Midland	030-0051	221
Payne House, near Marshall	ca. 1830	Orlean	030-0507	131
Payne House, near Orlean	ca. 1872	Orlean	030-0720	138
Peake House	1810–40	Middleburg	030-0599	113
Peters, Henry, House *Peters-Eskridge Property*	ca. 1830	Somerville	030-0587	223
Pleasant Vale	1810–20	Upperville	030-0680	68
Pleasant Valley	1820–40	Rectortown	030-0024	98
Poehlmann Log House	ca. 1830; ca. 1840	Warrenton	030-0383	183
Porter Log House *Weaver Cabin*	ca. 1810	Rectortown	030-0639	93
Porter Place	ca. 1790	Warrenton	030-0351	179
Priestly Farm	ca. 1879	Orlean	030-0245	139
Prospect Acres	1855	Catlett	030-0267	202
Prospect Hill	1934	Jeffersonton	030-0926	174
Puller House	ca. 1831	Rectortown	030-0609	100
Rector House	1850–80	Orlean	030-0898	136
Redman House	ca. 1810	Middleburg	030-0547	113
Reed-Hansborough House	ca. 1850; ca. 1880	Midland	030-0096	220
Reid, George, House	ca. 1920	Jeffersonton	030-0360	174
Ridgelea	1921	Warrenton	030-0084	191
Ridgeville	ca. 1890	Upperville	030-0882	83
Riley Cabin	ca. 1875	Orlean	030-0242	138
Riley House	ca. 1830	Orlean	030-0241	131
Road Island	ca. 1830	Marshall	030-0197	147
Robinson House	ca. 1850; ca. 1875	Remington	030-0469	214
Rock Cliff	1910	Upperville	030-0846	84
Rock Valley	1800–1840	Marshall	030-0525	143
Rockburn	ca. 1867	Rectortown	030-0214	106
Roland	1840–50; 1940s	Thoroughfare Gap	030-0075	164
Rose Bank *Rosebank*	ca. 1875	Upperville	030-0101	82

Name of Resource	Date	USGS Quad Name	VDHR File no.	Page
Rose Hill	1750–70	Upperville	030-0073	62
Rosedale *Bronough Farm*	ca. 1830	Warrenton	030-0413	183
Rosemont *Orange Hill*	1801; 1848; 1935; 1977	Rectortown	030-0652	91
Rumsey House *Bishop-Glascock House, Smith House*	ca. 1810	Rectortown	030-0668	93
Runnymede *Davis Place*	ca. 1896	Orlean	030-0824	140
Russell House	ca. 1872	Orlean	030-0719	138
Rutledge	ca. 1812; 1856	Upperville	030-0514	69
Ryan Cabin *Rappahannock Mountain Log House*	ca. 1835	Marshall	030-0228	149
Saint Bride's Farm	1916	Upperville	030-0857	85
Saint Leonard's	1940	Warrenton	030-0304	196
Saint Stephen's Farm	1883	Catlett	030-0456	206
Sands Log House	ca. 1840	Orlean	030-0875	134
Sanker House	1865	Jeffersonton	030-0389	171
Scarborough	1915	Marshall	030-0632	155
Seaton Farm	ca. 1840	Upperville	030-0049	75
Settle Cottage *Canterbury Cottage*	ca. 1780	Warrenton	030-0346	177
Seven Oaks	1880–1910	Catlett	030-0476	205
Shacklett, George W., House *Myers House*	ca. 1819; ca. 1830	Orlean	030-0657	127
Shirland Hall	ca. 1800; 1833	Rectortown	030-0706	90
Shumate House	ca. 1860	Catlett	030-0273	203
Shumate, Lewis, House *Foxmoor Farm*	1870	Warrenton	030-0478	185
Silver Spring Farm	ca. 1840	Orlean	030-0556	134
Sky Meadows *Mount Bleak*	ca. 1835	Upperville	030-0283	73
Smith, Enoch, House	ca. 1875	Marshall	030-0281	153
Smoot House	ca. 1865	Jeffersonton	030-0390	171
Snow Hill	ca. 1790; late 19th cen.	Thoroughfare Gap	030-0887	158
Snowden *Hart-Stinson House*	ca. 1820	Jeffersonton	030-0340	168
Southern View	ca. 1815	Marshall	030-0663	145
Spring Farm	ca. 1770; ca. 1810	Richardsville	030-0152	228

Name of Resource	Date	USGS Quad Name	VDHR File no.	Page
Spring Hill Farm	1856	Catlett	030-0441	202
Spring Valley Farm	1840–50	Upperville	030-0679	77
Springfield	ca. 1805	Middleburg	030-0810	112
Springfield Farm	ca. 1840	Thoroughfare Gap	030-0908	163
Stanley House	ca. 1830; ca. 1890; 1970	Catlett	030-0473	200
Stevens-Maddux House	ca. 1820	Germanna Bridge	030-0938	227
Stoneleigh	1830	Rectortown	030-0904	99
Strother, James, House *Molly's Folly*	1780s(?); 1830–50	Marshall	030-0661	141
Strother-Hart Farm *Parkinson Home–Malwin Hill*	ca. 1870	Jeffersonton	030-0352	171
Sudley	1870–90	Marshall	030-0081	153
Sulphur Springs	ca. 1850	Midland	030-0616	221
Summerfield	1837	Marshall	030-0489	150
Sumption-Shacklett House *Shacklett-Hatcher Property*	1874	Upperville	030-0536	82
Sunnyside	1936	Warrenton	030-0422	195
Sutphin House	1830–50	Jeffersonton	030-0374	168
Tannery Farm *Tan Yard Farm*	1830–50	Rectortown	030-0660	100
Tantivy	ca. 1900	Warrenton	030-0323	187
Taylor House	ca. 1880	Catlett	030-0433	205
Teneriffe	1800–1840	Nokesville	030-0270	207
Thorpe House	1830	Orlean	030-0737	130
Tirvelda Farm *High Meadows*	1931	Middleburg	030-0626	117
Toll House	ca. 1840	Middleburg	030-0624	116
Triplett House	ca. 1889	Linden	030-0105	61
Utterback-Foster House *Turnby*	ca. 1870; 1950s	Rectortown	030-0608	107
Valley View *Gibson House, Linden Goose Creek Farm, The Anchorage, Belle Meade Farm*	ca. 1820; 1938	Linden	030-0836	59
Vernon Mills	1840–60	Orlean	030-0799	135
Vivian *Old Catlett House, Silver Brook Farm*	ca. 1840; 1870s	Catlett	030-0254	201
Walnut Hollow	1890–1900	Orlean	030-0718	140
Water Dale *Riverview*	ca. 1820	Remington	030-0154	212

Name of Resource	Date	USGS Quad Name	VDHR File no.	Page
Watery Mountain Cabin *Hesperides Cabin*	1848	Warrenton	030-0399	185
Waveland	1833	Marshall	030-0512	149
Waverley	ca. 1787; 1890	Remington	030-0891	211
Waverley	ca. 1790; ca. 1830; 1940s	Middleburg	030-0226	111
Waverly *Turner Adams House*	ca. 1812; 1851	Upperville	030-0057	69
Waverly, near Warrenton *Moreborne*	1920	Warrenton	030-0337	191
Wellington	ca. 1820	Remington	030-0772	213
West View	ca. 1835; 1910	Rectortown	030-0893	101
West View *Chestnut Hill*	ca. 1840	Marshall	030-0528	151
Western View	1800–1810	Rectortown	030-0571	91
Western View *Castle of Hope*	ca. 1840	Upperville	030-0253	75
Western View *Denton*	1857	Rectortown	030-0570	105
Weston	1780–1800; 1840–60	Catlett	030-0058	198
Westwood	ca. 1835	Orlean	030-0555	132
Wheatland	1830–60	Marshall	030-0501	148
Whiffletree Farm	1940	Warrenton	030-0319	196
Whitehall	1947	Marshall	030-0542	157
Whitewood	ca. 1818	Rectortown	030-0561	96
Wine, Marshall, House	ca. 1840	Upperville	030-0817	76
Winmill-Nelson House	1870; 1930s	Warrenton	030-0381	185
Winter's Retreat *Fisher House*	1815; ca. 1890	Remington	030-0425	212
Wolf's Crag	1822	Upperville	030-0097	70
Woodbourne	ca. 1820; 1925	Warrenton	030-0322	180
Woodland Croft	ca. 1850	Jeffersonton	030-0393	170
Woodside, near Bristersburg	1830–50	Somerville	030-0153	224
Woodside, near Delaplane	ca. 1850	Upperville	030-0059	79
Woodstock	1870–90	Catlett	030-0454	204
Wyndham *Walker House*	1912	Warrenton	030-0303	180
Yew Hill *Watt's Ordinary*	ca. 1760	Upperville	030-0060	63

Glossary

Selected glossary data are from Paul Baker Touart, *Somerset: An Architectural History* (Maryland Historical Trust and Somerset County Historical Trust, Inc., 1990), used with permission; from *Old House Dictionary*, (c) 1994, Steven J. Phillips; and from Jeffrey Marshall O'Dell, *Inventory of Early Architecture and Historic and Archeological Sites, County of Henrico, Virginia* (Richmond, 1976), by permission of the County of Henrico.

Arcade   A series of arches supported by columns or pillars; a covered passageway.

Architrave   The lowest of the three main parts of the entablature; also, more loosely, the molded frame surrounding a door or window.

Art Deco (1920–40)   An architectural style characterized by: an overall linear, angular, vertical appearance; stepped facade; extensive use of zigzags, chevrons, lozenges, and volutes as decorative elements; and vertical projections above the roofline.

Balustrade   A short post or pillar in a series supporting a rail or coping and thus forming a balustrade.

Bargeboards   Projecting boards that are placed against the incline of the gable of a building and hide the ends of the horizontal roof timbers; sometimes decorated.

Batten   A wood strip placed over a flush seam between two adjacent boards.

Bay   A vertical division of the exterior or interior of a building marked not by walls but by fenestration, buttresses, units of vaulting, etc.; also, a projection of a room usually pierced with many windows.

Bay window   A window structure of angular plan projecting from a wall surface.

Bead   The convex, rounded end of a decorative member.

Board-and-batten   A type of wooden siding composed of vertical boards nailed to the house frame with a narrow strip placed over each joint. The battens were sometimes molded.

Box stair   A stairway enclosed by walls or partitions. Generally a box stair has a door opening at each floor level. Synonyms: boxed-in stair, closed stair.

Brackets   Small supporting pieces of wood or stone often formed of scrolls or volutes to carry projecting weight.

Catslide   A roof having a longer slope at the rear than at the front; especially, a roof whose rear slope continues in a single plane from the ridge to cover a rear addition.

Center-hall plan   Plan incorporating a central passage, usually containing a stairway, flanked by rooms of equal or approximately equal dimension.

Chair rail   A wall molding fitted around a room to prevent chairs, when pushed back against the walls, from damaging the surface.

Classical Revival   A term used to describe architecture and ornament from the late eighteenth to the early twentieth century that is based on ancient classical forms and details.

Colonial Revival   A style of American architecture that generally dates between 1870 and 1920 and reflects a renewed interest in pre-Revolutionary designs.

Corbel   A projecting block, usually of brick or stone, supporting a beam or other horizontal member.

Corner blocks   Blocks positioned at the corners of either window or door casings; often treated with design elements such as paterae (oval disks).

Cornice   A horizontal molded projection that crowns or completes a building or wall. Also, the uppermost part of the entablature.

Crenellation   Any decorative element that simulates the squares (merlons) and the spaces (embrasures, crenels) of a defensive parapet; moldings so decorated are said to be crenellated moldings or embattled moldings. Exterior trim, such as bargeboards, may also be crenellated.

Cupola   A dome, especially a small dome on a circular, square, or polygonal base crowning a roof or turret.

Dentil   A small square block used in rows to decorate cornices.

Distyle   An architectural term describing a portico or porch with two columns.

Doric order   Separated into two distinct types, the Greek and Roman, which have a similar treatment of the frieze. The most distinguishing feature is that the Roman Doric order was set on a base while the Greek Doric order was not.

Double pile   Term used to refer to a house two rooms deep.

Dry-laid   Masonry laid without mortar.

Ell   A wing of a building at right angles to the main structure.

Entablature   The upper section of a classical order resting on the capital and including the architrave, frieze, and cornice.

Facade   A face of a building; especially, a face that is given distinguishing treatment.

Fanlight   A window, sometimes semicircular, over a door in Georgian and Federal-style buildings, with radiating muntins to suggest a fan.

Federal style   A style of American architecture that followed the Revolutionary War and generally dates from the early 1780s to the 1820s. Paralleling the neoclassical designs popularized in England by the Adam brothers, the American version of neoclassicism often included patriotic symbols that reflected the birth of a new nation.

Fenestration   The design and placement of windows in a building.

Finial   An ornament fixed to the peak of an arch or an arched structure.

Fish-scale shingles   Wooden shingles of varying shapes (rounded, pointed, etc.) used to sheath late nineteenth- and early twentieth-century houses in various patterns.

Flemish bond   In this pattern of arranging bricks, headers and stretchers alternate in each course with the center of each header over the center of the stretcher directly below it; more decorative but structurally weaker than English bond.

Fluting   A series of parallel concave gouges used as a decorative technique. This type of decoration contrasts with reeding.

Foursquare. In architecture a house form which was common in the early to mid-twentieth century in which the overall shape is square and the number of interior rooms on the first floor is four.

Frieze A plain or decorated horizontal part of an entablature between the architrave and the cornice.

Gable A roof form triangular in section, with two slopes of equal pitch and length. Also, the triangular end of an exterior wall in a building with a ridged roof.

Gable roof A sloping (ridged) roof that terminates at one or both ends in a gable. Synonymous: pitched roof, ridge roof, comb roof.

Gambrel A ridged roof with two slopes on the front and back, the lower with a steeper pitch.

Georgian A general term used to identify the prevailing style of eighteenth-century architecture in Great Britain and the North American colonies. The style, named after George I, George II, and George III, rulers of Great Britain from 1714 to 1820, was derived from classical, Renaissance, and Baroque stylistic forms.

Gothic Revival One of the imitative styles of medieval architecture popularized during the mid-nineteenth century. An architectural style characterized by: overall picturesque cottage or castle appearance, steeply pitched roof with cross gables, extensive use of ornamental bargeboards, hood moldings over windows, doors and windows incorporating the Gothic arch, and the wall on the gable ends being uninterrupted.

Greek key A geometric ornament of horizontal and vertical straight lines repeated to form a band in the stylized shape of a key.

Greek Revival A mid-nineteenth-century style that closely followed architectural forms and details common to buildings of ancient Greece.

Hall-and-parlor plan Dwelling plan consisting of a larger room usually containing the stair and main exterior entrance (hall), which joins a somewhat smaller room (parlor). This plan was common in one- and one-and-a-half-story vernacular dwellings in the Chesapeake region in the eighteenth and early nineteenth centuries.

Hipped roof A roof that has four sloping sides usually of equal angle.

Hyphen The intermediate section of a house that connects the main block with an adjacent wing.

I-house Term coined in the 1930s by a geographer to denote a two-story, gable-roofed, usually center-hall-plan house type commonly seen in the Midwest states of Illinois, Indiana, and Iowa—hence the name—but occurring in all other parts of the United States as well.

Ionic order Originating in Asia Minor about the middle of the sixth century b.c., the order is distinguished in Roman examples by the voluted capital and dentils in the cornice.

Italianate Architectural revival style popular in the United States in the second half of nineteenth century, in which Italian Renaissance forms such as decorative eave brackets were employed.

Jacobean Revival A medieval revival style found in twentieth-century American architecture, generally domestic, that either copied or translated forms and details from sixteenth-century English Jacobean buildings.

Lean-to   A small, shallow building or extension having a single-sloped roof whose rafters pitch or lean against another building or wall. Also called a shed.

Lintel   The horizontal top piece of a window or door opening.

Lunette   A crescent-shaped or semicircular space, usually over a door or window, that may contain another window, a sculpture, or a mural.

Mansard roof   A roof with two slopes on all sides, the lower one being very steep and the upper one nearly flat.

Massing   In architecture a term describing the three-dimensional aspect of a building; i.e., temple-form massing refers to a building rectangular in plan and having a temple-form front elevation with blocklike side walls; low-lying massing refers to a building that has horizontal emphasis; asymmetrical massing refers to a building that has an irregular plan and roofline, etc.

Moldings   Continuous decorative band; serves as an ornamental device on both the interior and exterior of a building or structure; also often serves the function of obscuring the joint formed when two surfaces meet.

Mortise-and-tenon joint   A tightly crafted joint consisting of a cavity that is prepared to receive a similarly shaped projection (tenon) of another piece with an intersecting pin to hold the two members together.

Neoclassical   A revival of classical aesthetics and forms in art, architecture, music, and literature.

Neo-Georgian   A twentieth-century rendition of the Georgian style of architecture.

Nogging   Masonry (usually brick) infill between the timbers of a (usually exterior) wall.

One-and-a-half stories   Refers to a building either with corner windows on its upper floor or with a raised attic with floor-level front windows.

Order   In classical architecture a column with base (usually), shaft, capital, and entablature, decorated and proportioned according to one of the accepted modes—Doric, Tuscan, Ionic, Corinthian, or Composite.

Palladian   In reference to the mid-nineteenth-century architectural style derived from the designs of the Renaissance architect Andrea Palladio (1518–1580). Palladian designs and motifs were used frequently in large formal buildings in Virginia in the mid-eighteenth century.

Parapet   A low wall, sometimes battlemented, placed to protect any spot where there is a sudden drop, for example, at the edge of a bridge, quay, or housetop.

Pattern book   An architectural building manual which ranged from expensive treatises to carpenters' handbooks, showing the construction of doorways, cornices, windows, mantels, and other details.

Pavilion   A projecting room off a larger building, usually square in plan, connected to the main building by a hyphen and often forming a terminating wing of the main facade of the building. Also, an ornamental freestanding building used as a pleasure house or summerhouse in a garden.

Pediment   A crowning feature of porticoes, pavilions, doorways, or other architectural features, usually of low triangular form, sometimes broken in the center to receive an ornament. A triangular section framed by a horizontal molding on its base and two raking (sloping) moldings on each of its sides.

Pent closet   A small enclosed space for storage that projects from the exterior wall of a building but is reached from the interior by closet doors and is covered with a pent (shed) roof.

Pier   A squarish supporting member usually of wood, brick, or concrete block.

Pilaster   A flat rectangular column with a capital and base set into a wall as an ornamental motif.

Porte cochere   A covered entryway or porch large enough to accommodate vehicles.

Portico   A roofed space, open or partially enclosed, forming the entrance and centerpiece of the face of a temple, house, or church, often with columns and a pediment.

Queen Anne style   An eclectic late nineteenth-century style characterized by irregularity of plan and massing and a wide variety of surface textures.

Quoins   The dressed stones at the corners of buildings, usually laid so that their faces are alternately large and small.

Rafters   Structural timbers rising from the eaves to the ridge and supporting the roof covering.

Raised basement   A basement whose upper portion is raised considerably (more than about 18 inches) above grade. Also referred to as an elevated basement or an English basement.

Return   A piece of trim that finishes the side projection for a stair tread, mantel, or cornice.

Romanesque Revival   A late nineteenth-century revival of pre-Gothic architecture featuring heavy rock-faced stone or brick walls and round-arched windows and doors.

Rosette   Any round ornament that is carved, painted, or molded so as to resemble a flower; used as ornamental nailheads or screwheads, as decorative plaques in joinery, or simply as a means of embellishing a wall or ceiling.

Shed roof   A single pitched roof often used for dormers and simple kitchen additions.

Side-hall plan   Plan of a dwelling featuring at one gable end a passage which runs the full depth of the house and contains the principal exterior entrances and the stair; this side passage opens into one or more rooms on one side. This plan type was common in Virginia dwellings of the late eighteenth century and the first half of the nineteenth century.

Sidelight   A framed area of fixed glass alongside a door or window opening.

Single-pile   Refers to a house plan a single room in depth.

Sleeping porch   A double-story porch, generally projecting off the side walls of a house; the second floor or upper part of the porch often contained chambers connected to the upper floors of the house which functioned as service or sleeping rooms. A common feature of southern domestic architecture beginning in the mid-eighteenth century.

Soffit   The surface of the underside of an architectural feature.

Spindle   A turned baluster or a short turned decorative member.

Summer kitchen   An outbuilding used in the hotter months of the year for the principal cooking services of a household; sometimes attached to the main house by a colonnade or breezeway.

Surround   The border or casing that frames a window or door; also called an architrave.

Swag   A molding in the form of a garland or festoon representing flowers, fruit, or fabric.

Telescope house   A term to identify houses that were built with a stepped profile, usually, but not in all cases, decreasing in height from the main block to the kitchen.

Tenon   A narrow extension on a wood member that is inserted in a cavity or mortise to form a secure joint.

Tetrastyle   An architectural term describing a portico having four columns.

Tie beam   A horizontal beam that joins the front and rear walls.

Transverse hall   A hall lying in a cross direction.

Triglyphs   The group of three vertical bands found on the Doric frieze or its derivatives; alternates with the metopes.

Tudor (1890–1940)   An architectural style characterized by: steeply pitched end-gabled roofs, gabled entryway, multipaned narrow windows (usually in bands of three), tall chimneys (often with chimney pots), masonry construction, and decorative half-timbering in many cases.

Turned   Refers to a post, baluster, or finial which has been turned on a lathe for decorative effect.

Turret   A small ornamented tower or tower-shaped projection on a building.

Tuscan order   The simplest order, supposedly derived from Etruscan temples; recognized easily by a smooth column surface and largely undecorated entablature.

Tympanum   The recessed, ornamental space or panel enclosed by cornices of a triangular pediment.

Vernacular architecture   A broad multidisciplinary field of study centering around regional environments and their components. Vernacular buildings are viewed as those structures built in response to the everyday needs of a certain populace without the professional assistance of trained architects. Personal priorities and technologies change with time, and as a result vernacular buildings frequently do not conform to the architectural style or styles currently in vogue.

Victorian   A general term used to identify buildings pertaining to or dating from the period of Queen Victoria's reign over Great Britain and Ireland (1837–1901).

Water table   A projecting ledge or molded base capping the foundation of a building and designed to throw rainwater away from the walls of the building.

Weatherboards   Overlapping horizontal boards covering a timber-frame wall. These sawn boards are wedge-shaped in section, and the upper edge is thinner. It was a standard practice to finish the lower edge of the board with a decorative bead.

Weathering   The sloping portion of a chimney stack that carries the larger dimension of the base to the smaller dimension above. The surface is usually covered with brick, though in some cases it is covered with clay, tile, or stone.

Bibliography

Ackerman, James S. *The Villa: Form and Ideology of Country Houses.* Princeton, N.J., 1990.

Benjamin, Asher. *The American Builder's Companion.* 6th rev. ed. New York, 1969.

Brownell, Charles E., Calder Loth, William M. S. Rasmussen, and Richard Guy Wilson. *The Making of Virginia Architecture.* Richmond, 1992.

Buchanan, Paul E. "The Eighteenth-Century Frame Houses of Tidewater Virginia." In *Building Early America,* ed. Charles E. Peterson, 54–72. Radnor, Pa., 1976.

Carson, Cary. "The Virginia House in Maryland." *Maryland Historical Magazine* 69 (1974): 185–96.

Chappelear, B. Curtis, Esq. *Maps and Notes Pertaining to the Upper Section of Fauquier County, Virginia.* Warrenton, Va., 1954.

Craig, Lois A., and the Staff of the Federal Architecture Project. *The Federal Presence: Architecture, Politics, and Symbols in United States Government Building.* Cambridge, Mass., 1978.

Day, Annie G. *Warrenton and Fauquier County.* 1908. Rept. Warrenton, Va., 1970.

Downing, Andrew Jackson. *The Architecture of Country Houses.* New York, 1858. Rept. New York, 1969.

Farrar, Emmie Ferguson, and Emilee Hines. *Old Virginia Houses: The Piedmont.* Charlotte, N.C., 1975.

Fauquier County, Virginia, Historical Notes. Warrenton, Va., 1954. Supplement to map of Fauquier County.

Fauquier County, Virginia, 1759–1959. Warrenton, Va., 1959.

Fauquier County Land Records, Warrenton, Va.

"Fauquier's 200 Years." *Virginia Calvacade* 9:1 (Summer 1959): 21–29.

Fitch, James Marston. *American Building.* Boston, 1948.

Girouard, Mark. *Life in the English Country House.* New Haven, 1978.

Glassie, Henry. *Folk Housing in Middle Virginia.* Knoxville, Tenn., 1975.

Gott, John K. *High in Virginia's Piedmont: A History of Marshall (Formerly Salem), Fauquier County, Va.* Marshall, Va., 1987.

Gowans, Alan. *The Comfortable House: North American Suburban Architecture, 1890–1930.* Cambridge, Mass., 1986.

———. *Styles and Types of North American Architecture.* New York, 1992.

Groome, H. C. *Fauquier during the Proprietorship.* Richmond, 1927.

Harrison, Fairfax. *Landmarks of Old Prince William.* 1924. Rept. Berryville, Va., 1964.

Hewitt, Mark Alan. *The Architect and the American Country House, 1890–1940.* New Haven, 1990.

Historic American Buildings Survey, Fauquier County, Virginia, Library of Congress.

Jackson, Joseph. *American Colonial Architecture: Its Origins and Development.* Philadelphia, 1924.

Jefferson, Thomas. *Notes on the State of Virginia.* Ed. William Peden. Rept. New York, 1972.

Kaynor, Fay Campbell. "Thomas Tileston Waterman: Student of American Colonial Architecture." *Winterthur Portfolio* 20:2/3 (Summer/Autumn 1985): 103–47.

Kennedy, Roger G. *Greek Revival America.* New York 1989.

Kidney, Walter C. *The Architecture of Choice: Eclecticism in America, 1880–1930.* New York, 1974.

Kimball, Fiske. *Domestic Architecture of the American Colonies.* 1922. Rev. ed., New York, 1966.

Koeper, Frederick, and Marcus Whiffen. *American Architecture.* Vol. 1. Cambridge, Mass., 1981

Lane, Mills. *Architecture of the Old South: Virginia.* Savannah, 1987.

Loth, Calder, ed. *The Virginia Landmarks Register.* 3d ed. Charlottesville, Va., 1987.

McAlester, Virginia and Lee. *A Field Guide to American Houses.* New York, 1985.

McCarty, Clara S., ed. *The Foothills of the Blue Ridge in Fauquier County, Virginia.* Warrenton, Va., 1974.

MacLeod, Cynthia A. Survey of Fauquier County, Virginia, for the Virginia Historic Landmarks Commission, 1979–83, VDHR Archives, Richmond.

Morrison, Hugh. *Early American Architecture.* New York, 1952.

National Register of Historic Places Inventory Nomination Forms, U.S. Department of the Interior
Ashleigh, 1973
Boxwood, 1976
Melrose, 1982
Oak Hill, 1973
Oakley, 1982
Waverly, 1976

Noble, Allen G. *Wood, Brick, and Stone.* Amherst, Mass., 1984.

O'Dell, Jeffrey Marshall. *Inventory of Early Architecture and Historic and Archeological Sites, County of Henrico, Virginia.* Richmond, Va., 1976.

Pierson, William H., Jr. *American Buildings and Their Architects: The Colonial and Neo-classical Styles.* Garden City, N.Y., 1976.

Russell, T. Triplett, FAIA. "Country Places in Fauquier County, Virginia." Inventory, 1985.

———. "Country Places in the Northern Virginia Piedmont." Manuscript prepared for the Fauquier County Board of Supervisors, 1985.

Scheel, Eugene M. *The Guide to Fauquier: A Survey of the Architecture and History of a Virginia County.* Warrenton, Va., 1976.

Upton, Dell. "Vernacular Domestic Architecture in Eighteenth-Century Virginia." In *Common Places: Readings in American Vernacular Architecture,* ed. Dell Upton and John Michael Vlach, 315–35. Athens, Ga., 1986.

Waterman, Thomas Tileston. *The Mansions of Virginia, 1706–1776.* Chapel Hill, N.C. 1946.

Index

Note: Italicized page numbers refer to illustrations in the Historical Overview.

Payne, Emily Jayne, 138

Payne, James, 224

Payne, Capt. James, 227

Payne, John Barton, 196

Payne, Thomas Withers, 131

Payne, W. Wood, 33, 138

Payne, William, 135, 180, 182

Payne, Withers, 133

Payne family, 135

Payne House (Midland Quad, 030-0051), 221; (Orlean Quad, 030-0507), 135; (Orlean Quad, 030-0720), 138; (Orlean Quad, 030-0735), *32, 33,* 131

Peake, John, 113

Peake House, 113

Pearle, William, 87

Pearle House. *See* Fields House

Pendleton, Henrietta Randolph, 74

Pendleton, Rev. W. H., 74

Peters, Henry, House, 223

Peters family, 220

Peters-Eskridge property. *See* Peters, Henry, House

Peyton, Sen. Henry, 145

Philadelphia (Pa.), 48

Phillips, Adm. and Mrs. Neill, 83

Phillips, William A., 109

Phipps, Henry, 88

Phipps, John S., 88, 104

Pickett, Rev. John Sanford, 113

Pickett, Col. Martin, 182, 184

Pickett, William Sanford, 113

Piedmont Station, 47, 80. *See also* Delaplane

Piedmont Vineyards, 111

Pierce, Albert, 174

Pierce, Mandley, 104

Pignutt Mountain, 144

Pilson, Maurice, 190

Plains, The (Va.), 41, 96, 99, 105, 111, 114, 116, 147, 160, 162, 164

Plantation, in Virginia, 7, 22; economy, 34; houses, 40. *See also* Westover

Pleasant Vale, 68, 77; Church, 83

Pleasant Valley, 98

Poelhmann Log House, 183

Point Lookout Prison, 97

Polk-a-Dot Farm. *See* Locust Grove (Rectortown Quad, 030-0740)

Pool, William Henry, 184

Pool house, 109

Poorhouse Branch, of South Run, 131, 135

Porte Crayon, 14, *15,* 63

Porter, Samuel, 179, 186

Porter, Samuel, Jr., 161

Porter family, 179

Porter Log House, 93

Porter Place, 179

Portman, Frederick A. B., 183

Post office, 92, 135, 219

Potomac River, 5, 7, 176,

Powell, Col. Leven, 88, 98

Powell family, 92

Priest, Henry, 96

Priestly Farm, 139

Prince William County (Va.), 201, 228

Princeton University, 196

Prospect Acres, 202

Prospect Hill, 51, *53,* 174

Puller, Samuel, 100

Puller House, 100

Quadrangle, U.S. Geological Survey, 56

Quarters, in Virginia plantations, 22, 34. *See also* Slave quarters

Queen Anne style, in Fauquier County, 46, 47; examples, 82, 84, 108, 124, 140, 173, 204

Racetrack, 72

Railroads, 5; in Fauquier County, 43–47, 71, 80–82, 155, 208

Rapidan River, 8

Rappahannock Mountain Log House. *See* Ryan Cabin

Rappahannock River, 5, 7, 8, 179, 212, 213, 215; early settlements on, 7–8; canals along, 43

Rattlesnake Mountain, 122

Rawlings, John Will, 157

Rawlingsdale. *See* Flint Hill

Rayton, community of, 187

Rector, Caleb, 97

Rector, John, 94, 106

Rector, Thomas, 137

Rector, William, 94

Rector House, 97, 136. *See also* Crossroads Farm

Rector Store, 137

Rector's Crossroads, 97

Rectortown (Va.), 16, 60, 87, 88, 89, 90, 92, 94, 104, 107; map of, 86; Quadrangle, 86–110

Rectortown Post Office, 92

Red Oak Farm Log House. *See* Mountain View Log Building

Red Oak Mountain, 76

Redman House, 113

Reed, Washington, 127, 153

Reed Inn, 220

Reed-Hansborough House, 220

Reid, Alfred, 103

Reid, George, House, 174

Reid Place. *See* Kinross

Remington (Va.), 210, 227; map of, 210; Quadrangle, 210–15

Revolutionary War, 62, 64, 65, 72, 112, 142, 154, 178. *See also* American Revolution

Richardsville (Va.), 228; map of, 228; Quadrangle, 228–29

Richmond (Va.), 2, 5, 49, 64, 74, 196

Richmond County (Va.), 231

Ridgelea, 51, 191

Ridgeville, 77, 83

Riley, Wesley, 138

Riley Cabin, 131, 138

Riley House, 131, 138

Rinehart, Mary Roberts, 203

River port, 212, 213

Riverview. *See* Water Dale

Road Island, 147

Roads, development of in Fauquier County, 5, 13, 28, 48. *See also* Turnpikes

Robinson, Jesse B., 214

Robinson, Samuel, 214

Robinson family, 214

Robinson House, 214

Rockburn, 104, 106

Rockburn Stud Farm. *See* Oakley

Rock Cliff, 84

Rock Hill, 112

Rock Spring. *See* Belvoir

Rock Valley, 143

Roland, 24, 27, 164

Romanesque style, 43

Romantic Revival style, in Fauquier County, 43–47

Root cellar, 186

Rose, Alexander F., 210

Rose Bank, 47, 70, 82

Rose Hill, 10, 36, 62

Rosebank. *See* Rose Bank

Rosedale, 183

Rosemont, 91

Rose's Chippewa Farm. *See* Chippewa

Rout, John, 62

Rumsey House, 93

Rumsey House property, tenant house on, *28*

Runnymeade, 140

Russell, Alfred, 33